Slaves of the Passions

Long claimed to be the dominant conception of practical reason, the Humean theory that reasons for action are instrumental, or explained by desires, is the basis for a range of worries about the objective prescriptivity of morality. As a result, it has come under intense attack in recent decades. A wide variety of arguments have been advanced which purport to show that it is false—or surprisingly—even that it is incoherent. *Slaves of the Passions* aims to set the record straight, by advancing a version of the Humean theory of reasons which withstands this sophisticated array of objections.

Mark Schroeder defends a radical new view which, if correct, means that the commitments of the Humean theory have been widely misunderstood. Along the way, he raises and addresses questions about the fundamental structure of reasons, the nature of normative explanations, the aims of and challenges facing reductive views in metaethics, the weight of reasons, the nature of desire, moral epistemology, and most importantly, the relationship between agent-relational and agent-neutral reasons for action.

Mark Schroeder is an Associate Professor of Philosophy at the University of Southern California.

THANKS AGAIN MARC! I HOPE I'LL SEE YOU SOON, AT THE GRADUATION MAYBE

Slaves of the Passions

Mark Schroeder

OXFORD
UNIVERSITY PRESS

OXFORD

UNIVERSITY PRESS

Great Clarendon Street, Oxford OX2 6DP

Oxford University Press is a department of the University of Oxford.
It furthers the University's objective of excellence in research, scholarship,
and education by publishing worldwide in

Oxford New York

Auckland Cape Town Dar es Salaam Hong Kong Karachi
Kuala Lumpur Madrid Melbourne Mexico City Nairobi
New Delhi Shanghai Taipei Toronto

With offices in

Argentina Austria Brazil Chile Czech Republic France Greece
Guatemala Hungary Italy Japan Poland Portugal Singapore
South Korea Switzerland Thailand Turkey Ukraine Vietnam

Oxford is a registered trade mark of Oxford University Press
in the UK and in certain other countries

Published in the United States
by Oxford University Press Inc., New York

British Library Cataloguing in Publication Data
Data available

Library of Congress Cataloging in Publication Data
Data available

Typeset by Laserwords Private Limited, Chennai, India
Printed in the UK
on acid-free paper by
MPG Books Group

ISBN 978–0–19–929950–8 (Hbk.)
ISBN 978–0–19–957572–5 (Pbk.)

For my parents, Barney and Carol Schroeder

Preface

In 1739 Hume's *Treatise of Human Nature* announced that 'Reason is, and ought only to be the slave of the passions'. It was a bold thesis, and one that has organized many generations of philosophers who have been inspired by Hume in direct or indirect ways. It was a thesis about Reason—in the singular—the rational capacity that we have to reason—the verb. This book is neither about Reason in the singular, nor about reasoning the activity, except indirectly. It is not even—disappointingly, perhaps—about Hume. It is, rather, about reason*s* in the plural—the pros and cons which count in favor of and against things to do. It is a defense of a *Humean* view, in a very broad sense—not necessarily a view that Hume himself held, but a view that has been held by many philosophers at least loosely inspired by Hume, or who took Hume to be an intellectual forebear. It is a defense of the view that all reasons for action are ultimately explained by desires. It is the view, not that Reason is beholden to the passions, but that *reasons* are.

I didn't begin thinking about these issues as one sympathetic to this Humean idea. I began by thinking that it was false—that reasons are in no way beholden to our passions. But I take it to be a guiding principle of philosophical investigation that we can never know which theory we should take, without pushing each view in order to see how it might most profitably be developed. So sometimes rational investigation, I take it, requires figuring out how to develop some view, even if we disagree with it. And so as I encountered more and more anti-Humean arguments in the literature, I found myself constructing a more and more sophisticated Humean view in order to respond to these objections—even though I disagreed with it.

At some point, however, I started wondering why I thought this theory was false. Having developed responses to some of the main objections in the literature on behalf of the Humean, I began to see how the Humean view I was developing could solve other sorts of problems. And at some point I found myself believing it—at least in essentials. And so here we are. I still believe this same theory—in essentials—and it is set out in the following pages. The theory comes with a fair amount of detail as well, and in some of these details I am much more confident than in others. But the basic ideas behind the picture are, I think, essentially right, or at least point in the most promising direction that I know of.

Like most books, this one has both an overt and a covert agenda. Its overt agenda is to understand and defend the Humean Theory of Reasons, a view that I explain in more detail in Chapter 1. Intuitively, the Humean Theory of Reasons is the familiar view that reasons are in some sense *desire-dependent*, and as such, it is at the heart of what has often been referred to as 'the dominant conception of practical reason'. Despite being so often billed as 'the dominant conception', however, the Humean Theory has had very few explicit or careful defenses, and most of the immense literature critical of it focuses on its statement in a paper by Bernard Williams from 1981, if on any actual statement of the view at all, rather than simply attacking 'The Humean' or 'The Instrumentalist', without any further mention of who the target is supposed to be. I think the project of understanding the Humean Theory and whether it really suffers at the hands of these withering attacks is a worthwhile one, and my considered view is that the Humean Theory is, despite all this, true—a view that I develop and defend in this book.

Yet it is the covert agenda of the book which has driven my enthusiasm for the project. The covert agenda of the book is to explore some of the hidden and unevaluated background assumptions that moral philosophers make as a matter of course, to point out the ways in which those background assumptions affect issues of general importance, and to show how to begin to go about evaluating those background assumptions in their own right. In several cases, the views I discuss are typically taken for granted without even being articulated by the people who accept them. If moral philosophy is to become a mature discipline, it is my view that we need to do better at articulating and evaluating the many background assumptions that we make—something that in many areas of moral philosophy, I think people are getting worse at, rather than better.

Questions about these background assumptions don't have the glamour of those which initially attract our philosophical interest, but they are not merely dry questions of only technical interest. Though they may be dry, they are the questions which drive our answers to the glamorous questions with which we begin, and they are the ones we need to solve, if we are to come to rational, principled, and well-supported answers to those questions. It is my hope that this book makes some small contribution toward thinking about how to pose these questions, even if my efforts toward progress in answering them are ultimately (or rapidly) rejected.

I hope that you will read this book looking for a sophisticated contemporary defense of a Humean view about reasons. My overt agenda is to provide such a view, though I expect to persuade few to adopt it in every detail. But I also hope, and this is my covert agenda, that you will go away with an enlarged conception of the basic issues at stake in evaluating whether anything like the Humean Theory of Reasons, or any other theory of reasons, for that matter, is true. As I'll suggest in Chapter 11, I think many of the suggestions that I make on behalf of the Humean Theory can be taken on board for many other purposes, as well.

Acknowledgements

What I think of as the main ideas in this book were developed in 2001–2, during my first two years of graduate school at Princeton, though some, including the basic response to the Too Few Reasons objection, predate that period, and several others, in particular the details of the recursive account of the weight of reasons, were developed or at least substantially refined later on. It has gone through many quite different forms, and my confidence that it has settled on the right form is boosted somewhat by the fact that it now looks more like the book I originally planned to write as a second-year graduate student, than it did through many stages in between. I'm only too well aware of many of its faults, but it nevertheless represents my best attempt to assemble my considered views on these topics into a single, coherent package.

Because the development of my ideas on these topics spans my philosophical career, there are something over a decade's worth of people who deserve thanks for the role they have played in the development either of the ideas specifically developed in this book or in my development as a philosopher. I owe special thanks to Jennifer Manion, who taught three of my first four philosophy courses as an undergraduate at Carleton College, inspired me about philosophy, and encouraged me to pursue my interest in ethics in a way that is informed by metaphysics and the philosophy of language. Keith Lehrer, as a teacher, was an important early example in the *how to* of philosophy, and the biggest pieces of progress that I've made as a philosopher are owed to generalizing the maxim taught to us at Carleton as *Iseminger's Law*: that no great philosopher is a damn fool. In advising my undergraduate senior thesis, Dale Jamieson taught me half of what I know about how to write philosophy—though he can't be blamed for my prose style.

I developed key ideas now appearing in this book in seminars at Princeton with David Sussman, Gideon Rosen, Gilbert Harman, and Karen Bennett, and they were informed by discussions with or feedback over many years from, of those I can remember, Karen Bennett, Be Birchall, Peter Carruthers, Amy Challen, John Cooper, David Copp, Mimi Cukier, Stephen Darwall, Jamie Dreier, Ant Eagle, Andy Egan, Adam Elga, David Enoch, Joshua Gert, Gilbert Harman, Zena Hitz, Jeff Horty, Dan Jacobson, Anja Jauernig, Mark Johnston, Simon Keller, Sean Kelly, Tom Kelly, Matt King, Sari Kisilevsky, Colin Klein, Vera Koffman, Barry Lam, Hendrik Lorenz, Mike McGlone, Chris Mole, Michael Morreau, Mark Murphy, Philip Pettit, Jim Pryor, Peter Railton, Gideon Rosen, Gillian Russell, Kieran Setiya, Michael Smith, David Sobel, Jeff Speaks, David Sussman, Jay Wallace, Nate Williams, Mark van Roojen, and Michael Young.

Gideon Rosen was the best adviser I could have asked for, providing a constant sounding board, drawing me out on the range of my ideas, and always pressing me on what I would say about different new questions. But I have learned the most about the subject matter of this book by struggling directly with the ideas of Christine Korsgaard, Michael Smith, and Tim Scanlon. No doubt they will all wish that I had studied harder and learned more. And I owe a special debt of gratitude to Scott Soames as teacher, friend, colleague, and philosophical exemplar, but most of all for believing in me when I needed it.

More than to anyone else, I owe many of the original ideas in this book to discussions with Nate Williams—who, as I understand things, enjoys successful surprise parties thrown in his honor. The influence of discussions with him is visible in half the chapters of the book, and in a few cases I've borrowed his ideas or formulations shamelessly. He remains one of my favorite moral philosophers. A major turning point in the development of my ideas about the weight of reasons was my discussion with Jay Wallace after his colloquium talk at Princeton in October of 2001. I hope to now be able to better explain why Jay was mistaken to think that a reason for your friend to p must also be a reason for you to not interfere with his p-ing, a thesis which David Lewis, as I recall, found highly amusing at what was sadly his last departmental colloquium. The book has also benefited from feedback from reading groups at Brown University and the University of Maryland at College Park in 2006, organized by Michael Young and Matt King, respectively. And Dan Jacobson, Mark van Roojen, and especially Joshua Gert all provided enormously helpful feedback as referees for Oxford University Press.

Although I hope that it stands by itself, this book is not a stand-alone project; many of my arguments find further support and elaboration in a variety of connected papers, sometimes mentioned in the footnotes. But the book bears particularly close connections to three papers published previously. Large parts of Chapter 4 draw on 'Realism and Reduction: The Quest for Robustness', published in *Philosophers' Imprint* 5(1), <www.philosophersimprint.org/005001/>. Chapter 4 does not address all the issues raised in the paper, but it constitutes a more advanced statement of my position. The positive motivation in sections 11.3 and 11.4 builds on 'The Humean Theory of Reasons', published in *Oxford Studies in Metaethics* 2: 195–219. My treatment here is abbreviated, but fits better into the context of my overall position, as explained in the earlier chapters. And the principal moves of Chapters 5 and 6 are anticipated in 'Weighting for a Plausible Humean Theory of Reasons', published in *Noûs* 41(1): 138–60. The treatment here supersedes that in the paper, particularly given my recursive treatment of the weight of reasons in Chapter 7.

Finally, the book is dedicated with love to my parents, Barney and Carol Schroeder, who rightly taught me that the fact that I want it isn't always a reason for me to get it, among many other Important Things, and sparked and fueled my interest in ethics from the beginning.

Contents

1

Reasons and the Humean Theory

1.1 Introduction

Tonight there is going to be a party, and everyone is invited. There will be good food, drinks, friendly chat, music—and dancing. Ronnie and Bradley, like everyone else, have been invited to the party. But while Ronnie loves to dance, Bradley can't stand it. Not only does he not like dancing, he prefers to stay away from where it is going on, lest he come under pressure to be shown up in his awkward maneuvers by those with fewer left feet than he. So while the fact that there will be dancing at the party is a reason for Ronnie to go, it is *not* a reason for Bradley to go. Far from it; the fact that there will be dancing at the party is a reason for Bradley to stay away. Ronnie's and Bradley's reasons therefore differ—each has a reason that the other does not. Moreover, it's not hard to see *why* Ronnie's and Bradley's reasons differ, at least at a first pass—this is something to do with their respective psychologies. It is because of what they *like, care* about, or *want*. Ronnie likes to dance, but Bradley does not; he likes to stay away from where there is dancing going on.

It's largely uncontroversial—even among philosophers—that at least *some* reasons are like Ronnie's and Bradley's, in that whether they are reasons for some particular person depends on some feature of that person's psychology, such as what that person desires, wants, likes, or cares about.[1] And according to one time-honored tradition often taken to be vaguely inspired by Hume, *all* reasons are at some basic level pretty much like Ronnie's and Bradley's in this way. They are explained in some way by the psychological features of the agents for whom they are reasons—by the psychological features that explain the difference between Ronnie and Bradley.

---

[1] Of course, there is *great* disagreement about *which* of these psychological states, or others, such as intentions, *ends*, or 'valuings', can explain a difference in reasons.

It is not hard to see why this is a natural idea. If it is uncontroversial that reasons are *sometimes* explained by psychological features, then assuming that we all have the same sense of 'explanation' in mind, perhaps there can be a *unified* explanation of why people have the reasons that they do only if *all* reasons are explained by this kind of psychological feature. At least, this should be a good initial candidate for such an explanation. When seized by our philosophical moods, we may seek to achieve some kind of deep understanding or appreciation of what reasons are, how they fit into the world as we encounter it through our experiences, or where they come from. If there is any unified story about this, and it *sometimes* works by appealing to psychological features of some kind, the Humean thought is that it must *always* work by appealing to psychological features of that kind.[2]

This book is a systematic and sympathetic exploration of this simple 'Humean' thought. My task is to explore the viability of what is known as the Humean Theory of Reasons:[3]

> **HTR***   Every reason is explained by the kind of psychological state that explains Ronnie's reason in the same way as Ronnie's is.

Importantly, the Humean Theory of Reasons is a *parity* thesis. By itself, it does not tell us *how* Ronnie's reason is explained by the feature of his psychology that distinguishes him from Bradley, or even what feature of Ronnie's psychology this is. It merely says that *however* this explanation works, all reasons are explained by psychological states in this same way. Different *versions* of the Humean Theory of Reasons are distinguished by their distinctive theories about how Ronnie's reason *is* explained by his psychology. Since it is possible to take many different views about how Ronnie's reason is explained by his psychology, there are correspondingly many possible versions of the Humean Theory of Reasons.

Now one obvious way in which such views can differ, is with respect to what *kind* of psychological feature they hold is required in order to explain

---

[2] Obviously this is not a conclusive argument. But I'll develop the thought behind this kind of motivation further in Ch. 11.

[3] I call it the 'Humean Theory of Reasons' with strong reservations, since it would be a very substantive view to attribute this commitment to Hume. At best, it is merely vaguely inspired by him. Or perhaps it is simply most often held by those who are inspired by him in other respects. On a natural interpretation of Hume, he thinks that there are no reasons for action at all, because 'reason', properly speaking, governs only beliefs. See e.g. Korsgaard [1997], Rawls [2000], and Setiya [2004].

the difference between Ronnie and Bradley. For example, according to one view it is Ronnie's *desires* that explain the difference between him and Bradley, but according to another it is what Ronnie takes *pleasure* in that matters. But as we'll see throughout the book, there are many other important questions on which different versions of the Humean theory can disagree. And every one of these differences can give rise to differences in the plausibility of the corresponding version of the Humean Theory of Reasons. For a toy example giving a general illustration of this point, consider a distinction among versions of the Humean Theory of Reasons which hold that Ronnie's reason is explained by a *desire*, between those which hold that this happens *holistically*, and those which hold that it happens *atomistically*.

Atomistic and holistic versions of the Humean Theory of Reasons differ in their theories about how Ronnie's reason gets explained by his desire in the following way: *atomistic* versions say that we need only *one* desire of Ronnie's in order to explain the difference between him and Bradley. But in contrast, *holistic* versions say that we have to look at all of Ronnie's desires in order to explain the difference. According to a simple holistic theory, there is a reason for Ronnie to go to the party only if going there will maximize the satisfaction of all of his desires *on balance*.[4] While according to a

---

[4] As I am conceiving the distinction, there are *many* holistic Humean theories in the literature, including many views which seem to posit only counterfactual connections between reasons and (atomistic) desires. For example, a theory of reasons modelled on the theory of rationality in Brandt [1979] might hold that there is a reason for X to do A only if doing A would promote a desire that X *would* have, after undergoing cognitive psychotherapy. Similarly, according to Smith [1994], there is a reason for X to do A only if, were X to achieve reflective equilibrium in her desires under full information, she would desire her actual (non-equilibrium) self to do A. Such views don't *seem* to claim that an actual feature of an agent's psychology is necessary in order to explain reasons—they seem to explain reasons by *counterfactual* desires.

But counterfactual views that are genuinely Humean don't hold that these counterfactuals are *ungrounded*. For example, according to Brandt, different people would desire different things after cognitive psychotherapy. So *which* things you would desire after cognitive psychotherapy must be grounded in your actual present psychology—not necessarily in some individual desire, but in holistic features of your psychology which ground the truth of the relevant counterfactuals. This is where Smith's view differs from Brandt's, with which it bears so many surface similarities. Smith does not believe that different people will have different desires after achieving reflective equilibrium under full information—he thinks that under such conditions agents will have identical desires, no matter where they start from. Or at least, he thinks that this must be true in order for there to be any reasons at all. So in Smith's view, these counterfactuals are *not* grounded in actual features of the agent's psychology. Compare Smith [1994: 164–74].

This difference between Brandt's and Smith's views is important. Counterfactual views such as Brandt's are Humean (though holistic); counterfactual views such as Smith's should not be classified as Humean at all. I therefore hold that there are not two kinds of Humean views: actual and counterfactual.

simple atomistic theory, there is a reason for Ronnie to go to the party only if Ronnie has at least *some* desire that going there will satisfy—regardless of whether he has other, stronger, desires that it will frustrate.

It follows from their different theories about how Ronnie's reason is explained by his desires, that these two versions of the Humean Theory of Reasons have different commitments when it comes to explaining other kinds of reasons. So consider the case of Ryan. Katie needs help, and intuitively that is a reason for Ryan to help her. According to the Humean Theory of Reasons, that can only be so if his reason can be explained in the same way as Ronnie's reason is. The holistic version of the Humean Theory of Reasons tells us that this can be so only if helping Katie maximizes the satisfaction of Ryan's desires on balance. So intuitive counterexamples to the holistic theory are easy to come by. All that we have to imagine is that Ryan cares more about his own time than about Katie's welfare, and we have a case in which there is no reason whatsoever for him to help Katie. In contrast, the atomistic version of the Humean Theory of Reasons tells us that reasons are easier to come by. All that need be the case in order for Ryan to have a reason to help Katie is that he have *some* desire that would be promoted by helping her. So to construct a counterexample to the atomistic version of the Humean Theory, we need to imagine that no desire of Ryan's whatsoever would be satisfied by his helping her. Cases like this are at least more unusual.

So this atomistic version of the Humean Theory of Reasons is subject to less obvious counterexamples than this holistic one. That makes it a better view about reasons like Ryan's, and that, in turn, makes it a better hypothesis about the uniform explanation of all reasons. But on the face of it, the atomistic theory is also a better theory, even when we consider only Ronnie's case. According to the holistic theory, if Ronnie desires to dance, but desires to hang out with Bradley *more*, the fact that there will be dancing at the party is no reason at all for Ronnie to go there. For Bradley predictably fails to be co-located with dancing. But that result is already wrong. On the face of it, even if Ronnie has *better* reasons *not* to go to the party, those reasons don't change the fact that he also has a reason to *go*—they merely *outweigh* it. So not only is the atomistic view in a better

There are only actual Humean views—though some of these, like Brandt's, may employ counterfactuals in order to *pick out* the right holistic feature of an agent's psychology. So conceived, counterfactual theories are just one kind of holistic Humean theory; the one considered in the main text is another.

position to account for Ryan's reason, it is also in a better position to account for Ronnie's.

These remarks don't suffice to show that the holistic version of the Humean Theory of Reasons is false; nor do they suffice to show that the atomistic version is not refuted by such counterexamples. And both of the example views just sketched are artificially schematic, for the sake of the illustration. But what this discussion does show is that different theories about how Ronnie's reason is explained lead to important differences in the commitments of different versions of the Humean Theory of Reasons. And in this case, the view that leads to a better account of Ryan's reason is also already a better account of Ronnie's reason.

That is what this book is about. The Humean Theory of Reasons has come under a great deal of fire in recent years. Many philosophers have offered arguments which claim to show that no version of the Humean Theory of Reasons could possibly be true. Some of these arguments claim to pose insuperable objections to the Humean theory, or to point out that it leads to intolerable consequences. Others claim to show that any version of the Humean Theory of Reasons is necessarily incoherent, because committed to theses that are flatly inconsistent with one another. These arguments are resourceful, and their variety is rich. But as I will argue, each and every one of these arguments makes best sense against a set of substantive assumptions about how Ronnie's reason is explained by his psychology. On every score, I will show how to isolate these assumptions, explain why they are substantive, and explain how to reject them. Moreover, as in the illustrative example of holistic and atomistic theories, in each case I will argue that the view that leads to a more successful version of the Humean Theory of Reasons is also the view that leads to a better account of Ronnie and Bradley's case, considered by itself.

The way that I will illustrate these points is simple. In this and following chapters I will lay out, explain, and defend a *version* of the Humean Theory of Reasons that I call *Hypotheticalism*, adopting Kant's term for an imperative which, like Ronnie's reason, is contingent on an agent's psychology.[5] Like all versions of the Humean Theory of Reasons, Hypotheticalism is

---

[5] In Kant's view, the relevant psychological feature happens to be the agent's *ends*. Kant, importantly, distinguishes ends from desires. And for Kant, ends are apparently not features of a merely empirical psychology. But Kant's account of hypothetical imperatives is apparently what he would appeal to, in order to explain the difference between Ronnie and Bradley.

distinguished by its distinctive theory about how reasons like Ronnie's *are* explained by desires.[6] What it shares with all other versions of the Humean Theory of Reasons is the view that all reasons must be explained in the same way. What I claim for Hypotheticalism is simple: (1) that it is immune to every objection to the Humean Theory of Reasons of which I am aware, (2) that in any case it gives us the best account of how Ronnie's desire explains his reason, and (3) that this means that the Humean Theory of Reasons is a viable and serious contender in ethical theory, rather than a naïve or outmoded dogma.

1.2 Desires and the Classical Argument

I've characterized the Humean Theory of Reasons as a *parity* thesis. In itself, I've claimed, it does not make any particular claims about *how* Ronnie's reason is explained by his psychology—not even to take a view about what kind of feature of Ronnie's psychology it is, that does the explaining. But most philosophical discussions of the Humean Theory of Reasons understand the view much more narrowly. They assume that to be a Humean, you have to take a view about what kind of psychological feature explains the difference between Ronnie and Bradley. They assume that a Humean must hold that this psychological state must be a *desire*.

The best philosophical reason for limiting our discussion to Humean views which hold that the difference between Ronnie and Bradley has to be explained by a desire, is that this seems to be entailed by the argument that Humeans most often use to motivate their theory: the *Classical Argument*.[7]

---

[6] I don't claim that there is any intuitive difference between the semantic fields of 'the Humean Theory of Reasons' and of 'Hypotheticalism' that merits this difference in use. On the contrary, the philosophical literature has as yet no settled term for the Humean Theory of Reasons, and 'Hypotheticalism' is as good a term as any, and certainly much better than 'the internal reasons theory', which too easily confuses the view with another important thesis—existence internalism about reasons (see section 1.2). But I need a way of distinguishing the specific view I'll be defending from the more general view, and so I claim the right to stipulate a name for my view. I don't think that the name is *entirely* undescriptive; I like it because of the connection between the thesis of Ch. 2 and the passage at [4: 421] of the *Groundwork*, in which Kant explains why it is possible to demonstrate the possibility of hypothetical imperatives by analytic means, but synthetic means are necessary in order to prove that there is a categorical imperative. Hypothetical imperatives, Kant says, are 'based on a presupposition'—which is what I say about Ronnie's reason in Ch. 2. See Schroeder [2005b].

[7] See e.g. Williams [1981a], Bond [1983], Darwall [1983], Korsgaard [1986], Millgram [1997], Hubin [1999], and Heuer [2004] for discussion of this argument.

The Classical Argument for the Humean theory has two premises. First, *Existence Internalism about Reasons*, which says that if there is a reason for someone to do something, then it must be possible to motivate her to do it for that reason. And second, the *Humean Theory of Motivation*, which says that motivation requires a desire. If having a reason requires motivation, and motivation requires a desire, then having a reason requires having a desire. As Elijah Millgram puts it succinctly,[8] 'How could anything be a reason for action if it could not motivate you to actually *do* something? And what could motivate you to do something except one of your desires?'

If the Classical Argument is the best reason to believe the Humean Theory of Reasons, then that would tell us a great deal about what *shape* the Humean Theory of Reasons might take. Then we could use this knowledge about the possible shape of viable versions of the Humean theory in order to evaluate the viability of the theory as a whole. And this is, in effect, a charitable way of understanding the strategy of many purportedly general discussions of the Humean Theory of Reasons in the literature, which really focus on specific features of a small number of versions of the Humean theory, and most often exclusively on that of Bernard Williams in 'Internal and External Reasons' in particular, as though what goes for Williams's idiosyncratic view must go for all Humean theories.[9]

But I don't think that the Classical Argument is a particularly good argument for the Humean Theory of Reasons, and I certainly don't think that it is what really gives the Humean theory its deep philosophical appeal. As I'll argue in Chapter 11, I think that the Humean Theory of Reasons should be broadly appealing for *many* different reasons, some of which I think are much deeper than that proposed by the Classical Argument.

So my parity-thesis formulation of the Humean Theory derives from healthy skepticism about the success of the Classical Argument, and from the idea that what properly motivates the Humean Theory is the premise that we know something about what *does* explain Ronnie's reason, even

---

[8] Millgram [1997: 3].

[9] For a sampling of literature focused on Williams's view, see Korsgaard [1986], Hooker [1987], Quinn [1993*b*], McDowell [1995], Smith [1995], Millgram [1996], Kriegel [1999], T. Price [1999], Lillehammer [2000], Copp [2001], Cordner [2001], Gert [2001], Hurley [2001], Sobel [2001], Thomas [2002], Brunero [2003], Robertson [2003], Tiffany [2003], Fitzpatrick [2004], Hamilton [2004], Heuer [2004], Shelton [2004], and Moreau [2005]. Book-length treatments are often less preoccupied with Williams, but see Hampton [1998] and the appendix to Scanlon [1998]. If anything, the attention paid to Williams's view seems to be accelerating.

though it is by no means uncontroversial *which* psychological feature does this explaining. But more importantly, the main general philosophical reasons to want to know whether the Humean Theory of Reasons works are reasons which don't discriminate between versions which say that reasons must be explained by *desires*, and those which say that reasons must be explained by some other psychological feature.

The most general philosophical reason to be interested in the prospects for the Humean Theory of Reasons—and the reason for which it has attracted so much attention—is that it seems to license a certain kind of doubt about the objective prescriptivity of morality. For it is plausible that what makes morality objectively prescriptive is that it entails the existence of reasons—this makes it *prescriptive*—which are reasons for absolutely anyone, no matter what she is like—which makes this prescriptivity *objective*. But if whether a reason is a reason for some individual must always be explained by some psychological feature of that agent, then it is more than puzzling how it could be that *anything* is a reason for absolutely everyone, no matter what she is like. So it is puzzling how morality could be objectively prescriptive.

For these reasons, some have held that moral claims are systematically false, since they *purport* to be objectively prescriptive, but are not. On one viable reading, this is how to understand Mackie's 'queerness' argument,[10] and Richard Joyce has more recently advocated this argument as the best argument for moral error theory.[11] Others have concluded for identical reasons that the prescriptivity of morality must not be objective after all. So this is, for example, Gilbert Harman's principal argument in favor of his brand of moral relativism.[12] And still others have been led by this argument to conclude that the objectivity of morality is not, after all, prescriptive, in the sense of entailing reasons. So this is, for example, Philippa Foot's argument in 'Morality as a System of Hypothetical Imperatives' that though moral norms *apply* to everyone, they must do so in some other way than by providing them with reasons.[13] And it is easy to see how to expand this argument in order to use it to argue for a moral fictionalism, as Joyce does, or for a revisionary expressivism, as Mackie is sometimes thought to accept, or for indexicalist or contextualist views about moral language.[14] It

---

[10] Mackie [1977].   [11] Joyce [2001].   [12] Harman [1975], [1978], [1985].
[13] Foot [1975].   [14] Such as those in e.g. Dreier [1990], [1999], and Timmons [1999].

appears to be a very powerful argument, given the truth of the Humean Theory of Reasons.

The Humean Theory of Reasons has rightly received a great deal of attention in the last twenty-five years, largely because it is seen to potentially have precisely these kinds of vast implications about morality. But notice that nothing in these skeptical arguments hinged on making any assumptions about what kind of psychological state is needed in order to explain reasons. *Whatever* kind of psychological state this is, it will be puzzling how it could be that *anyone* has the right kind in order to explain some reason, *no matter what she is like*. So if we are really interested in the Humean Theory of Reasons because we are concerned about these kinds of possible implications, then we should cast our nets *wide*—we should be interested in any version of the Humean Theory of Reasons, and not simply ones which hold that the psychological state needed to distinguish Ronnie and Bradley is a desire. And so anyone interested in defending the objective prescriptivity of morality should be just as concerned to defend it against any version of the Humean Theory of Reasons, broadly construed as a parity thesis.

Nevertheless, I'm going to adopt a bit of stipulative terminology, and introduce the term 'desire' as a stipulative abbreviation for 'the kind of psychological state, whatever it is, that ultimately explains the difference between Ronnie and Bradley'. This orthographical conceit allows us to state the Humean Theory of Reasons more concisely and familiarly:

HTR   Every reason is explained by a desire in the same way as Ronnie's is.

My choice of stipulative term is not without point; I will eventually argue, in Chapter 8, that desires in this technical sense really are desires in at least something more like the ordinary philosophical usage. So I do, ultimately, think that the best versions of the Humean theory are 'desire-dependence' views. But though my argument for this thesis in Chapter 8 depends on part of my argument in Chapter 2, everything in Chapters 2 through 7 is independent of the conclusions of Chapter 8. So everything that I have to say in those chapters speaks to the viability of *any* version of the Humean Theory of Reasons *broadly conceived*—even those which hold that the difference between Ronnie and Bradley is explained by an intention, a whim, a craving, a pleasant sensation, or a valuing.

But before we can start looking for explicit theories about how Ronnie's reason *is* explained by his desire (in this stipulative sense), we need to lay some groundwork for how to talk about reasons, which can sometimes be distractingly complicated. Indeed, I hold that much substantive disagreement can be attributed simply to some easily isolated complications in talk about reasons.[15]

1.3 Reasons: Objective, Subjective, Motivating, Explanatory

It is important to get clear on the different senses of 'reason' and on a few preliminary questions: in which sense is the Humean Theory a theory about reasons? what sort of thing are reasons in this sense? and so on. This is important both to avoid confusions and in order to set aside the residual uneasiness that some philosophers have with talk about reasons. Philosophers who experience this uneasiness are sometimes bothered enough by the different ways in which the word 'reason' is used to feel that there is no interesting thing that it is about, but only a context-dependent mess. And sometimes they are bothered enough by the fact that philosophers never began talking about reasons until the middle of the twentieth century to wonder whether the sense of 'reason' which the Humean Theory is about is simply a recent philosopher's invention, out of this context-dependent mess.

On the second score, I think these philosophers are clearly wrong. Reasons, in the sense in which we will be primarily interested, are not a philosopher's invention, but are very much the property of ordinary common sense, whether or not philosophers managed to get interested in them prior to the middle of the twentieth century. Reasons in this sense are commonly mentioned in popular music, appear often in the titles of legal documents going back for centuries, and appear repeatedly in very old uses in the *Oxford English Dictionary*. Unfortunately, as the *OED*'s entry on 'reason' also suggests, the uses of 'reason' *are* many and diverse. And so skeptics about the notion of a reason are right to be cautiously suspicious about untutored intuitions about what is and is not a reason. So

---

[15] See my [2007*b*], 'Reasons and Agent-Neutrality' and [2008], 'Having Reasons'.

it is my aim in this section to make several distinctions between different legitimate senses of 'reason' in order to set aside the one in which we will be interested, and in order to set out some substantive background views that I will be taking about reasons in a preliminary way. The idea is both to demonstrate that there is a natural way to carve up the domain in such a way that the various uses of 'reason' all turn out to make sense and to be about interesting things, and to give us tools for keeping in view which of these senses we have in mind, the better to tutor our intuitions about reasons.

So setting aside a traditional sense in which 'reason' is used in the singular as a name for the human faculty of reasoning, or as a certain source of rational obligations, and the sense in which it is used as a verb, 'to reason', which are easy to distinguish, let us focus on senses in which it is used as a count noun, of which there are still several uses in English. One way that we can use it is in citing facts that figure in explanations of why something is the case. For example, we can say that the reason why the dinosaurs went extinct is that a large meteorite hit the earth sixty-six million years ago. The word 'reason', used in this way, does not necessarily have to pick out one of the *causes* of the thing being explained. Whether we think that it does depends on whether we believe in non-causal explanation. Suppose, for example, that we think that we can explain why there can't be circles with some points further away from their centers than others. We might think that this is so because what it is *to be* a circle is simply to have all of one's points equidistant from one's center. If we think this, then we will think that this fact is the reason *why* no circle has some points further from its center than others. Whatever sort of thing we think is appropriate to figure in the 'because' clause of an answer to a question of the form, 'Why is *P* the case?' is going to count as a reason why *P* is the case in this *explanatory* sense of 'reason'.

The word 'reason' also has a *normative* sense. In this sense, we can say that one reason for Ronnie to go to the party is that there will be dancing there, even if Ronnie does not actually go to the party. This is the sense in which Ronnie differs from Bradley. Philosophers sometimes distinguish this sense by saying that it is the sense in which reasons *count in favor* of what they are reasons for. I think this way of talking is slippery, so let us think about this sense of the word 'reason' as follows: if we suppose that neither Ronnie nor Bradley is aware that there will be dancing at the party tonight, the fact that there will be dancing there still counts, in this sense, as a reason for Ronnie but not for Bradley to go there. When context requires, I'll distinguish by calling this the 'objective normative' or 'objective' sense of the word 'reason'.[16] It is the sense in which Hypotheticalism holds that reasons are explained by desires. For most of this book, when I use the word 'reason', it will therefore be this sense which I have in mind.

Another commonly distinguished sense of 'reason' is exhibited by all of the following kinds of claim:

1   The reason for which Bianca took a sip is that her glass contained gin and tonic.
2   The reason for which Bernie took a sip is that he believed that his glass contained gin and tonic.
3   The reason why Bianca took a sip is that her glass contained gin and tonic.
4   The reason why Bernie took a sip is that he believed that his glass contained gin and tonic.

Philosophers typically call these claims about *motivating* reasons. The first thing to notice about motivating reason claims is that they are *not* merely explanatory reason claims. Suppose that I tell you that the reason why Bernie took a sip is that he believed that his glass contained gin and tonic, but continue: 'and he has a special kind of virus that causes him to move his hand toward his mouth and make swallowing motions whenever the word "tonic" pops into his head'. In the sense in which we had an answer to why the dinosaurs went extinct, I've answered the question, 'why did Bernie take a sip?' But I haven't properly made a claim about motivating reasons. Such claims require something more.

Although the locutions in English by which we make claims about motivating reasons constitute an interesting class, I don't think that motivating reasons constitute a deep ontological category. For it looks like they are merely a special case of a broader category. Suppose that Bernie does not, in fact, take a sip, but that he is somewhat moved to take a sip, in the sense of experiencing some *pro tanto* motivation to take a sip.[17] We can't

---

[16] The appropriateness of this terminology is an unfortunate consequence of etymology, as objective reasons, on my view, are no more *objective* than subjective reasons, distinguished below. As I know of no better terminology, I will stick with this one.

[17] Compare the kind of *pro tanto* motivation to which Michael Smith's version of motivational internalism appeals in Smith [1994].

talk about the reason *why* Bernie took a sip, because he didn't take a sip. But we can talk about the reason why he was moved to take a sip. Here we seem to be making the same *kind* of claim. Now take a step further back. Suppose that Bernie is standing there, holding the glass he believes to contain gin and tonic, and wanting to drink a gin and tonic, but he hasn't done anything yet. There is a sense in which he has a reason to take a sip, even if something distracts him and he is never even slightly motivated to take a sip. Intuitively, the reason that he has to take a sip is that he believes that his glass contains gin and tonic. Moreover, if he is somewhat moved to take a sip, it is this reason for which he will be somewhat moved. And if he actually goes on to take a sip, the reason why he took a sip will have been the same—that he believed that his glass contained gin and tonic.

So I hold that motivating reasons are a subclass of reasons in this broader sense of 'reason'. I do not, however, hold that they are a subclass of *objective normative* reasons. For the sense in which Bernie has a reason to take a sip is not the objective normative sense that we distinguished earlier. Whether he has such a reason seems not to depend on how things are, independently of his beliefs, but on what he believes, independently of whether it is true. Suppose that Bernie's glass does not, in fact, contain gin and tonic, but rather gasoline. This does not change our judgment about whether, in the sense presently at issue, he has a reason to take a sip. After all, we can reasonably expect him to take a sip, we can reasonably criticize his deliberations if he does not take a sip, and if he does take a sip, we can say that he did so for a reason. All this new information about Bernie gives us is another sense—the objective sense—in which there is a reason for Bernie to set the glass down without taking a sip.[18]

Objective normative reasons, then, depend on how things are independently of the agent's beliefs (even when the relevant way things are

[18] As I noted, Hypotheticalism is an account about *objective* normative reasons. But some 'Humean' views are really only accounts of *subjective* normative reasons. For example, standard decision theory seems to be such an account—at least, it seems to be an account of the corresponding subjective sense of 'ought'. So for a long time, many philosophers assumed that *all* versions of the Humean Theory of Reasons work in this way. One of the main contributions of Williams's seminal paper, Williams [1981a], was to point out that it is possible to give a Humean account of *objective* normative reasons. That is the reason for which he originally introduced the gin and tonic example. (Unfortunately, there is also good evidence that Williams thought his account applied *equally* well to subjective and to objective reasons, subsuming them under a single category, which may have confused the issue again.) See Williams [1981a: 102–5], [2001: 92–3].

is a matter of what the agent believes[19]). Subjective normative reasons depend on what the agent believes, independently of how things actually are. Explanatory reasons are not normative at all; they are only the reasons why something is the case. On my account, assertions about motivating reasons are assertions about both subjective normative reasons *and* about explanatory reasons:

> **Motivating**   For R to be the (motivating) reason for which X did A is for the fact that R was a subjective normative reason for X to do A to constitute an explanatory reason why X did A.[20]

The three most fundamental senses of 'reason', then, on this view, are the explanatory sense, the objective normative sense, and the subjective normative sense.[21]

I also, however, favor a simple theory about the relationship between the objective and subjective normative senses of the word 'reason'. It's a substantive theory, but it's quite natural, and I think it is relatively standard. According to this theory, subjective reasons are to be understood in terms of objective reasons. Bernie counts as having a reason to take a sip by virtue of believing that his glass contains gin and tonic, on this view, because the content of this belief is the right kind of thing to be an objective reason for Bernie to take a sip—were it true:

> **Subjective**   For R to be a subjective reason for X to do A is for X to believe R, and for it to be the case that R is the kind of thing, if true, to be an objective reason for X to do A.

This formula, I think, is only roughly correct.[22] But I hold that some claim like it is going to be true.[23]

---

[19] This sounds strange, but facts about what an agent believes may themselves be objective normative reasons for her to act. For example, the fact that Jon believes that he is Napolean may be an objective normative reason for him to seek psychological counseling.

[20] This account will plausibly still require further restriction—my aim here is only to articulate the broad picture that I think is correct.

[21] Not: three kinds of reason. There is no further sense of 'reason' in which these are three kinds of reason, in the way that it is controversial whether there are both epistemic and practical reasons for belief, and relatively uncontroversial that there are both moral and prudential reasons for action.

[22] Amendments are necessary in light of a distinction that I'll make in section 2.1 between reasons and background conditions.

[23] 1. This is a substantive claim, for which I won't argue here. According to a quite different view, subjective reasons are basic. On this view, for R to be an objective reason for X to do A is for R to be

If Motivating and Subjective are both true, then the fundamental sense of 'reason' that is relevant in all but purely explanatory contexts is the objective normative sense. It is this sense in which there is a reason for Ronnie but not for Bradley to go to the party tonight, and so it is this sense of 'reason' in which Ronnie's reason appears to be explained by his desires. The Humean Theory of Reasons claims that all objective normative reasons are explained in the same way as Ronnie's. Hypotheticalism, as a version of the Humean Theory of Reasons, has a particular story about *how* Ronnie's reason is to be explained by his desires. This is what gives it its particular story about how all reasons are to be explained by desires. So if we grant the truth of Motivating and Subjective, Hypotheticalism amounts to a comprehensive explanation of where reasons come from, in all of these senses of the word 'reason'. And that is what Hypotheticalism aspires to do.

1.4 Reasons To, Reasons For, and the Reasons that are To and For

But even focusing on the case of objective normative reasons, there are still a number of ways that we use the word 'reason'. A small sampling:

5   The fact that there will be dancing at the party is a reason for Ronnie to go to the party.

6   There is a reason for Ronnie to go to the party.

true, and for it to be the case that were X to believe that R, R would be a subjective reason for X to do A. This alternative view takes a very different explanatory strategy. And according to my interpretation of Dancy [2000] (which he has accepted in personal conversation), he thinks that neither objective reasons nor subjective reasons are basic, but that both objective and subjective reasons are accounted for in terms of some third thing: 'there are just two questions which we use the single notion of a reason to answer' [2000: 2]. Moreover, even among those who accept that subjective reasons should be accounted for in terms of objective reasons, there are several distinct views about how to do this.

2. Objection: on this view, claims 1 and 3, the Bianca sentences, semantically express propositions that are true, but claims 2 and 4, the Bernie sentences, semantically express propositions that are false. But this is no great cost. For on any viable view, one or the other of these pairs of sentences will semantically express falsehoods. Suppose that you ask Bernie what reasons he has to take a sip. He will tell you that his reason is that his glass contains gin and tonic. If you ask me, however, I will tell you that his reason is that he *believes* that his glass contains gin and tonic. But clearly Bernie and I are not, in fact, in disagreement about what his reason is. We are only in disagreement about whether his glass does, in fact, contain gin and tonic. So any view that we take about what subjective reasons are must explain why either Bernie or I have to utter a sentence which semantically expresses a falsehood. I think it's easier to explain my utterance in this way than to explain Bernie's—and if that is right, it *supports* the account just given. But nothing turns on this point in what follows.

7 The fact that Katie needs help is a reason to help Katie.

8 There is a reason to help Katie.

Ascriptions of objective normative reasons still vary in two significant dimensions. On the one hand, they can make reference to what the reason is for someone to do something, or they can merely say that there is some reason for her to do it. On the other, they can say that the reason is a reason for some particular agent or agents in some particular group to perform the action, or they can say merely that it is a reason to perform that action, *simpliciter*.

Let us take the first difference first. On the face of it, 'there is', in 'there is a reason for Ronnie to go to the party', is an existential quantifier. On the face of it, it is true that there is a reason for Ronnie to go to the party because there is something—namely, the fact that there will be dancing at the party—that is a reason for Ronnie to go to the party. Claim 6 is true, that is, because claim 5 is. I'm going to proceed throughout this book on the natural assumption that this is correct, and that claims about there being a reason for someone to do something are merely existential generalizations of claims to the effect that something or other is this reason.[24] This assumption will come up more than once, but I hold that we should need a very good argument in order to be persuaded to reject it.

Now compare claims 5 and 6, on the one hand, with claims 7 and 8, on the other. 5 and 6 seem to express a relation that is *agent-relational*,[25] in the

---

[24] Thomas Nagel, notably, seems to reject this assumption in his [1970], and Raz [1975: 28] comes close, even though he is committed to accepting it. I'll discuss one possible motivation for doing so in section 2.3. In fact, *many* theories about reasons seem to be indirectly committed to this view. For many theories of reasons give accounts of what it is for there to be a reason for X to do A which don't tell us what it is for R to be a reason for X to do A. For example, compare the account of Michael Smith in his [1994: 151–77]. Yet if the former were an existential quantification into the latter, then surely a correct account *has* to proceed by telling us what it is for R to be a reason for X to do A. But while I think that Nagel does have reasons for taking this approach, I suspect that most others who are implicitly committed to this kind of view simply haven't completely thought out these implications of their views.

[25] Notice that the way that I am using this terminology, for a reason to be agent-relational is for it to be a reason *for* someone. So it follows that a reason can be both agent-relational and agent-neutral. 'Agent-relative' is officially the term used in the literature for reasons that are agent-relational but not agent-neutral (Nagel [1970: 90–5]), but this is complicated by the fact that philosophers interested in this distinction typically follow Nagel [1970: 47] in making an artificial assumption about what *kind* of action a reason can be in favor of—that it can only be of the form, *promote state of affairs p*. It is this artificial assumption that enables the use of the uncontroversial distinction between agent-relative and agent-neutral reasons to play the role that it usually does in distinguishing consequentialism from deontology. Compare McNaughton and Rawling [1991], who recognize this and therefore insist on

sense that it has an agent for one of its relata. This relation is a three-place relation between the thing that is the reason,[26] the agent for whom it is a reason, and the action-type that it is a reason to perform. (Although 6 looks as though it only has two places, recall that we've just decided that it is an existential quantification into this three-place relation.) But 7 and 8 seem to express a relation that is *agent-neutral*, in the sense that it has no space for an agent as one of its relata. This relation is a two-place relation between the consideration that is the reason and the action that it is a reason to perform.

Philosophers take many different views about the relationship between this triadic 'reason' relation and the dyadic one.[27] According to one class of views, the dyadic relation is basic, and the triadic relation is to be understood in terms of it. Some philosophers seem to hold, for example, that when we say that R is a reason for X to do A, the 'for X' part works like a sentential operator of some kind. According to this view, when R is a reason for X to do A, this is because *from X's point of view* R is a reason to do A, or because for X it is *as if* R is a reason to do A. This approach is compatible with many different ways of understanding how the 'point of view' operator is to be understood. According to another view in this same class, *actions* are not the proper relatum of the agent-neutral reason relation at all. Rather, this relation is a relation between considerations and *propositions*, or considerations and *states of affairs*. It is open to someone who holds this view[28] to claim that to say that R is a reason for X to do A is to say that R is an agent-neutral reason counting in favor of the state of affairs, *that X does A.*

According to yet a third similar view, agent-relational reasons exist for an agent to perform those actions which are *means* to, or *ways* of doing, something that there is an agent-neutral reason to do. On this view, there is some set of actions that there is reason to do, and individuals have reasons to do things other than these because doing so is a means to doing

---

making the relative/neutral distinction in a different way. See my 'Teleology, Agent-Relative Value, and "Good" ', for further discussion.

[26] Scanlon uses the handy fudge-word 'consideration' for the category of things that can stand in this place of the relation and of which it can properly be said that they are reasons [1998], so I'll use that term from time to time. We'll discuss what kind of things these are more fully below.

[27] The following views are discussed in detail in Schroeder [2007b].

[28] Some who hold that propositions or states of affairs, rather than actions, are the relata of the *reason* relation don't take this view. They still hold that the basic relation is triadic and has an agent-place. John Broome apparently holds this view, for example. See Broome [1999: 399–401], Wedgwood [2006]. I catalogue a few objections to each of these ways of treating reasons as taking propositions in Schroeder [2004].

the things that there is reason to do.[29] And on yet a fourth view, the agent-relational reason relation is merely illusory, and the only sense in which reasons are relative to agents is the subjective sense. All these views hold that the agent-relational reason relation is in some way derivative from the agent-neutral reason relation.

I've argued against all these interesting views elsewhere; I introduce them here in order to illustrate that the view I will take is substantive and controversial, even though I think it is also extremely natural. This natural view is that the agent-neutral relation is to be analyzed as a universal quantification into the agent-place of the agent-relational relation. One attractive feature of this account is that it lets us assimilate agent-neutral reason ascriptions like 7 to cases such as the following: we're deciding whether to go to the party tonight, we all like to dance, and our plans are independent of Bradley's. Someone says, 'one reason to go to the party is that there will be dancing there'. She isn't asserting that there is a reason *simpliciter* to go to the party—she knows full well that this is not a reason for Bradley to go there. All she means to assert is that it is a reason for *us* to go there. On my view, agent-neutral ascriptions—sentences such as 7 and 8—*all* work like this:

> **Agent-Neutral** For R to be a reason to do A is for R to be an agent-relational reason for all of [us] to do A.

As I understand Agent-Neutral, context can determine who counts as one of 'us' for the purposes of the utterance. In contexts in which it is clear that we are leaving Bradley out (since he obviously doesn't like to dance, and isn't with us, anyway), we can say that the fact that there will be dancing at the party is a reason for us to go there but not implicate him. But in other contexts, particularly moral contexts, it will be clear that *everyone* counts as one of 'us'. If the fact that Katie needs help is a moral reason *simpliciter* to help Katie, then it is a reason for each and every one to help her. In this way, Agent-Neutral treats the agent-neutral sentences that are obviously merely elliptical for agent-relational sentences in the same way as it treats those which are not. I like this result.

---

[29] This view will play a very important role in Ch. 3. It is a very old view, and was explicitly advocated and defended by Ralph Cudworth [1731] and Richard Price [1948].

So this is my account of these matters: the basic objective normative reason relation has three places, as in the relation expressed in 5. But we commonly existentially quantify into the consideration-place—the place for the thing which counts as the reason. This gives us locutions like that in 6. We also commonly universally quantify into the agent-place. When we do so, we do so under a restriction that can vary from context to context. In some contexts, including ones in which moral considerations are salient, this restriction is trivial, and so the quantification is over all agents or perhaps even over all possible agents. This is how we get claims like 7. And finally, if we do both of these things, the result is a locution like that in 8. But in all cases, it is the three-place objective normative reason relation that is basic.

These claims, though substantive, are extremely natural and less precise versions of them are in fact fairly widely (although not universally!) accepted. I am not going to provide further argument for them here, other than to note that they seem to deal nicely with the surface phenomena regarding these kinds of 'reason' locutions.[30] What I want to be clear on for present purposes is this: you can argue against the views that I develop in later chapters, and against my arguments for those views, by arguing against these basic assumptions. But an argument that simply *assumes* different answers to these questions simply begs the question against Hypotheticalism. The analytic framework employed by Hypotheticalism is part of the view.

Since it holds the natural view that the triadic relation is basic, it is this relation that Hypotheticalism hopes to elucidate or to explain. This should not be a great surprise. Hypotheticalism, like the Humean Theory of Reasons generally, starts by noticing when it is that a consideration is a reason for one agent but not for another—as in such cases as Ronnie and Bradley's. In Ronnie and Bradley's case, it is not that there is *no* reason for Bradley to go to the party. On the contrary, the fact that there will be good food there may well be a reason for him to go. The relevant datum in Ronnie and Bradley's case is that the very thing which is the reason for Ronnie to go is not a reason for Bradley to go. And this is a datum in which both the

---

[30] I do argue that this provides the best way of understanding the connection between the agent-relational and agent-neutral reason relations in my paper, 'Reasons and Agent-Neutrality' [2007*b*], and I support my views about the connection between objective and subjective normative reasons in 'Having Reasons' [2008].

consideration that is the reason, and the agent for whom it is a reason, are relevant. So it is no surprise that it is the *triadic* relation that Hypotheticalism, like every version of the Humean Theory of Reasons, seeks to explain.

Finally, since we are taking seriously the idea that when we say that there is a reason to do something, we really mean that *there is* something that is this reason, it is worth getting clear on what sort of things can be reasons. This is important because at a first pass, anything can count as an objective normative reason for someone to do something. The height of the Empire State Building is a reason not to jump off. Obesity is a reason to eat well and exercise regularly. Bas van Fraassen is a reason to study philosophy of science at Princeton University, Schrödinger's wave equation is a reason for physics students to study partial differential equations (as well as for the non-mathematically-inclined to stay out of physics), and the flu is a reason to get your flu shot. It's no wonder that philosophers tend to use the ontologically unloaded fudge-word 'consideration' in referring to the kind of thing that reasons are.

But every time that we can cite one of these things as a reason for someone to do something, it is also true that there is a fact or true proposition in the neighborhood which we could cite equally well. Suppose that I've just explained to you that the height of the Empire State Building is a reason not to jump off, but you're still undecided about your course of action. Will you be convinced after I tell you that another reason not to jump off is that it is so high? Intuitively, I've given you the same reason all over again. Now in my view, it is a poor methodological rule, in counting reasons, to think that two reasons are the same reason just because we ought not to weigh them separately in our deliberations.[31] So I don't think that this by itself proves anything about what reasons are. But I do think that in every case in which something can be cited as a reason for someone to do something, there is some fact or true proposition which can be cited equally well. And I do not think that there is a person or an equation or a disease which can be cited equally well as the reason not to jump off the Empire State Building.

So if any unified kind of thing is going to be a candidate for the sort of thing that reasons are, I take it that it will either have to be true

---

[31] I'll explain this further in Chs. 2 and 7.

propositions or facts, if we distinguish them. In my view, things go more smoothly if we say that reasons are true propositions than if we say that they are facts, but none of our discussion will turn on that question. What *is* important, is to observe how claims that something *other* than a fact or true proposition is a reason need to be understood. If what I've just said is right, then these claims are not alternatives to taking a stand on which fact or true proposition is a reason. Most pertinently, if we say that someone's reason is her desire, then we can be plausibly reinterpreted as meaning that her reason is the fact that she has that desire.[32] This will be important in Chapter 2.

1.5 Organization

Our task, then, to return to the main thread, is to look for answers to the question of how Ronnie's reason is explained by his desire (in the stipulative sense), see how some views about this question can facilitate certain kinds of apparently general objection to the Humean Theory of Reasons, and show how rejecting these views can let Hypotheticalism give a better account of Ronnie and Bradley's case, in the first place. In Chapters 2 through 4, we'll examine some very general, high-level theories about how the explanation of differences in reasons works, and some very interesting, sophisticated, objections to the Humean Theory to which these theories can lead. In Chapters 5 through 7 we'll turn to some more obvious objections to the Humean theory—that it is extensionally incorrect, either allowing for too many reasons or allowing for too few (or both!), and consequently raises troubles for the objectivity of morality. In Chapter 8 I fill in a Hypotheticalist account of desire, in Chapter 9 I illustrate some potential advantages of Hypotheticalism for normative epistemology and the theory of motivation, and in Chapter 10 I turn to address some more general objections to the Humean Theory, relating to the accusation that

---

[32] A very common and, as I'm now arguing, misleading way of characterizing the Humean theory is as the view that reasons *are* desires, or that desires *provide* reasons. Consider, for example the title of Ruth Chang's recent paper, 'Can Desires Provide Reasons for Action?', or its first sentence: 'On a widely accepted story of human agency, *all* reasons for acting, intending, and desiring are provided by the fact that the agent wants something or would want it under certain conditions' [2004: 56]. This suggests a particular view not only about what *explains* someone's reasons, but about *what* her reasons are—a view that it will be the purpose of Ch. 2 to reject.

it is *instrumentalist* in some objectionable sense. Finally, in Chapter 11, I return to reconsider why it is that Hypotheticalism makes such an attractive view, and what challenges this poses us, if we remain resolute in our anti-Humean predilections. As I noted earlier, I don't claim to have a conclusive argument for Hypotheticalism, but I *do* aim in Chapter 11 to illustrate the diversity of its attractions.

2

Background Conditions

2.1 The No Background Conditions View

Ronnie's and Bradley's reasons differ *because* of the difference in their desires: the fact that there will be dancing at the party tonight is a reason for Ronnie to go there because he desires to dance. That Ronnie desires to dance is part of *why* this is a reason for him to go there. But different versions of the Humean Theory of Reasons differ with respect to their theories about *how* Ronnie's reason is explained by his desire. One obvious way in which they may differ is with respect to what they think all of this 'because' and 'why' talk is *about*, and it is this kind of difference that we'll consider in Chapters 2 through 4.

According to a very common theory that I'll call the *No Background Conditions* view, there is only one way for the fact that Ronnie desires to dance to explain why there is a reason for him to go to the party. It is for this fact to be *part* of the reason for Ronnie to go to the party. So, for example, many philosophers say that the fact that there will be dancing at the party isn't *really* a reason for Ronnie to go there, all by itself—but only in *combination* with the fact that Ronnie desires to dance.[1] Similarly, Thomas Nagel claims that properly speaking, the reason for someone to do something has to be a modally sufficient condition for it to be the case that there is a reason for her to do it.[2] So on Nagel's view, anything that has

---

[1] 'A complete reason consists of all the facts stated by the non-redundant premises of a sound, deductive argument entailing as its conclusion a proposition of the form "There is a reason for *P* to *V*"' Raz [1999c: 228]. Dancy [2004: 97–8] gives a good statement of some of the central reasons why the 'deductive' part of Raz's view needs to be replaced with an explanatory requirement. This modification would identify Raz's view with the denial of background conditions on 'complete' reasons. See also Crisp [2000: 36–40].

[2] Nagel [1970: 90–5]. This assumption is actually necessary for Nagel's original distinction between agent-relative and agent-neutral reasons (which he calls 'subjective' and 'objective', ibid.) to work. So that is obviously a theory-laden way of making the distinction.

to be appealed to in order to explain the difference between Ronnie and Bradley has to be *part* of the reason for Ronnie to go to the party.

The No Background Conditions view is an interesting theory. It tells us something informative about the *way* in which Ronnie's desire explains his reason. It explains it, on this view, simply by the fact that he has this desire being *part* of his reason. And it is clearly a substantive theory. For it denies a distinction with respect to reasons that is a perfectly good distinction in many other domains. Although being inaugurated is a necessary condition for someone to be president of the United States, and the fact that George W. Bush was inaugurated less than four years ago is part of why he is president, the fact that Bush was inaugurated isn't part of the president of the United States. It is merely a background condition on George W. Bush being president of the United States. Similarly, in order to be a piece of corn on the cob, a vegetable must have grown on a maize plant. But the fact that this particular yellow, buttered, and salted tasty morsel was grown on a maize plant isn't part of the piece of corn on the cob that I'm eating—the piece of corn on the cob is just the yellow, buttered, and salted tasty morsel itself.[3] So in general, we have no trouble distinguishing between the facts necessary in order to explain why something is an *F*, and what the thing is, which is the *F*. The No Background Conditions view denies this distinction with respect to reasons, and that is how it comes by its name.

The No Background Conditions view is not the kind of theory that philosophers usually make explicit. It is the kind of view which sympathizers are apt to take for granted.[4] But like many such assumptions, it is actually very important, and it is going to resurface again throughout this book. But to get an idea for some of its implications, I want to consider its

[3] There are also, it is true, cases in which this distinction has proved to be hard to maintain—e.g. in the literature on causation. What we'll eventually need, in order to defend the robustness of this distinction, is a further criterion for what sort of things reasons are that will discriminate between typical reasons and typical background conditions—for example, between the fact that there will be dancing at the party tonight, and the fact that Ronnie likes to dance. Hypotheticalism's criterion will be the subject of section 2.3.

[4] Here is what Ulrike Heuer [2004: 53] says: 'If all this is right, there must be something wrong with the Humean account of reasons. The claim that it is never a reason for an action that it satisfies a desire *directly contradicts* the conclusion of the argument from motivation that a person has a reason to act precisely if the action leads to the satisfaction of one of her desires' (italics added). Since these two theses come into conflict only if we assume that there is no distinction between reasons and background conditions, Heuer's claim that they *directly contradict* one another underscores the extent to which she takes the denial of this distinction for granted.

role in motivating a hard version of one of the standard objections to the Humean Theory of Reasons: that it makes practical reasoning out to be Objectionably Self-Regarding. Now the naïve version of the Self-Regarding objection to the Humean theory is an old one, and does not itself presuppose the No Background Conditions view. But as we'll see shortly, the most sophisticated version of this objection *does* presuppose this view.

The naïve version of the Self-Regarding objection arises like this. One feature of Ronnie and Bradley's case is that each has a desire that is about himself—Ronnie desires that *he* go dancing, and Bradley desires that *he* stay away from dancing. One possible version of the Humean Theory of Reasons—the *self-interest* theory—claims that this feature of Ronnie and Bradley's case generalizes to the case of all other reasons. According to the self-interest theory, all reasons are to be explained by *self-interested* desires. And in some natural sense, the self-interest theory makes practical reason out to be objectionably self-regarding. On the self-interest theory, even if Ryan cares more about Katie's well-being than about his own chances to go dancing, the fact that Katie needs help is not a reason for him to help Katie, unless helping her serves some self-interested desire of his, such as the desire that *he* gets his picture in the paper for saving her life.

The self-interest theory, like the version of the global Humean Theory discussed in Chapter 1, gives us a good model for the relationship between Hypotheticalism and other versions of the Humean Theory of Reasons. Most versions of the Humean Theory of Reasons don't hold that the fact that Ronnie's and Bradley's desires are self-interested is an essential feature of their case. Most such views hold that what is important is only that they are *desires*. These desires need not be self-interested; they might be completely altruistic. For all that most versions of the Humean Theory of Reasons tell us, all desires might be completely altruistic. What is important is that reasons are to be explained by interests *of* the self, not that they are to be explained by interests *in* the self. Hypotheticalism adopts this view, and is therefore weaker than the self-interest theory. This version of the 'self-regarding' objection therefore does not get a grip.

Astute critics, however, are unsatisfied by this move. They hold that the Humean Theory of Reasons still makes practical reason out to be objectionably self-regarding in some way. It is useful on this score, as on many, to think about how Thomas Nagel sets things up in *The Possibility of Altruism.* In that book, Nagel wants to understand how it could be possible for an agent to act for reasons that are genuinely altruistic. But Nagel defines altruism in such a way that being motivated by genuinely other-regarding desires does not count as being *purely* altruistic.[5]

Why does Nagel think that being motivated by altruistic, other-regarding desires should not count as altruism? Nagel, as I've observed and we'll see in more detail in section 2.3, does not distinguish between reasons and background conditions. So he holds that if the reason for Ryan to help Katie needs to be explained, in part, by one of Ryan's desires, then that desire must be mentioned in the complete statement of Ryan's reason to help Katie. So on Nagel's view, the reason for Ryan to help Katie must be, strictly speaking, that Katie needs help *and* that Ryan wants Katie to have whatever she needs.[6] On this view, there is still a sense in which Ryan's reason to help Katie is self-regarding. It would not be a reason for Ryan unless Ryan got mentioned as part of the reason.

There is a further very natural assumption which strengthens this result. That assumption is that when Ryan is reasoning well, the kinds of thing about which he should be thinking are his reasons. Call this the *Deliberative Constraint.* So suppose that Ryan is reasoning well. Can the thought that Katie needs help motivate him to go help her? On Nagel's understanding of the Humean Theory of Reasons, it cannot. For it isn't really a reason for him to help her. The only reason for Ryan to help Katie, on this view, is that she needs help and Ryan wants her to have whatever she needs. So if Ryan is reasoning well, on this view, he will have to think about whether or not he wants Katie to have whatever she needs.

Nagel assumes that there are No Background Conditions on reasons, and accepts the Deliberative Constraint. From the No Background Conditions assumption it follows that if the Humean Theory of Reasons is correct, then Ryan must get mentioned as part of his reason. But from the Deliberative Constraint, it then follows that Ryan must think about his own desires in deliberating about whether to help Katie. On such a view, practical

---

[5] Nagel tells us that 'by altruism I mean not abject self-sacrifice, but merely a willingness to act in consideration of the interests of other persons, without the need of ulterior motives' [1970: 79]. And he allows that motivation by benevolence or sympathy satisfies this account. But then he tells us that what he *really* wants to demonstrate is the possibility of *pure* altruism. *Pure* altruism is 'the direct influence of one person's interest on the actions of another, simply because in itself the interest of the former provides the latter with a reason to act' [1970: 80].

[6] Or whatever we assume Ryan's altruistic desire about Katie to be.

reasoning really does turn out to be objectionably self-regarding. It is *objectionable* to think that when Ryan is thinking about whether to help Katie, his reasoning is somehow flawed or even enthymematic, if he does not take a moment to reflect on whether he wants Katie to have what she needs. Such a view commits agents who are deliberating well and non-enthymematically to taking what Mark Johnston calls the *pornographic attitude*: they are moved only by considerations about the satisfaction of their own desires—even when these desires happen to be other-directed.[7] This is why Nagel hopes for the possibility of altruism in a much stronger sense—not reasons to act which derive from purely altruistic motives, but reasons to act which don't derive from motives at all. He holds that this is the only way in which one's reasoning can avoid being self-regarding.

2.2 Background Conditions

By focusing on Ryan's case (in which the explanatory connection between reason and desire is at best not obvious) this discussion creates the impression that there is a tension between the Humean Theory of Reasons, the No Background Conditions view, and the Deliberative Constraint. But the role of the Humean Theory of Reasons in creating this tension is illusory. Even in Ronnie's case, there is a tension between the latter two ideas. The fact that Ronnie desires to dance has to be mentioned in the complete explanation of why it is the case that there is a reason for Ronnie to go to the party. But even Ronnie is acting in a manner that is objectionably self-regarding if the thought that there will be dancing at the party doesn't move him to go there, until he remembers that he desires to dance. If Ronnie genuinely desires to dance, then *all it should take* for him to be moved to go to the party is the thought that there will be dancing there.[8]

---

[7] Johnston [2001].

[8] Stephen Darwall's discussion of *The Possibility of Altruism* in his book, *Impartial Reason* [1983], is an excellent illustration of the tension between the No Background Conditions assumption and the Deliberative Constraint. Darwall takes the latter idea as the cornerstone for how to think about reasons, and so this is why he finds some of the things that Nagel says about agent-relative and agent-neutral reasons ('objective' and 'subjective', in Nagel's terminology) to be confusing. Nagel's discussion is also illuminating. Although Nagel takes the first idea as his cornerstone for how to think about reasons, the second also clearly shapes the way the entire book is framed. I think of Darwall's discussion as demonstrating that we can't think about normative reasons in *both* these ways. And unlike other defenders of the Humean Theory of Reasons, I hold that it is better to give up the former than the latter. As we'll see later, Hypotheticalism also solves many other problems by doing so.

And such reasoning is not merely enthymematic. Since Ronnie's and Bradley's reasons are explained by their desires, this shows that the problem lies not with the Humean Theory of Reasons at all, but with one of the other two theses.[9]

This leaves any view that is trying to fill in the explanation of what is going on in Ronnie and Bradley's case, including any version of the Humean Theory of Reasons, with a choice: either you give up the Deliberative Constraint, or you give up the No Background Conditions assumption. The standard move, both for those who accept the Humean Theory of Reasons and for those who do not, is to continue to deny the distinction between reasons and background conditions and reject the Deliberative Constraint.[10]

These versions of the Humean Theory of Reasons *accept* the result that on their accounts, Ryan's practical reasoning when he does not think about his own desires is enthymematic. There are many explanations of why it may be that Ryan can reason well without thinking about his reasons, or by thinking about only part of his reasons, but I still think that this is an odd thing to say. Moreover, I think that of these two theses, *this* is the right one to concede to the critics. The most outspoken critics of Hypotheticalism are worried about how well it treats lots of obvious, intuitive data, such as that reasoning involves thinking about reasons. The way to respond to these critics is not to claim that reasoning need not involve thinking about reasons after all, but to offer an account like that of Hypotheticalism, which gets *more* of the intuitive data correct. On Hypotheticalism's account, it is

---

[9] One possible move at this point in the dialectic is to claim that if it really does sound objectionably self-regarding for Ronnie to have to think about his own desire to dance in being moved to go to the party, then Ronnie's case is really not one of the uncontroversial cases of a reason being explained by a desire after all. I take it that this is the argument of T. M. Scanlon in the first chapter of *What We Owe to Each Other*. I understand Scanlon as using the same argument as that in the paragraph in the main text in order to argue that even lots of reasons that we think are to be explained by desires are really better explained in some other way. But this is simply to deny my premise that there really are uncontroversial cases such as Ronnie's and Bradley's in which reasons are to be explained by some psychological state. Moreover, this argument has the structure of using a particular assumption about how reasons are to be explained by desires in arguing that Ronnie's reason may not be explained by his desire after all. But when evaluating the Humean theory in the abstract, it should be up for grabs how the explanation of Ronnie's reason will work.

[10] Compare, for example, Railton [1984]. Railton isn't defending the Humean Theory of Reasons, but consequentialism. But he is defending it from a very similar kind of objection—that if consequentialism is right, then someone who is reasoning well about what to do will be objectionably focused on the good as such. I take it that Railton's line is essentially to defend the view that a good agent can reliably reason in ways that are enthymematic, and to explain why that could be so.

not strictly false to say that the fact that there will be dancing at the party is a reason for Ronnie to go there. So by making a distinction between reasons and background conditions, Hypotheticalism actually sticks closer to the intuitive data.

The Hypotheticalist account of Ronnie's case is simple. There is something that Ronnie likes—dancing. There is an action which Ronnie could do—going to the party—which can help bring it about that Ronnie goes dancing. Certain features of the world—for example, the fact that there will be dancing at the party—help explain *why* this is the case. And these are the reasons for Ronnie to go to the party. They are reasons for Ronnie to go to the party, because they help to explain why his going there can help bring it about that he has a chance to dance, and because dancing is something that he likes to do.

In general, according to Hypotheticalism, the objective normative reasons for X to do A are the things which help to explain why X's doing A *promotes P*, where P is the object of one of X's desires.[11] And the fact that R helps explain why X's doing A promotes P isn't part of the reason—only R is the reason. And R needn't mention X at all. So there is a distinction between reasons and background conditions.

Reason* For all propositions r, agents x, and actions a, if r is a reason for x to do a, that is because there is some p such that x has a desire whose object is p, and the truth of r is part of what explains[12] why x's doing a promotes[13] p.[14]

---

[11] Recall that I still haven't said anything about what kind of psychological state desires are, and won't until Ch. 8. Until then, I'm using the word 'desire' in only a technical sense, to refer to whatever kind of psychological state does explain the difference between Ronnie's and Bradley's reasons.

[12] Just to be clear, I do not understand explanation to be an epistemic notion. *Explaining* things is an activity that we engage in, of trying to understand things, and is epistemic. But I take there to be facts about what is true because of what, and these facts are facts about explanations, as I am using the term.

[13] For now, think of X's doing A's *promoting P* as a matter of its helping to bring about P. I do think that there is an intuitive notion in the neighborhood, but we'll return to a discussion of *promotion* in Ch. 6.

[14] A technical point about terminology: discussions of desire often use 'p' as a schematic letter standing in for a sentence, so that 'the desire that p' is well-formed. Similarly, discussions of reasons often use 'ϕ' as a schematic letter standing in for a verb, so that 'a reason to ϕ' is well-formed. I've elected to use 'p' as a variable ranging over propositions, and 'a' as a variable ranging over actions, so that I can quantify into those positions. This requires me to sometimes use more circuitous locutions: for example, I write of 'a reason to do A' rather than 'a reason to A', which is not well-formed, and 'a desire whose object is p', rather than 'a desire that p', which is not well-formed. I reserve lower-case letters for variables and upper-case letters for schematic letters standing in for names.

On this view, Ronnie has the desire that he go dancing. It is because there is dancing at the party that Ronnie's going there will allow him to dance. So the fact that there will be dancing at the party is a reason for Ronnie to go there. This fact is Ronnie's reason to go to the party, and Ronnie does not get mentioned as part of this fact—he is mentioned only as part of the explanation of why this fact satisfies the necessary conditions in order to be a reason for Ronnie. So Ronnie can satisfy the Deliberative Constraint and take all his reasons into account *without* thinking about himself or his own desires. All he has to think about is dancing. And the same goes for Ryan, assuming that the fact that Katie needs help helps to explain why helping her will promote p, for some p, the object of one of Ryan's desires.[15]

Now consider Susan. Susan wants a cup of coffee, and there is coffee in the lounge. Intuitively, we can say a lot about Susan's reasons:

1   The fact that there is coffee in the lounge is a reason for Susan to go to the lounge.

2   The fact that by going to the lounge she can get some coffee is a reason for Susan to go to the lounge.

3   The fact that Susan desires a cup of coffee is a reason for Susan to go to the lounge.

We understand the claim that Susan wants a cup of coffee as suggesting that Susan desires[16] that she have some coffee. Her going to the lounge will allow her to get some coffee, and this is because there is coffee there. This is how Hypotheticalism captures 1 as literally true.[17] The fact that there is coffee in the lounge is part of *why* it is true that going to the lounge

---

[15]   Whether this is, in fact, the case will have to wait until Ch. 6 to be resolved.

[16]   Again, nothing that I say until Ch. 8 will turn on what kind of psychological state desires are. I'm *assuming* that whatever they are, they can take propositional objects. But the account could be re-worked without that assumption. This would merely require revisions in how to think about the *promotion* relation.

[17]   Rather than as false or merely elliptical, as the No Background Conditions view is committed to claiming. Don't get distracted by the fact that Susan shouldn't weigh the fact that there is coffee in the lounge and the fact that by going to the lounge, she can get some coffee *separately* in her deliberations about whether to go to the lounge. It is true that the second doesn't add extra *weight* to the first. But weighing reasons is complicated. We need a *theory* in order to let this convince us that the sentence, 'The fact that there is coffee in the lounge is a reason for Susan to go there' is literally false. And it seems to me that a good theory might as well make the things that we ordinarily say, like this one, come out to be true.

is a way for Susan to get some coffee. The literal truth of 2 is also easily captured by Hypotheticalism. The fact that by going to the lounge Susan can get some coffee serves as a trivial explanation of itself—it is the limiting case of what could count as such an explanation. If we can say this, then Hypotheticalism captures 2 very neatly.

Hypotheticalism does not, however, provide direct support for 3—at least, it doesn't obviously[18] come out to be true, just because Susan desires to have a cup of coffee. This result is intentional. It may be that the fact that Susan desires a cup of coffee is a reason for her to go to the lounge. But it should not be explained by her desire for a cup of coffee. If it is a reason for Susan, it must be explained by some *other* desire. This is not a problem for my view; I'll now explain why this is the kind of view that we should expect a Humean to take.

Recall that most versions of the Humean Theory of Reasons are traditionally motivated at least in part by the Classical Argument, which begins with two ideas. First is the idea that the normative reasons for Susan to go to the lounge are the sort of thing which could move Susan to go to the lounge. And second, the idea that in order to be moved to go to the lounge, Susan must have some desire which would move her to go.[19] Now, if Susan desires a cup of coffee, this may move her to do lots of things. If she thinks that there is coffee in the lounge, it may move her to go to the lounge. If she thinks that it is Karen's turn to make the coffee, it may move her to stop by Karen's office to remind her. If she thinks that Small World has the best coffee around here, then it may move her to head out to Small World. But there is one kind of motivation that it would be very strange to expect of Susan. It would be very strange to expect that Susan's desire *for coffee* would move her to go to the lounge *because she thinks that she desires some coffee.*[20]

---

[18] Whether it *unobviously* can be explained by Susan's desire to have a cup of coffee depends on some of the results from Ch. 6. My view is that it can. See Ch. 6.

[19] See section 1.2.

[20] See Darwall [1983: 37]. Darwall notes this point in arguing that this motivation does not support the Humean Theory of Reasons. I'm using it to motivate the view that holding the fact that Susan desires to have some coffee to be one of Susan's reasons to go to the lounge should not be thought to be one of the commitments of the Humean Theory of Reasons in the first place. Compare the distinction that Pettit and Smith [1990] make in the theory of motivation between desires as figuring in the *foreground* of deliberation, versus desires as figuring in the *background*. The Humean Theory of Motivation holds that a desire is always implicated in motivation, but Pettit and Smith show that it doesn't follow that desires must figure in the foreground—the most natural Humean thought is that

Grant, then, the common assumption that the Humean Theory of Reasons is supposed to posit a robust connection between objective normative reasons to do A and the kind of desires which would motivate someone who was aware of those reasons to actually do A. It follows that if the fact that Susan desires to have some coffee is a reason for her to go to the lounge at all, it must be because of some *other* desire that Susan has, such as the desire to do what promotes her desires. It is not because of Susan's desire to have some coffee. This is compatible with Hypotheticalism. Hypotheticalism doesn't say that the fact that Susan desires to have some coffee is *not* a reason for Susan to go to the lounge. It merely says that if it is, the desire that explains it is not her desire to have some coffee.[21]

According to Hypotheticalism, 1 and 2 are both literally true. But a simple argument is widely supposed to show that 1 and 2 cannot both be literally true. The argument starts by assuming that if R is a reason for X to do A and Q is a reason for X to do A, then R and Q together must be a better reason for X to do A than either separately. But, the argument notes, the fact that there is coffee in the lounge and the fact that by going to the lounge she can get some coffee are not, together, a better reason for Susan to go to the lounge than either is separately. So, the argument infers, at most one of these can be a reason for Susan to go to the lounge.

A similar argument purports to show that the fact that there is a reason for X to do A cannot itself be a reason for X to do A. After all, this existential fact must be true only because there is some R such that *it* is a reason for X to do A. But R and the existential fact do not, together, make a better reason for X to do A than R alone. So, the argument infers, the existential fact must not itself be a reason for X to do A. It is this argument that leads philosophers to believe that Buck-Passing accounts of value, which say that facts about value are to be analyzed as existential facts

---

desires figure in the background of motivation. Here is the connection between Pettit and Smith's distinction and the one I've drawn between reasons and background conditions: if on the most natural version of the Humean Theory of Motivation desires figure only in the background, and if the Humean Theory of Reasons is motivated by the Humean Theory of Motivation, then the Humean Theory of Reasons should hold that desires are not *part* of the reason, but only part of its background conditions. This is the view taken by Hypotheticalism.

[21] A caveat: pending complications in Ch. 6, I eventually want to allow that it may be that Susan's desire for coffee *can*—non-obviously—explain this reason. But this is only because *any* desire could explain it—not that this desire is in any way distinctive. See n. 16.

about reasons, are committed also to holding that facts about value are not, themselves, reasons.

On each count, I think these arguments are flawed. It is true that 1 and 2 are not *independent* reasons for Susan to go to the lounge. Their weights do not add up separately, and her deliberation would be flawed if she treated them as separate considerations in favor of going to the lounge. Similarly, it is true that R and the existential fact that there is a reason for X to do A are not *independent* reasons for X to do A. Their weights do not add up separately, and X's deliberation would be flawed if she treated them as separate considerations in favor of doing A. So the argument gets *something* right. But I hold that we do better to explain this in terms of how these reasons' weights *add up*, rather than by forcing us to accept views about which one is a reason and which one is not.

In support of this view, recall that the Deliberative Constraint says that one's reasons are the kinds of thing that one ought to pay attention to in deliberating. But a good account of deliberation should not distinguish between whether Susan should pay attention to the fact that there is coffee in the lounge, or only the fact that by going to the lounge she can get some coffee. Moreover, in the case of the existential fact, we can even construct a case in which the agent's ability to deliberate on the basis of each consideration comes apart. So consider the case of Nate, who hates all parties except for successful surprise parties thrown in his honor. Given Nate's situation, the fact that there is a surprise party waiting for him now at home is a reason for him to go home. But it isn't a reason that Nate could know about or act on. Still, someone Nate trusts might tell him that there is a reason for him to go home now.

In such a case, Nate can reasonably deliberate about whether to go home. He won't—and can't—think about the surprise party, because he does not know about it (and can't, without the reason going away). But he can and will think about the fact that there is a reason for him to go, and act on this reason. So the Deliberative Constraint and the combination of Subjective and Motivating from Chapter 1 both suggest that we should think that the existential fact about Nate's reasons is itself a reason for Nate to go.[22] In general, therefore, I think that we should take our attributions

---

[22] I think that this is compatible with Reason*—for the fact that there is a reason for Nate to go into the living room, on the view I will defend in section 3.4, is just the fact that there is some true

of reasons at face value—the things that we call reasons are the same things that we pay attention to in our deliberations. True, sometimes we call two things 'reason' or may pay attention to either of two things in deliberation that we should not treat as adding up to have a greater weight together than either separately. But that is something we should deal with when it comes to giving an account of the *weight* of reasons, and in particular how reasons' weights add up.[23]

2.3 What Motivates Denying the Distinction?

The No Background Conditions view rejects, in the case of reasons, a distinction that we can easily make in the case of presidents and pieces of corn on the cob. This is the distinction between a thing of a kind, and what is required in order to explain *why* it is a thing of that kind. In the case of reasons, it is the distinction between a reason, and what must be cited in a complete explanation of *why* it is a reason. As we've seen, rejecting this distinction plays an essential role in motivating a sophisticated version of the objection that the Humean Theory of Reasons makes practical reasoning out to be Objectionably Self-Regarding. But as I've also argued, the same objection can be leveled in Ronnie's case. And so I've suggested that this is good cause—in addition to the fact that it sounds true in ordinary language to say that the fact that there will be dancing at the party is a reason for Ronnie to go there—to distinguish between reasons and background conditions. And so I proceeded to say what Hypotheticalism takes the background conditions on a reason to be.

But now I think it is worth taking a closer look at what might have led philosophers to *deny* this obvious-sounding distinction in the first place. After all, the No Background Conditions view is pervasive among philosophers. It is so commonly presupposed that a helpful journal referee was recently able to explain to me that 'no clear thinker' would deny it. Yet

---

consideration r and some desire of Nate's with object p, such that Nate's going into the living room promotes p. This fact, I think, trivially explains why Nate has some desire with object p, such that his going into the living room promotes p. So as long as trivial explanations like this one can figure as a limiting case, then I think the claim that the existential fact is itself a reason is compatible with Reason*.

[23] See Ch. 7.

as I've just explained, this assumption that 'no clear thinker' would deny is clearly substantive. What motivates it? What is the suppressed argument that all 'clear thinkers' find compelling?

I suspect that the best reason for denying the distinction starts with something like the following consideration. It is commonly assumed that there is no distinction between the normative reason for someone to do something and the reason why it is the case that she ought to do it. On this view, the following claims are equivalent:

4 The reason for Lynne not to steal is that stealing is wrong.

5 The reason why Lynne ought not to steal is that stealing is wrong.

One way of understanding this view is as the theory that objective normative reasons are to be understood in terms of what people *ought* to do and explanatory reasons. In section 1.3 I offered Motivating as an account of motivating reasons in terms of subjective normative reasons and explanatory reasons and Subjective as a (provisional) account of subjective normative reasons in terms of objective normative reasons. It is natural to suppose that objective normative reasons and explanatory reasons are also related in some interesting way. Perhaps the objective normative reason for Lynne not to steal just is the explanatory reason why Lynne ought not to steal. This seems like a way of motivating the theory that anything that is part of the explanation of why Ronnie but not Bradley has a reason to go to the party must also be part of Ronnie's reason.

In his book, *Reason in Ethics,* Stephen Toulmin advocates this kind of analysis of objective normative reasons in terms of *ought* and explanatory reasons.[24] According to Toulmin, the reasons *for* someone to do something are the things which must be cited in an explanation of *why* she ought to do it. Toulmin's account allows us straightforwardly to equate 4 and 5.[25] But Toulmin's account is also straightforwardly problematic. For there can be no explanation of *why* something is the case, if it is not the case at all. Yet it is possible for there to be an objective normative reason for someone to do something, even though she ought not to do it. Suppose, for example, that Ronnie ought not to go to the party. It may be, for example, that it is his wife's birthday, and she has made dinner reservations for them during

---

[24] Toulmin [1950], ch. 11. John Broome also advocates the analysis in Broome [2004: 34].

[25] I don't think that Toulmin offers his account in the spirit of a substantive theory; I think that he takes it for granted that 4 and 5 are equivalent. Still, it makes for an interesting theory.

the party. It doesn't follow that there is no reason for him to go to the party, just that it is outweighed by the reasons for him to have dinner with his wife instead. So the natural view equating 4 with 5 can't be correct.[26]

The most natural way of amending Toulmin's view goes like this: if there can be reasons for someone to do something that she ought not to do, then perhaps normative reasons are not the reasons why someone *ought* to do something. Perhaps they are instead the explanatory reasons why there is a *reason* for her to do it. And this leads us directly to the view of Nagel in *The Possibility of Altruism*. According to Nagel, for R to be a reason for X to do A is for R to be the complete sufficient condition for it to be the case that *there is* a reason for X to do A.[27]

However, if we understand this account, like Toulmin's, as giving us an account of objective normative reasons in terms of explanatory reasons, it commits us to a surprising result. This account analyzes 'R is a reason for X to do A' in terms of 'there is a reason for X to do A'. But one might have thought that 'there is', in 'there is a reason for X to do A', is an existential quantifier. And if so, then what it is for there to be a reason for X to do A is just for there to be something, R, such that *it* is a reason for X to do A. But these can't both be true, for this analyzes 'there is a reason for X to do A' in terms of 'R is a reason for X to do A'. For this reason, I think that Nagel's story must get things the wrong way around. Because 'there is' expresses an existential quantifier, we can't use 'there is a reason for X to do A' in order to explain what it is for R to be a reason for X to do A.

On a story like Toulmin's or Nagel's, whatever explains why the fact that there will be dancing at the party tonight is a reason for Ronnie (but

---

[26] Acknowledging counterexamples like mine, Broome decides that 'reason' is really ambiguous, and divides into an *all-things-considered* sense of which the Toulmin account provides an analysis, and a *pro tanto* sense, which requires another analysis. I find Broome's argument for this ambiguity hard to credit. It is compelling to think that 5 entails 4—and that is like the No Background Conditions view—but it isn't compelling to think that 4 entails 5—on any sense. If Broome is right, then in cases in which there is a reason for someone to do something which she nevertheless ought not to do, it should make sense to say things like, 'well, in one sense there is a reason for her to do it, but in another sense there is no reason for her to do it'. Or at least like, 'there is no reason for her to do it'. But these claims *don't* make sense. So this isn't much of an argument for an ambiguity in 'reason'. And there are enough ambiguities in 'reason' that we *do* have to acknowledge (recall Ch. 1) that it should take a pretty *good* argument to force us to acknowledge another.

[27] Strictly speaking, Nagel says that the reason for X to do A is the (weakest) *predicate*, R, such that $\Box \forall x (Rx \rightarrow$ there is a reason for x to do $A)$, and X satisfies R. He might as well have said, however, that it is the fact that X satisfies R, or the true proposition that $R(X)$. Although Nagel has been criticized for identifying reasons with predicates, that part of his view is immaterial for this issue.

not Bradley) to go there would have to be part of Ronnie's reason to go there—or at least, a further normative reason for Ronnie to go there. But I've argued that we should think about the relationship between reasons and what we ought to do differently. Though it is true that the reasons for someone to do something are among the reasons why it is the case that she ought to do it (assuming that she ought to do it), I hold that we should leave room for the conceptual possibility that there may be *background conditions* on something being a reason for someone to do something. Background conditions on reasons are explanatory reasons *why* some consideration is a reason for someone to do something, and hence derivatively part of the reason why it is the case that she ought to do it. But they are not among her normative reasons *for* doing it.

I'm *not* claiming that ordinary English marks this distinction well. In fact, I think that in certain contexts, one can systematically use the locution, 'is that really part of *why* he ought to do it?' to ask whether it is really among his objective normative reasons for doing it. But the same goes for motivating reasons and 'why' questions. I can ask 'what is the real reason *why* he did it?' and not be satisfied if you tell me something about a virus that he has which causes his body to make certain movements. In the first case we use a 'why' question to ask about an objective normative reason, and in the second we use a 'why' question to ask about a motivating reason. In neither are we merely after an explanatory reason. On the other hand, if I ask, 'is that really part of why *it is the case that* he ought to do it?' or 'what is the real reason why *it is the case that* he did it?' these interpretations are less compelling. Here it no longer seems obvious that someone who is asking these questions is looking for an objective normative reason for him to do it or for his motivating reason for doing it. But it is hard to see why we should find this difference, if both objective normative reasons and motivating reasons are merely special cases of explanatory reasons.

2.4 The Wrong Place Objection

This provides what we need in order to answer another hard objection to the Humean Theory of Reasons, which I call the *Wrong Place* objection. According to any version of the Humean Theory of Reasons, all reasons are to be explained by desires on the same model as Ronnie's reason to go to the party. So if Katie needs help, and there is a reason for Ryan to help her, this must be in virtue of, or *because* of, some desire of Ryan's. The Wrong Place objection says that it doesn't matter whether or not we grant that Ryan has such a desire. Even if he does, this is simply the wrong answer to the question, '*Why* is there a reason for Ryan to help Katie?' According to the Wrong Place objection, it is simply *intuitive* that the Humean Theory of Reasons finds the answer to this question in the Wrong Place.

Distinguish the Wrong Place objection from some related objections that will have to wait until Chapter 6. One such objection to the Humean Theory of Reasons is that it *can't* explain reasons like Ryan's reason to help Katie, because in some cases the agent will not have the right kind of desire. For now, we're granting that Ryan does have the right kind of desire for an explanation like that of Ronnie's reason to go through. Another objection to the Humean Theory of Reasons is that it does not get the right *modal* results about Ryan's reason to help Katie, because Ryan would have his reason to help Katie even if he did not have the desire that the Humean Theory of Reasons uses to explain it, whatever that desire is. A large part of the force of the Wrong Place objection stems from this modal objection, but like the objection that the Humean Theory of Reasons can't account for Ryan's reason at all, I want to leave this objection to be treated in Chapter 6.

I think that the Wrong Place objection has a force that is independent of the modal objection. It derives simply from the thought that we *do* have some intuitive idea of why it is that there is a reason for Ryan to help Katie, and it says nothing about whether or not Ryan desires that Katie gets whatever she needs. We know that the fact that Katie needs help is part of why there is a reason for Ryan to help her, and we *just know* that this is not because of one of Ryan's desires. It doesn't matter, for this objection, how we get this knowledge. It just matters that it is obviously true.

Compare the version of this same objection leveled against act-utilitarianism. Act-utilitarianism says that when someone ought to do something, this is always because her doing so will bring about the greatest happiness. Consider an intuitively hard case for act-utilitarianism, such as the case in which a judge is confronted with the choice between framing and hanging an innocent man, or setting the mob waiting outside loose on a riot which will certainly result in much more loss of innocent life.

Some act-utilitarians will try to explain how they get the intuitively right results in such a case, by claiming that if such a deliberate framing by the judge were to be discovered, the costs would be so great that even though such an event is unlikely, in realistic cases the risk of these potential costs still outweigh the benefits of framing the innocent man. But people often think that it doesn't matter whether the act-utilitarian can get the 'right' results. They think that even if the act-utilitarian is right about all possible cases—that in any realistic case, discovery is probable enough that its potential costs still outweigh the likely benefits to be gained—this gives the wrong answer about *why* the judge ought not to frame the innocent man. Surely the reason *why* the judge ought not to frame the innocent man, this thought goes, is simply that he is *innocent*.

I think that the persistence of these kinds of arguments is evidence that there is a datum here that existing versions of the Humean Theory of Reasons have importantly neglected. So I hold that there is a genuine sense in which we *do* know that the fact that Ryan desires that Katie gets whatever she needs is not part of *why* there is a reason for Ryan to help Katie. But I hold that this is simply the sense in which it is not actually part of the objective normative reason *for* Ryan to help Katie. It is only part of its background condition.

Recall that I've just agreed that there is a reading of 'the reason *why* Ronnie ought to help Katie is that he wants her to have what she needs' on which it serves to attribute an objective normative reason, and to say the same thing as 'the reason for Ronnie to help Katie is that he wants her to have what she needs'. The same goes for the claim that 'Ryan ought to help Katie *because* he wants her to have what she needs'. Hypotheticalism does not hold that the fact that Ryan wants Katie to have what she needs is part of Ryan's normative reason to help Katie. It does not hold that it is a further, more basic, reason from which Ryan's reason is derived. It merely holds that it is a background condition on Ryan having the reason that he does. But the words 'why' and 'because' don't *always* serve to ascribe objective normative reasons. In fact, in most contexts, they serve only to ascribe *explanatory* reasons. And as I've already said, when Hypotheticalism says that the fact that Ryan wants Katie to have what she needs is part of why the fact that Katie needs help is a reason for Ryan to help Katie, it intends this only in this general explanatory sense.

Not all versions of the Humean Theory of Reasons make the distinction between reasons and background conditions. But according to Hypotheticalism, the theories which don't make this distinction *do* locate Ryan's reason in the wrong place. They make claims about *why* Ryan ought to help Katie that are patently wrong, since they are intended not merely as explanations of why it is the case that there is a reason for Ryan to help Katie, but as further specifications of that reason. And it is simply not true, in part for the reasons discussed in sections 2.1 and 2.2, that Ryan's reason makes reference to his desire. Hypotheticalism could easily be misunderstood as making such a claim, since it purports to help explain *why* Ryan ought to help Katie. That is why we have to be careful in stating Hypotheticalism to distinguish the different senses in which this claim might be taken. Though on Hypotheticalism's view there is a *sense* in which this is true, in the sense driving the Wrong Place objection it is most emphatically false.

But if this latest bit is right, and in ordinary English we really can use phrases like, 'is that really *why* there's a reason for him to do it?' in order to ask whether it is itself an objective normative reason for him to do it, then it is easy to see why the No Background Conditions assumption forms the basis for an attractive *theory* about what we are doing, when we ask what explains the difference in Ronnie's and Bradley's reasons. It is an attractive theory because this is often what our answers to 'why' questions in normative contexts *are* trying to do. But as we've seen, it is also a substantive theory, and one which leads to unfortunate results, in conjunction with the Deliberative Constraint, even when it is applied to Ronnie's case. So in my view Ronnie's case is all the motivation that we need in order to follow Hypotheticalism in rejecting the No Background Conditions view.

3

Incoherence and Chauvinism

3.1 The Standard Model for Normative Explanations

According to the No Background Conditions view, when we say that there is a reason for Ronnie to go to the party because Ronnie desires to dance, what follows the 'because' tells us not just what explains *why* there is such a reason, but tells us part of what that reason is. If we reject that view, then the fact that Ronnie desires to dance must be able to explain how something else—the fact that there will be dancing at the party—is a reason for Ronnie to go there. But there are still many views that we might take about how it does that. In this chapter I will articulate and examine a very common implicit theory about how explanations of reasons, like that of Ronnie's, must work. The theory needs to be articulated, because those who accept it usually take it for granted and unexplicitly. But it cannot be taken for granted when discussing the Humean Theory of Reasons, because it is a theory that Hypotheticalism rejects. And like each view that Hypotheticalism takes, I will argue that rejecting this theory can be motivated on purely independent grounds, for the theory gives a bad account of what is going on in Ronnie's case.

The theory that I want to consider is best motivated by consideration of what seems like a typical or ordinary case of an explanation of a reason, as happens in Rachel's case. Rachel is a liberal arts undergraduate whose poetry professor has given her the following assignment: every morning, she is to spend an hour writing about whatever she happens to be thinking about that morning. So it is natural to think that each morning, here is something there is a reason for Rachel to do: to write about what she is thinking about that morning. And the reason for her to do so is clear: it is that it has been assigned by Professor Smith, who teaches her poetry class.

Now, on Monday Rachel rolls out of bed onto the floor, fumbling with the snooze button on her clock radio, her head a haze of thoughts about feather pillows and dread over drifting off to sleep in poetry lecture. On Monday, there is a reason for Rachel to write about feather pillows, since that is what she is thinking about. Whereas on Thursday, Rachel leaps out of bed half an hour before her alarm goes off, her mind racing with anticipation of her weekend plans. So on Thursday, there is a reason for Rachel to write about Phil's smile, for that is what figures so prominently in her weekend plans. On the face of it, Rachel's case is much like that of Ronnie and Bradley. Ronnie and Bradley give us a case of two individuals whose reasons differ at the same time, due to some non-normative difference in their situation. Rachel gives us a case of a single agent whose reasons differ across two different times, due to a non-normative difference in her situation at those two times. Just as Ronnie's reason is due to, or explained by, the difference between him and Bradley—that he and not Bradley desires to dance—Rachel's reason on Monday is due to the difference between her situation on Monday and her situation on Thursday—that on Monday but not on Thursday she is thinking about feather pillows.

If this much is right, then it pays to examine Rachel's case closely, as an illustration of how differences in reasons might be explained. Indeed, I think that we can tell a great deal from Rachel's case. The very first observation that I drew about Rachel's case was that even if Rachel's reasons to write about feather pillows and to write about Phil's smile differ between Monday and Thursday, there is one reason that Rachel has on both mornings—to write about what she is thinking about that morning. We agreed that this was one reason that Rachel had, and we were even able to say what the reason was: it was that the soporific Professor Smith had given it as an assignment.

It is more than natural to think that it is no accident that on Monday when Rachel finds herself thinking about feather pillows, she acquires a reason to write about feather pillows, given that she already has a reason to write about what she is thinking about. After all, the fact that she is thinking about feather pillows explains why writing about feather pillows is a way to write about what she is thinking about, and that is something that she has a reason to do. Similarly, it is more than natural to think that it is no accident that on Thursday when Rachel finds herself thinking about Phil's smile but *not* about feather pillows, she has a reason to write about Phil's smile rather than one to write about feather pillows. For the facts about what she is thinking about alter her situation by altering which actions are *ways* or *means* for her to do something that she *already* has a reason to do, independently of what she is thinking about on Thursday—namely, to write about whatever she is thinking about.

If these things are no accidents, then it looks like the difference in Rachel's situation on Monday and Thursday helps to explain the difference in her reasons only with the help of a further reason that she has on both days. It looks like she needs to have this further reason, in order for the explanation to work. Rachel's case therefore gives us a model for how an explanation of a difference in reasons can work. It can work, by appealing to a further reason that is really the same—a reason for both Ronnie and Bradley, or for Rachel at both times. On this model, the fact that Rachel is thinking about feather pillows on Monday helps to explain why on Monday there is a reason for Rachel to write about feather pillows, because it explains why writing about feather pillows is on Monday a *way* or *means* for her to do the things which she is assumed to already have a reason to do. Because Rachel's case seems to be typical, or *standard*, and because this is such a natural idea about the explanation of differences in reasons—and about normative explanations generally—I call this model the *Standard Model* for normative explanations.[1]

Standard Model   The explanation that there is a reason for *X* to do *A* because of *P* follows the *Standard Model* just in case it works because there is (1) some further action *b* such that there is a reason for *X* to do *b* and (2) not just because of *P* and (3) *P* explains why doing *A* is a *way* for *X* to do *b*.

---

[1] Both Ralph Cudworth's *A Treatise Concerning Eternal and Immutable Morality* [1731] and Richard Price's *A Review of the Principles Questions of Morals* [1948] explicitly advocate the Standard Model as enabling explanations of normative differences, though neither discusses reasons explicitly. Cudworth and Price take the view that morality is literally *immutable*: obligations and reasons don't *ever* change, and can't. What changes is only what actions are *means* to do the things which are immutably required. So the Standard Model is how Cudworth and Price get away with saying that moral obligations can never change, even though promises, commands, and other things can *apparently* seem to alter what we ought to do. It is also, as I have argued elsewhere, crucial in the central argument which leads them to believe that morality *must* be immutable in the first place. See Schroeder [2005d].

The Standard Model *Theory*, then, is the theory that *all* normative explanations—or at least, all explanations of reasons—follow the Standard Model:

> **SMT** For all *x*, *a*, and *p*, if there is a reason for *x* to do *a* because of *p*, that explanation must follow the Standard Model.

In particular, it follows from the Standard Model Theory that the explanation of Ronnie's reason follows the Standard Model, and hence that when we say that there is a reason for Ronnie to go to the party because he desires to dance, the role that the fact that he desires to dance is playing is that it is explaining why going to the party is a way or means for Ronnie to do something that there is an antecedent reason for *both* Ronnie and Bradley to do. And it explains the difference between Ronnie and Bradley because, since Bradley does not desire to dance, going to the party is *not* a way for Bradley to do this thing that both he and Ronnie have a reason to do.

As noted, the Standard Model Theory is a very natural theory. But it is important from the very beginning to see that it is a *substantive* theory. It is not, for example, simply a statement of the simple truth that it cannot follow from the fact that Rachel is thinking about feather pillows that there is a reason for her to write about feather pillows unless the following is true:

> 1 If Rachel is thinking about feather pillows, then there is a reason for her to write about feather pillows.

Nor is it simply a statement of the still relatively uncontentious view that some *quantified* version of this claim is needed, from which we can suppose 1 to follow:

> 2 For all topics *x*, if Rachel is thinking about *x*, then there is a reason for her to write about *x*.

Both 1 and 2 are *conditional* claims. Neither actually postulates a reason for Rachel to do anything, except conditionally on what she is thinking about. If Rachel is not thinking about anything, then so far as 1 and 2 go, it doesn't follow that she has any reasons at all. But in a *Standard Model* explanation—and this does seem to correctly describe Rachel's case—both 1 and 2 are explained by the existence of a reason for Rachel that is not itself contingent on what she is thinking about:

3   There is a reason *r* for Rachel to write about whatever she is thinking about.

It is easy to see that 3 is a stronger claim than 2. It is also easy to become confused about this, if we ignore the fact that 'there is', in 'there is a reason for *R* to do *A*', expresses an existential quantifier. I don't believe that we were confused about this in Rachel's case, because I observed that 3 was true before I even considered what might explain the difference between Rachel's reasons on Monday and on Thursday.

But it's important to see that however typical Rachel's case might seem, and however natural the Standard Model may seem, it is not at all obvious that explanations of reasons *have* to work in this way. *Logically* speaking, 2 could certainly be true even without 3, because it is logically weaker. Moreover, we would find it more than a little puzzling if someone told us that *non*-normative explanations had to work in this way. Consider a simple example. Though I am in Washington right now, Marcus is in Milwaukee. So Marcus is north of Chicago, but I am not north of Chicago. This difference in what places we are north of—Marcus and I—is due to the difference in the places that we occupy. We might explain it in this way. It is because Marcus is in Milwaukee, that he is north of Chicago. In general,

4   For all individuals *x*, if *x* is in Milwaukee, then *x* is north of Chicago.

This quantified conditional explains why Marcus is north of Chicago. But there is no reason to think that there must be some further place that Marcus is north of, which makes this conditional true of him. The scope of 4 certainly includes even people who are at the South Pole—they, just as much as Marcus and I, will be north of Chicago, if ever they go to Milwaukee. But since there is no place that they are north of, this conditional truth about where they might be north of simply *can't* be explained by their already being north of some place. So when it comes to being north of a place, we only need *conditional* claims like 4 to explain the difference between people, and not categorical claims about where people are already north of.[2] Standard Model cases are cases in which things

[2] Of course, we may need to advert to the fact that *Milwaukee* is north of Chicago. But *that* explanation doesn't have the form of the Standard Model. The Standard Model explanation of 2 by 3 explains why everyone satisfies an open conditional by postulating an open categorical claim of the category appearing in the consequent, which is also satisfied by everyone.

seem to be otherwise, with reasons. And according to the Standard Model *Theory*, things *have* to be otherwise, with reasons.

3.2 Incoherence and Chauvinism

The consequences of the Standard Model Theory for the Humean Theory of Reasons are disastrous. For according to the Standard Model Theory, it is not possible for Ronnie's reason to go to the party to be explained by his desire to dance, except with the help of some further, antecedent reason to do something that given this desire, going to the party is a way for Ronnie to do. The natural idea is that it is a reason to *pursue his desires*. If we apply the Standard Model to Ronnie's case, it is because there is a reason for Ronnie to pursue his desires, that facts about what Ronnie desires can make a difference in what he has reasons to do. If he desires to dance, then going dancing becomes a *way* for Ronnie to pursue his desires, and hence something that there is a reason for Ronnie to do. And if there will be dancing at the party, then going to the party becomes a way for Ronnie to go dancing, and hence something that there is a reason for Ronnie to do. So the explanation of Ronnie's reason by his desire has to advert to a further reason—the reason for Ronnie to *pursue his desires*.

This is an unfortunate result for a Humean to accept. For according to the Humean Theory of Reasons, *all* reasons must be explained by a desire in the same way as Ronnie's. But consider the reason for Ronnie to pursue his desires, which according to the Standard Model is needed in order for the explanations of reasons by desires to *work*. Can this reason be explained by a desire? For it to be explained by a desire in the *same way*, it would have to be explained by itself. And that would surely be circular. No reason can explain itself. It can't be because there is a reason for Ronnie to pursue his desires that there is a reason for Ronnie to pursue his desires. Since it *can't* be explained in this way, it follows from the Standard Model Theory that the Humean Theory of Reasons is committed both to saying that this reason *can* be explained by a desire, and that it *cannot*. So if the Standard Model Theory is right, then the Humean Theory of Reasons is literally incoherent.

Exactly this objection has been leveled against the Humean Theory of Reasons—that it cannot help but be literally self-inconsistent. Actually, there are at least five interesting versions of the objection that the Humean

Theory is literally incoherent, and this is only the most striking.[3] But it is this version of the objection that Jean Hampton seems to be making, when she argues:

Note that this norm, which is implicitly involved in what it means to be instrumentally rational, is stated in a way that makes it categorical rather than hypothetical. Kant's position on the nature of hypothetical imperatives **must** be construed (contra his explicit wishes) such that understanding the bindingness of a hypothetical imperative is no easier than understanding the bindingness of a categorical imperative. My interpretation cannot save Kant's belief that the former is more straightforward than the latter; indeed, my argument is that Kant's belief is wrong. The **only** way to analyze Kant's analyticity claim is to do so in a way that locates in hypothetical imperatives the same mysterious objective authority that attends the categorical imperative. Even more strikingly, I have argued that the force of hypothetical imperatives is dependent on, and *is at least in part constituted by*, the force of some antecedent categorical imperative that is in part definitive of instrumental rationality.[4]

Hampton claims that a reason or imperative that is not explained by psychological features in the way that Ronnie's is *must* be appealed to in order to explain Ronnie's reason. And she claims that this establishes not only that the Humean Theory is incoherent, but even that Kant's own view is. Kant himself is clearly not shy about postulating reasons or imperatives that are *categorical*, and consequently unexplained by psychological states—ends or desires—in the way that Ronnie's reason is. But Kant at least held that it was conceptually possible that there might be only reasons like Ronnie's, and that more philosophical work was needed, in order to establish the existence of the kind of reasons or imperatives which he believed are required for morality.[5] If even Kant's view turns out to be incoherent, the Humean Theory of Reasons certainly does as well.

Of course, even if the Standard Model Theory is right, there does remain one way to extricate the Humean from literal incoherence. We can interpret him as having exaggerated just slightly when he said that *every*

---

[3] The other four, leveled by Korsgaard [1997], Darwall [1983], another possible reading of Hampton [1998], and on a possible reading, Quinn [1993b] and Scanlon [1998], will be the topic of section 5.2.

[4] Hampton [1998: 165–6]. Boldface added for emphasis but italics in original.

[5] 'On the other hand, the question as to how the imperative of *morality* is possible is undoubtedly the only one needing a solution, since it is in no way hypothetical and the objectively represented necessity cannot therefore be based on any presupposition, as in the case of hypothetical imperatives' Kant [1997: 4: 419].

reason had to be explained in the same way as Ronnie's. Obviously, since this simply can't be the case, what he must have meant was that every reason *but one* has to be explained in this way. Surely his account isn't supposed to apply to the reason to pursue your desires! So on this interpretation, the Humean theory was never really about a uniform explanation of all reasons at all—that was just bluster. It was simply about a *subsumption* of all reasons under one—the reason to pursue one's desires.

This way of thinking about what is at stake between Humeans and non-Humeans is a familiar one from the literature, and Christine Korsgaard is one of its chief proponents:[6] 'Most philosophers think it is both uncontroversial and unproblematic that practical reason requires us to take the means to our ends . . . The interesting question, almost everyone agrees, is whether practical reason requires anything *more* of us than this.'[7] According to Korsgaard, even the Humean Theory of Reasons accepts that there is a rational requirement to take the means to one's ends. The dispute between Humeans and non-Humeans is only over whether there are other such requirements. Rephrasing from talk about requirements to talk about reasons, the dispute is not about whether there is a basic agent-neutral reason for everyone to pursue one's desires—by the Standard Model Theory, even the Humean has to accept such a reason, and allow that it is not itself explained by a desire. According to Korsgaard, then, the dispute between Humeans and non-Humeans is simply about how *many* agent-neutral reasons there are which don't have to be explained by a desire. The Humean says one, and non-Humeans say more than one.

If this is the real issue about Humeanism, then in a natural sense, Humeans are really merely being *Chauvinist* when they are confronted with cases of intuitive reasons that they can't manage to explain by appeal to a desire.[8] For example, suppose that it turns out that no desire of Ryan's can explain why there is a reason for him to help Katie. The Humean has

---

[6] Although she is certainly not the only one. According to Doug Lavin, '[r]ecently it has become fashionable to speak of the *instrumental principle* and then to characterize cases of doing A in order to do B as following the instrumental principle, to characterize being suited to receive advice like "you ought to do A seeing as you propose to do B" as being subject to the instrumental principle, and along the same lines, to characterize the instrumentalist as holding that the instrumental principle is the only formal principle of practical reason' Lavin [2004: 433].

[7] Korsgaard [1997: 215].

[8] The Chauvinism of the Humean Theory of Reasons is also the focus of Korsgaard [1986], but there her argument is not a general one—it depends on assuming that the Humean Theory of Reasons is motivated by Williams's version of the Classical Argument (Williams [1981a]).

to accept the result that there is no reason for Ryan to help Katie. But a non-Humean will say: why can't there be *two* reasons that are unexplained by desires? One to pursue one's desires, and another to help people in need of help? Whatever could be wrong with that?

Korsgaard's Humean can have no principled way of answering this question. After all, he himself thinks that at bottom there is nothing philosophically problematic about there being a reason that is not itself explained by a desire. He himself believes in one! So what makes him so sure that there is only one of these? Merely a desire for theoretical economy? It surely wouldn't be *that* much more uneconomical to allow for two reasons unexplained by desires. Though Korsgaard's Humean claims to be skeptical about other kinds of reasons—for example, Ryan's—this can't really be for *principled* reasons. He must simply be a Chauvinist about some sorts of reasons—partial to ones to promote desires, but less ecstatic about moral reasons. And this objection of Chauvinism is a serious threat to the Humean Theory. For as we noted in section 1.2, the Humean Theory of Reasons is often used to motivate skepticism about the objectivity of morality.[9] If it isn't even *possible* for this kind of skepticism to be principled, then the Humean Theory of Reasons isn't at all what we might have thought.

This argument that the Humean Theory of Reasons is either incoherent or Chauvinist is a good argument. That is, it is a *valid* argument, if we take the Standard Model Theory to be one of its premises. But however natural or persuasive the Standard Model Theory may be, we've seen that it is nevertheless a substantive theory about how an explanation of a difference in reasons might work. I therefore hold that the Korsgaard–Hampton dilemma should teach us about what kind of theory about the explanation of Ronnie's reason a Humean ought to take. Humeans shouldn't think that the explanation of Ronnie's reason follows the Standard Model. So for these reasons Hypotheticalism rejects the Standard Model Theory, and holds that the explanation of Ronnie's reason by his desire must work in some other way—and *not* by subsuming going to the party under some action that there is antecedently a reason for Ronnie to do.

We still haven't arrived at a *positive* view for Hypotheticalism to take about how this explanation works—we'll get to that in section 3.4 and consider it at length in Chapter 4. But like the rejection of the No

---

[9] See e.g. Harman [1975], Foot [1975], and Mackie [1977].

Background Conditions view, finding such an alternative view is not, I think, solely a burden for Hypotheticalism and other versions of the Humean Theory of Reasons. For as I'll now argue, the Standard Model Theory is implausibly strong, and not particularly well suited to accounting for reasons like Ronnie's.

3.3   Brett and Vera: Against the Standard Model Theory

The Standard Model Theory is an appealing and natural view to take, and it is easy to see why someone could find it so natural and obvious as not to need articulating as a substantive assumption. But it is highly rejectable, and there are a number of reasons to find it highly suspicious. For one, it yields results that are surprisingly strong. If the Standard Model Theory is true, the same argument that shows that the Humean Theory of Reasons is incoherent will show the same thing about any other perfectly general explanatory theory of reasons of the form of Theory:

> **Theory**   For all propositions r, agents x, and actions a, if r is a reason
> for x to do a, that is *because r, x*, and a stand in relation $\mathfrak{R}$.

The incoherence argument will work in exactly the same way. By the Standard Model Theory, any such explanation must appeal to a further reason for x to do what she is related to by $\mathfrak{R}$, for some r. But such a further reason cannot be explained in the same way, because then it would be explained by itself. Since it follows from the Standard Model Theory that *any* explanatory account of the form of Theory is incoherent, that is grounds to think that the Standard Model Theory is too strong.

Another reason to think that the Standard Model Theory is too strong is that it renders incoherent not just general explanatory theories of reasons, but the very intelligibility of the possibility there might be agent-relational reasons but no agent-neutral reasons. The idea that such a possibility is intelligible is by far the mainstream throughout the history of moral philosophy. Even Kant, as Hampton pointed out, held that it was intelligible and could not be disproved by analytic means that there might be hypothetical imperatives but no categorical imperative. But on the assumption that all differences in reasons can be explained somehow, the Standard Model Theory makes this view incoherent. For according to the Standard Model Theory, all differences between agents' reasons must ultimately be explained in terms of reasons that are reasons for everyone. Since on this view there is no reason for anyone unless there is a reason for everyone, it is incoherent to suppose that there might be reasons for some but no reasons for everyone. But any view which makes a possibility that has been considered intelligible and real for most of the history of moral philosophy turn out to be incoherent should give us cause for suspicion. So again, quite plausibly the Standard Model Theory is simply too strong.

If the Standard Model Theory is too strong, there must be *some* explanations of *some* reasons which don't follow the Standard Model. So any evidence that cases like Ronnie and Bradley's are *more likely* to be cases that don't follow the Standard Model than other cases are, is evidence that the explanation of Ronnie's reason does not follow the Standard Model. In the remainder of this section, I will be offering two independent arguments directly for the conclusion that the explanation of Ronnie's reason does not follow the Standard Model. But if these arguments are unconvincing, there is an easy fallback. What Hypotheticalism needs in order to independently motivate its rejection of the Standard Model explanation of Ronnie's reason, is merely the result that Ronnie's reason is a *good candidate* to be one that does not follow the Standard Model. And so the following arguments can be thought of as contributing to that case.

If there is to be an explanation of Ronnie's reason to go to the party along the lines of the Standard Model explanation of Rachel's reason to write about feather pillows on Monday, then there must be some action that there is a reason for both Ronnie and Bradley to do, but which going to the party is only a way for Ronnie to do. And for this to be the case, there must be something, which is the reason for Ronnie and Bradley to do it. But I will now argue that there is no such action, and no such reason to do it.

Consider the case of Brett. Brett is passionate about becoming a rock star, but he's also keen on becoming a successful philosopher. For the sake of the example, let's follow Brett in assuming that these are not incompatible aims, even if the obvious means to them often are. To further his aim of becoming a rock star, Brett plays gigs with the Head Set at Mercury Lounge. And to further his aim of being a successful philosopher, he works diligently on his dissertation on the pragmatics of context-dependence.

Playing gigs with the Head Set at Mercury Lounge is not necessary for Brett to become a rock star. He might instead play with Helicopter, Helicopter, or choose to play gigs at The Cutting Room. Nor is writing a dissertation on the pragmatics of context-dependence necessary in order for Brett to become a successful philosopher. He might write about the pragmatics of belief-ascriptions instead, or even about the *Tractatus*. But despite not being necessary for Brett's aims, the means that he takes are still things that he has reasons to do.

Brett's band-mates in the Head Set are considering accepting a gig at Mercury Lounge for next Saturday. But Brett can't both play at Mercury Lounge on Saturday night *and* work on his dissertation then. I make three claims about this case. First, there is a reason for Brett to play with the Head Set on Saturday night. Second, there is a reason for Brett to work on his dissertation on Saturday night. And third, these two reasons are both paradigmatically of the kind that are, like Ronnie's, explained by features of the psychology of the person for whom they are reasons. Mike, who doesn't care to become a rock star, doesn't have the same reason to play with the Head Set, and Eleanor, who doesn't want to become a philosopher, doesn't have the same reason as Brett does to work on context-dependence. It doesn't matter to me at all whether you agree with my judgments about this case. What matters is that you can agree that there are structurally similar cases—cases in which there are reasons paradigmatically like Ronnie's, to do things which are not *necessary* for the accomplishment of the desires that explain them, and to do actions which can come into conflict with one another. These features of the case are enough to create strong pressure to think that there is no action that can explain all these reasons as *ways* of doing it.

Consider the action of doing *everything* that promotes one's desires.[10] This is the right kind of action to explain each of Brett's reasons to play at Mercury Lounge and to work on his dissertation. For given Brett's desires, each of these actions promote them. And so doing each of these things is necessary in order to do everything that promotes his desires. So it follows that if there were a reason for Brett to do *everything* that promotes his desires, that could easily explain a reason for Brett to do each of these things. And

---

[10] If you don't think that there is really any such action, then so much the better—the Standard Model explanation of cases like Ronnie's doesn't even get off of the ground, then.

that is what we want—we want a reason under which each of Brett's desire-explained reasons could be *subsumed*—which would suffice to explain them, given the facts about Brett's desires. But unfortunately, there simply can't be a reason for Brett to do everything that promotes his desires. His very situation shows that it is *impossible* for him to do everything that promotes his desires. So on a generalization of the principle that 'ought' implies 'can', we simply shouldn't accept that there is a reason for Brett to do this.

On the other hand, consider the action of doing *something* that promotes one's desires. Each action that Brett has a reason to do is *something* that promotes his desires, and it is certainly possible for him to do *something* that promotes his desires. So no generalization of the principle that 'ought' implies 'can' is going to force us to conclude that there is no reason for Brett to do this. But it is much less obvious that this reason could successfully *explain* all of Brett's reasons. Suppose that Brett is with the Head Set at Mercury Lounge, and they are in the middle of their first set. Even then, there is a reason for Brett to be working on his dissertation on context-dependence. That is how dissertations work. Once you get started on them and before you are finished, you always have some reason to be making progress, even if you often have better reasons to be doing other things—like sleeping. But while Brett and the Head Set are in the middle of their first set, he is *already doing something* that promotes his desires. So it is hard to see how a reason to do *something* that promotes his desires could explain why at that very time he has a reason to be working on his dissertation instead.

What a Standard Model explanation of Brett's case needs, is an action such as doing *anything* that promotes one's desires, that is distinct from both doing *something* that promotes one's desires, and from doing *everything* that promotes one's desires. But there is no such action. Compare:

Some   There is a reason for Brett to do *something* that promotes his desires.

All   There is a reason for Brett to do *everything* that promotes his desires.

Any   There is a reason for Brett to do *anything* that promotes his desires.

Some and All each have two scope disambiguations. The quantifier can be read as part of the action that Brett has a reason to do, or it can be read as quantifying over actions that Brett might have a reason to do. For example, in the case of All, the two readings are:

Easy For all x, if x promotes Brett's desires, then there is a reason for him to do x.

Required There is a reason for Brett to: do everything that promotes his desires.

To have a Standard Model explanation of Brett's reasons, we require Required, rather than simply Easy. Only Required posits an action that there is antecedently a reason for Brett to do. Easy simply states a true generalization. The true generalization posited by Easy is easy to come by. It is the thing that we are trying to explain when we posit cases such as Brett's. For the Standard Model to work, we need the reading of All on which it posits an action that there is antecedently a reason for Brett to do.

The problem with the Standard Model is that only Any can successfully explain each reason of Brett's, but there is no reading of Any that fits the Standard Model. Though Any looks as though it has the same form as Some and All, Any can unambiguously be read as Easy. And Easy doesn't get us what a Standard Model explanation of Brett's reason needs. If there is no good candidate for the action that Brett has a reason to do which explains each of his reasons to play with the Head Set and to work on his dissertation, then there can't be any successful Standard Model explanation of these reasons.

In my view, however, even if there *were* a good candidate for what this action might be, the Standard Model explanation of cases like Ronnie's would still run into trouble. For I don't think that there is any good candidate for what the reason to *do* it might be. For compare Brett to Vera. Since Brett wants to be a rock star, there is a reason for him to practice his bass. Vera wants to get better at chess. And so there is a reason for her to practice playing chess. It should be uncontroversially true that there are cases like this in which two different people have reasons to do two different things, which are nevertheless both reasons that are paradigmatically like Ronnie's, in that they are obviously contingent on the psychologies of the people for whom they are reasons. Any case like this will do.

It is *easy* to come up with candidates for what the reason is for Brett to practice his bass. For example, the fact that he needs to practice in order to get better seems to be such a reason. Similarly, it is easy to come up with candidates for what the reason is for Vera to practice playing chess. For example, the fact that *she* needs to practice, in order to get better, seems to be such a reason. But it's *hard* to see what consideration it could possibly be that counts in favor of all of these things: Brett's practicing his bass, Vera's practicing chess, and Brett's writing a dissertation on context-dependence. What feature of the world tells in favor *all* these? Not the fact that they *all* have to practice, in order to get better. Surely the fact that Brett has to practice the bass, in order to get better at playing the bass, has nothing to do with why there is a reason for Vera to practice playing chess. She would have the same reason to practice playing chess even if for some reason practice would make Brett worse.

If you like the Standard Model Theory, and agree that it is hard to think of what this reason *is*, you might still take some initial comfort in the fact that it is intuitively true that:

Intuitive   There is a reason for everyone to do what promotes her desires.[11]

So you might hope that that is evidence that there must be *some* such reason, even though you aren't exactly sure what it is. But that would be incautious. For Intuitive is multiply ambiguous.[12] It could mean any of:

5   For all agents x and actions a, if doing a promotes one of x's desires, then there is a reason r for x to do a.

6   For all agents x, there is a reason r for x to do whatever promotes one of x's desires.

7   There is a reason r for anyone to do whatever promotes one of her desires.

And of these readings, it is at best 5 that is obviously true. I've never encountered a good candidate for what the reasons postulated by 6 and 7 could be.[13] And given the ambiguity in Intuitive, I think it follows that

---

[11] For present purposes, I bracket the worry that there may be things which promote our desires which we have no reason to do.

[12] Granting, of course, that there is an action of 'doing whatever promotes one of x's desires' that can do the work for the Standard Model explanation.

[13] For my purposes here I'll content myself by leaving it at that. The very best candidate I've ever been able to come up with is the fact that the world is agent-neutrally *better* when more people do what promotes their desires. This, at least, is the kind of consideration that *could* be such a reason, that

confidence that there must be some such reason that is unaccompanied by equal confidence about what that reason is should be highly suspicious. And so I'm forced to conclude that the Standard Model does not seem to be particularly well suited to reasons like Ronnie's. It neither has a story about what *action* there is antecedently a reason for Ronnie to do, nor a story about what the antecedent *reason* to do this action is.

If you still find the Standard Model Theory attractive, it may be that none of this convinces you. But that's okay—I think that the Standard Model Theory is substantive and interesting. The point of arguing on independent grounds that it is false is to establish that the assumptions that Hypotheticalism makes about the explanation of Ronnie's reason are not ad hoc moves in order to get out of powerful objections, but can be independently well motivated.

3.4 Hypotheticalism as an Analysis

In this chapter and the last I've articulated and rejected two theories about how the explanation of Ronnie's reason by his desire works. These theories are commonly implicitly accepted, and that gives currency to the objections to the Humean Theory of Reasons that I've discussed—that it makes practical reasoning out to be Objectionably Self-Regarding, that it locates the explanation of reasons like Ryan's in the Wrong Place, that it is Chauvinist, and even that it is literally incoherent. The theories give currency to these objections, because the theories are precisely what we need in order for the arguments in favor of these objections to be successful. The proponents of these arguments haven't articulated them in this way, but I've shown that they are all *good* objections when so articulated, and I know of no other way to make these objections stick. And the assumptions about the explanation of Ronnie's reason on which they turn are incredibly

is suitably general in scope, and that could be a reason for everyone. But I take it that it does not take any enormous amount of reflection in order to see that this choice for the reason would seem to get many peculiar results—for example, in cases in which one agent can bring about many other agents doing what promotes their desires by *not* promoting her own, it does not predict any reason at all for her to do what promotes her desires. And that is surely wrong—even if it is always all things considered more reasonable to sacrifice your own aims for the pursuits of others (which it is natural to think that it is not!), surely in such situations it is merely that others' needs *outweigh* the reasons for you to do what promotes your own ends—not that you turn out to have no such reasons at all.

natural—it is easy to see why someone could accept these assumptions, and easy to see why she could take them for granted.

But I've been arguing all along that once we make the No Background Conditions view and the Standard Model Theory *explicit*, we can see that the obvious thing for a committed Humean to do is to reject these theories. So Hypotheticalism, my favored version of the Humean Theory of Reasons, rejects these theories about the explanation of Ronnie's reason. And in both cases, I've argued that rejecting them actually allows for a *better* explanation of what is going on in Ronnie's case—a better explanation of his reason to go to the party. So, I've argued, anyone has good grounds to reject them, Humean or not.

But those are only negative theses. None of this tells us, yet, what Hypotheticalism's theory *is*, about how the explanation of Ronnie's reason works. And it is not enough to stop with these negative theses. For the No Background Conditions view and the Standard Model Theory are such natural ideas that many philosophers have felt comfortable relying on them in philosophical argument without feeling the need to make them explicit. If these theories are so natural, then, it is important to get a clear substantive alternative on to the table, lest we find ourselves slipping back, unawares, into misunderstanding Hypotheticalism as committed to one or both of these theories.

It might be enough to say that according to Hypotheticalism, the difference between Ronnie's and Bradley's reasons is explained by the truth (or necessary truth) of this biconditional:

Biconditional   For all propositions *r*, agents *x*, and actions *a*, *r* is a reason for *x* to do *a* if and only if there is some *p* such that *x* has a desire whose object is *p*, and the truth of *r* is part of what explains why *x*'s doing *a* promotes *p*.

Using Biconditional, we could explain Ronnie's reason in this way: the fact that there will be dancing at the party explains why going to the party is a way for Ronnie to go dancing, and this is the object of one of Ronnie's desires. So it follows from the *if* part of Biconditional that the fact that there will be dancing at the party is a reason for Ronnie to go there. But Bradley has no desire such that the fact that there will be dancing at the party explains why going there is a way for him to promote that desire. So it follows from the *only if* part of Biconditional that the fact that there will be dancing at the party is not a reason for him to go there. And that would successfully explain the difference between Ronnie and Bradley.

This explanation allows for a distinction between reasons and background conditions, because in Biconditional, *r* is the reason, but everything on the right-hand side of the biconditional is part of the background conditions on *r* being a reason. And it avoids committing to the Standard Model Theory, because its explanations of reasons do not advert to a further reason, but only to Biconditional, which is merely a conditional thesis about reasons, and is consistent with there being no reasons whatsoever. So strictly speaking, the Biconditional explanation of Ronnie's reason is all that Hypotheticalism needs to accept, and a version of the Humean Theory of Reasons which took this view would escape each of the four objections leveled in the last two chapters.

But Hypotheticalism opts to say more about the explanation of Ronnie's reason. One reason why it is important to do so is because it is possible to Revive a version of Korsgaard's Chauvinism objection even without the help of the Standard Model Theory. Korsgaard's version of the Chauvinism objection was a problem for a Humean who accepted the Standard Model explanation of Ronnie's reason, but wanted to avoid allowing that his view was incoherent. This Humean was forced to accept that there is one reason that is not explained by a desire in the way that Ronnie's is, because this reason is needed in order to explain every other reason. And this was Chauvinist, because someone who is willing to accept one reason as needing no explanation by a desire might as well be willing to accept others. For there is no *principled* basis on which such a view could insist that there are no others.

The Revived Chauvinism objection admits that Ronnie's reason can be explained by Biconditional even if there is no further, antecedent, reason that explains the truth of Biconditional. But if the *if* direction of Biconditional itself needs no further explanation, we might ask, why couldn't there be *more* conditions under which someone has a reason to do something? Why couldn't this be true, for example?

Neighbor   For all propositions *r* agents *x* and actions *a*, *r* is a reason for *x* to do *a* if for some person *y*, *a* is the act of being friendly to *y*, and *r* is the fact that *y* is *x*'s neighbor.

It's not that a Humean who accepts the Biconditional explanation of Ronnie's reason has to reject Neighbor—whether he does depends on whether he thinks that Neighbor is a consequence of Biconditional, together with background facts about desires and what promotes them. But anyone who accepts the Biconditional explanation of Ronnie's reason has to allow that Neighbor is beholden to Biconditional, in a way that Biconditional isn't beholden to anything.

But now we can see how to Revive the Chauvinism objection. If this sort of Humean is happy to accept the *if* part of Biconditional as unexplained, then what makes him so confident in the *only if* direction? Why must it be that every other true conditional like Neighbor has to be explained by the *if* direction of Biconditional, but this does not, further, have to be explained by anything else? If there can be *one* basic such conditional, why not others? To deny that there can be others seems merely to express a deep kind of Chauvinism, when it comes to reasons that don't obviously depend on desires. This Revived Chauvinism objection, I think, is where a lot of the pressure to postulate a further explanation of Biconditional comes from.

To respond to the Revived Chauvinism objection, an account of how Biconditional explains Ronnie's reason needs to do two things. First, it needs a story about why it is that there can be only one basic conditional ultimately explaining the existence of reasons. Alternately put, this is a story about why the right-hand side of the biconditional ultimately explaining the existence of reasons cannot be disjunctive. And second, it needs an answer to why we should think that it is the *if* direction of Biconditional that is this basic conditional, rather than Neighbor, or some other conditional about reasons.

Hypotheticalism's positive account of the explanation of Ronnie's reason proposes to answer these two challenges posed by the Revived Chauvinism Objection. According to Hypotheticalism, Biconditional is true because it merely states *what it is* for R to be a reason for X to do A:

Reason   For R to be a reason for X to do A is for there to be some p such that X has a desire whose object is p, and the truth of R is part of what explains why X's doing A promotes p.

Since Reason tells us *what it is* for R to be a reason for X to do A, Biconditional follows easily. Something can't be a chair without satisfying *what it is* to be a chair. And if something satisfies *what it is* to be a chair, nothing else is required in order for it to be a chair. So similarly for reasons.

This idea, that Hypotheticalism gives us a *constitutive* account, or an *analysis* of what it is for *R* to be a reason for *X* to do *A*, also forms the basis for an answer to the first challenge posed by the Revived Chauvinism Objection. For there can be more than one disjunct in the basic biconditional explaining the difference between Ronnie and Bradley only if the *analysis* or fundamental account of *what it is* to be a reason is disjunctive. But that is like saying that reasons are like pieces of jade—that there is nothing distinctive that they have in common. And to accept that result would plausibly amount to a kind of skepticism about reasons. So if the basic biconditional that explains the existence of reasons is basic because it merely states the correct *analysis* of reasons, then plausibly there will be pressure to think that it is not disjunctive. And that is an initial sketch of my answer to the first challenge raised by the Revived Chauvinism objection, which I will build on in Chapter 4. My answer to the second challenge is that Reason provides a better theory of what reasons are than do competing accounts. Making good on this claim requires the remainder of the book.

So this is the view taken by Hypotheticalism: Ronnie's desire explains his reason, and desires have to serve in the explanation of *every* reason, because desires are part of the correct *analysis* of reasons. This analysis is a *reductive* one. It analyzes *reasons*, a normative category, wholly in non-normative terms. So taking this stance, in response to the Revived Chauvinism objection, places Hypotheticalism firmly in the camp of the reductive normative realists. Reductive views, however, are not popular in ethics. In Chapter 4 I will fill in the details of how I think about what reduction is, what motivates it, and what motivates thinking that the explanation of Ronnie's reason works in this way. It is one of the central pieces of Hypotheticalism's positive view about the explanation of Ronnie's reason.

4

Reduction of the Normative

4.1 What is Reduction?

In Chapters 2 and 3 we considered two interesting and substantive theories about what is going on when we say that the fact that there will be dancing at the party tonight is a reason for Ronnie to go there *because* he desires to dance: the No Background Conditions view and the Standard Model Theory. Hypotheticalism rejected both of these views, both because they lead to insuperable problems when conjoined with the Humean Theory of Reasons, and because doing so seemed to be motivated by consideration merely of how well they dealt with cases like Ronnie's, considered on their own. But this was only a negative view, so in section 3.4 I began to sketch a picture of what Hypotheticalism might say: that his desire explains Ronnie's reason because having such a desire is part of *what it is* for Ronnie to have a reason—that desires are part of the correct *analysis* of reasons. If so, then Hypotheticalism amounts to a *reductive* view about reasons. In this chapter I try to fill in the picture of what I mean by that: how I understand the interesting reductive project, why it is viable and interesting, and what should make us think that it makes for a good account of how it is that Ronnie's reason is explained by his desire.

Start by comparing how the Standard Model Theory would work, if we tried to apply it to non-normative explanations. Recall that a Standard Model explanation of a difference in reasons requires that it be explained by a further reason that it had in common. So consider the figure depicted at Fig. 4.1. It is a triangle. Moreover, it has three sides. Indeed, this is no coincidence; it is a triangle *because* it has three sides. In fact, this is all that it takes for it to be a triangle. So all figures, no matter what their shape, have this conditional property: if they have exactly three sides, then they are triangles. Even the ellipse at Fig. 4.2 has this *conditional* property. Now an analogue of the Standard Model would have it that since a difference in their three-sidedness explains a difference in their shape, there must be a further shape that both figures have in common and that explains why their three-sidedness can make this difference. But in the case of shapes, that sounds completely bizarre. On the contrary, most will find it obvious that being three-sided makes a figure a triangle not because there is any further shape that all figures have, but because that is just what triangles *are*: three-sided figures.

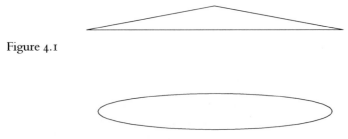

Figure 4.1

Figure 4.2

The idea behind Hypotheticalism's reductive explanation of Ronnie's reason is that it works in this same way. It is a *constitutive* explanation of why the fact that there will be dancing at the party is a reason for Ronnie to go there, because what it does is to tell us that the conditions obtain, in which that fact's being a reason for Ronnie to go to the party *consist*. Another explanation that is naturally interpreted in that way is that in Marcus's case, from section 3.1. Marcus is north of Chicago because he is in Milwaukee, and Milwaukee is north of Chicago. That explanation distinguishes Marcus from someone such as me (who is not north of Chicago) not because there is a further place that both Marcus and I are north of, but because of *what it is* to be north of a place. For a person X to be north of a place P, on a natural view, is just for X to occupy some place, Q, such that Q is north of P.[1] That is why being in Milwaukee, which is north of Chicago, explains why Marcus is north of Chicago. He could equally well have been north of Chicago by being in Racine, Kenosha, Sheboygan, or Green Bay. And that is because Racine, Kenosha, Sheboygan, and Green Bay are all places that are north of Chicago.

---

[1] This is not to say that this explanation is uncontroversial—it rests on substantivalism about space.

Constitutive explanations, I take it, are a ubiquitous phenomenon with which we need to be comfortable in order to understand a wide variety of phenomena. Figures are triangles *by* having three sides; they are not three-sided by being triangles. In Kit Fine's illuminating example, things are members of the unit set of Socrates *by* being Socrates, not Socrates by being a member of the unit set of Socrates.[2] Constitutive explanations are what get expressed by these 'by' claims, and they are something that we simply have to be comfortable with, even if we don't understand exactly how they work. So if there *are* any constitutive connections between reasons and things like desires, then we can use those connections to explain reasons in the same way that we use facts about who is located where in order to explain who is north of where, and facts about what has three sides in order to explain what is a triangle. I take it that the chief problem for applying such explanations to reasons should not be whether we understand what such explanations are claiming or what they are trying to do. Whatever that is, it is the same thing that is going on with triangles and with people being north of places.

I take it that the chief problem for applying such explanations to reasons will then be resistance to the idea that there *could be* any constitutive account of reasons in terms of desires—resistance to the idea that reasons, a normative relation, could ever be reducible to non-normative properties and relations, in the way that triangularity reduces to three-sidedness. Nevertheless, I'll now try in sections 4.1 and 4.2 to say more about what I think reduction is supposed to be, that it could play this kind of role in constitutive explanations, before I go on in sections 4.3 and 4.4 to explain why I think we should not be quite so pessimistic about whether there could be any correct constitutive account of a normative relation such as the *reason* relation in terms of non-normative properties.

The currently prevalent story about what reductive views do is that they state *property identities* between the properties of the reduced domain and the properties of the reducing domain; for example, that the property of being a triangle is identical to the property of having three sides. But this currently prevalent story does not do very much to help us make sense of constitutive explanations. The problem is that identity is symmetric. So

---

[2] Fine [1994].

it is unclear why an identity should underwrite the 'because' claims that we made, for example, about triangles. If what warrants the claim that our figure is a triangle because it has three sides was that being a triangle is identical to having three sides, then that seems equally well to warrant the claim that it has three sides because it is a triangle. So if reductions are to play a role in constitutive explanations such as that of why our figure was a triangle, then I think that we need to say more about what reductions are. In particular, I think that it should turn out that reduction is an *asymmetric* relation.

Another problematic feature of the proposal that reductive theses are merely property identities is that it makes reductive views out not to really be theses of metaphysics at all, but only in the philosophy of language or epistemology. It is no great surprise, after all, to find out that some property is identical to itself—everything is, after all. So if reductive theses are in any way informative, but they are constituted by property identity-statements, then where does that informative content come from? The literature contains two proposals. According to the first proposal, the informative content of those statements consists in the fact that they tell us that different terms of English turn out to pick out the same property.[3] According to the second proposal, the informative content of reductive theses consists in the fact that they tell us that the properties in the reduced class are *natural*, where being natural is a matter of the way in which we find out about them.[4] The problem with these proposals is that according to the first, reductive theses tell us more about English than about, for example, reasons. And according to the second, reductive theses tell us more about epistemology than about metaphysics. So I think that a proper understanding of the interesting reductive project in metaphysics should make clear why it is a metaphysical view, and not merely one about what words we can use to say what, or how we find out about something.

It's not that I want to *deny* that the property of being a triangle is identical to the property of having three sides. On the contrary, I think that that is right. But I think that focusing on the identity claim misses the point. What is interesting about this claim is not that it involves an identity, but that the term on the right-hand side of the identity elucidates something

---

[3] See e.g. Jackson [1997: 123].

[4] Compare the discussions of naturalism in Shafer-Landau [2003] and Huemer [2005] (though neither Shafer-Landau nor Huemer is a reductivist).

about the *structure* of triangularity—that it involves *sides*, and *three* of them, and so on. What makes the view that triangularity is the property of having three sides a constitutive or reductive account is not that it simply picks out that same property using a different term, but that the term that it uses to pick it out tells us something further about the nature of that property.

It used to be, after all, when reduction was conceived of as *conceptual analysis*, that reduction was thought of as an asymmetric relation. It was thought of as the relation of *analysis* among *concepts*, which were thought of as having structure. The theoretical role of concepts was to explain phenomena of *cognitive significance*. For example, if someone believes that she is seeing Hesperus but not that she is seeing Phosphorus, then it is said that she is deploying different *concepts*. But if that is the theoretical role of concepts, then it is easy to see that normative concepts such as that expressed by 'reason' are probably not plausibly analyzed in terms of non-normative concepts. For it is possible to believe that there is a reason for Ronnie to do something but not believe that he has a desire which his doing it would promote. So the work that concepts are supposed to do does not seem to call at all for an analysis of reasons in terms of something else—indeed, it seems to rule out any such analysis being plausible. And that is, very broadly, the lesson of Moore's Open Question argument.

This did not, however, lead philosophers to think that there was no interesting reductive project at all; rather, it led them to say that the interesting reductive claims were not claims about concepts at all, but about properties.[5] Yet in doing so, they actually made *two* moves. First, they switched from talk about concepts to talk about properties. And second, they switched from talk about analyses, to talk about *identities*. It is this second move that I think was a mistake. It is certainly not warranted by the observation that claims about concepts should stand or fall with phenomena of cognitive significance—that could at best warrant a move to substitute analyses of properties for analyses of concepts. The unwarranted move, I think, is to give up on the idea of an analysis altogether, substituting instead the symmetric relation of identity. Switching to talk of identities was what made reductive views symmetric and hence incapable of supporting constitutive explanations. And it was what made reductive views uninformative about the *nature* of the properties involved,

---

[5] For examples in ethics, compare Adams [1979], Railton [1986], Boyd [1989], and Brink [1989].

understanding them only as telling us something about how we talk about those properties, or about how we find out about them.

I think both these consequences are bad. I want reductive views to be able to underwrite constitutive explanations, such as that of why our three-sided figure is a triangle. And I think that in order to do so, they must be views in metaphysics, not merely views about how we use our words or how we find out about things. Both of these remain true if we understand reductive views as offering *analyses* of properties. As such, they are asymmetric—the reduction of *triangular* reduces it to *having, three,* and *sides,* by analyzing it in terms of them. But *having* does not get analyzed in terms of *triangular,* and neither do *three* or *sides.* Moreover, on this approach reductive views *do* tell us something about *triangularity,* and not merely about what words we can use to ascribe it to something. It tells us about its *structure.*

There is only one problem with this view. And it is presumably an important part of the reason why, once philosophers stopped thinking about reduction as a relation among concepts, they also stopped thinking that it was a kind of *analysis.* The problem is that it is not exactly clear what it means to say that a property is structured. In fact, according to many views about properties, properties are *not* structured, being individuated no more finely than by necessary equivalence. For example, according to Frank Jackson, a property is 'a way things might be'.[6] If these views are right, then we will not be able to make sense of the idea that reduction is a kind of *analysis* of properties. So in section 4.2 I will sketch a picture of what it means to say that properties are structured.[7] I will then argue that this conception of reduction makes sense of the connection between reduction and constitutive explanations, explains why the conjecture that the normative reduces to the non-normative should be an attractive hypothesis, and allows us to reassess the plausibility of reductive normative realism in a way that is friendly to its prospects.

---

[6] Jackson [1997: 126]. I should note that when Jackson first explains how he is going to use the word 'property', what he says is substantially weaker: 'Our notion of properties [...] is to be distinguished from the notion of properties allied to predicate or concept meanings' [1997: 16]. But for many purposes philosophers have found it convenient to *model* properties as sets of possible worlds (or, more generally, functions from worlds to truth-values), and this model is understood with metaphysical import for properties by many, following, for example, Lewis [1986].

[7] I intend the account that I'll be sketching to be broadly consonant with the kinds of ideas about essence developed in Fine [1994] and the ideas about analysis developed in King [1995], [1998], and [2002].

4.2 The Structure of Properties

According to Jackson, our grip on properties is that they are 'ways things might be'. That is why he thinks that if it is not possible for something to be one way but not another, then those are the same two ways of being, and hence the same property. But on a much older way of thinking about properties, they are features that things have *in common*. For example, compare the following figures:

    A: ■   B: ●   C: □   D: ■

There is something that A, B, and D have in common that is not shared by C—they are all shaded. There is also something that A, C, and D have in common that is not shared by B—they are all squares. And there is something that A and D have in common that is not shared by B or C—they are shaded squares. These are all properties, because they are features that different things have in common.

But the feature that A and D have in common—being *shaded squares*—is not, on the face of it, some mysterious and unrelated third thing, over and above the feature that A, B, and D have in common and the feature that A, C, and D have in common—being *shaded* and being *square*. On the face if it, being a *shaded square* is just both being *shaded* and being *square*. It is nothing over and above this. It is, I think, an example of a structured property, a property with parts. Its parts are *shaded* and *square*, and its structure is the conjunctive structure.

You may object that we might as well say that being *shaded* is simply being a *shaded square* or being a *shaded circle* or being a *shaded triangle* or . . . (and so on). After all, why is the account of *shaded square* in terms of *shaded* and *square* any better than the account of *shaded* in terms of *shaded square*, et al.? The answer is that properties are what things have *in common*. It may be that the open-ended disjunction is equivalent to *shaded*. But it doesn't tell us what shaded things have in common, because having some member of an open-ended disjunction is not having anything in common with other things that have some other member of the open-ended disjunction. On the other hand, understanding *shaded square* in terms of *shaded* and *square* does tell us what shaded squares have in common. They have more in common than shaded things, and more in common than squares. What they have in common is each of these things.

The shaded square case is only one example—the conjunctive example—of how properties can be structured. But there are other ways in which properties can be structured. For example, A, B, and C all have something in common that is not shared by D. They are all *left of D*. But what is this—being left of D? What kind of thing is that to have in common? I think that it is not hard to say. Besides looking at what individuals have in common, we can also look at what ordered *n*-tuples have in common—*relations*—of which we can take individuals to be a special case. There is something that <A,B>, <A,C>, <A,D>, <B,C>, <B,D>, and <C,D> have in common that the other pairs from among A, B, C, and D do not share. This is that the first of these pairs is *left of* the second. Given this, there is nothing surprising about what A, B, and C have in common that D does not—they all stand in this relation to D. That just *is* what they have in common: it is standing in the *left of* relation to some thing, where that thing is D.

This gives us a second way in which properties can be structured, over and above the conjunctive way, as with *shaded square*. But I think that the story is essentially the same. The structure of the property tells us what things that have it have in common, by appealing to other features that things can have in common. There are other kinds of structure that properties can have—I'm not going to try to enumerate them here. But if properties can have different kinds of structure in this way, that can explain why certain kinds of reductive view are possible that seem to be ruled out by the view that reduction is property identity.

For example, observing that a circle is the set of points in the plane equidistant from a fixed point, and that an ellipse is the set of points in the plane whose summed distance from each of two fixed points is the same, we might conjecture that all two-dimensional shape properties can be reduced to zero- and one-dimensional shape properties, along with logical and set-theoretical properties. But no two-dimensional shape property is a zero- or one-dimensional shape property, nor a logical property, nor a set-theoretical property. Nor are they obtainable merely by Boolean operations on such properties. So the view that the reduction of one set of properties to another requires that the properties in the first set either be in the second set or its Boolean closure fails to allow for interesting reductive views like that of the two-dimensional shape properties. Whereas the picture on which reduction is property analysis, where the structural relations involved in analysis are richer than Boolean operations, *can* allow for such interesting reductive views. That is another reason to prefer this account of reduction. After all, the idea that two-dimensional shape properties can be reduced in this way seems both intelligible and interesting.

What, then, does this have to do with constitutive explanations? I think that it has everything to do with constitutive explanations. Since there is no more to what shaded squares have in common than being shaded and being square, it follows that there is no other way, and no more is required, to be a shaded square than to be shaded and to be a square. So being shaded and being square is what explains why they are shaded squares. This is not a causal explanation—it is a constitutive one. So property analyses, on the model that I've sketched, seem to have everything to do with underwriting constitutive explanations.

Moreover, I claimed in section 3.4 that it would be undesirable to settle for a fundamentally disjunctive account of what it is to be a reason; we can now explain why. If what it is to be a reason were fundamentally disjunctive, then reasons would have about as much in common as pieces of jade, which, beyond being called 'jade', have no more distinctively in common than do moons of Jupiter and natural numbers smaller than 17.[8] If there *is* something that reasons have in common, then we should expect that the correct analysis of *reason* will not be fundamentally disjunctive in this way. And that answers the first problem raised by the Revived Chauvinism objection from section 3.4. The explanation of why the fundamental conditional explaining why people have the reasons that they do cannot be disjunctive, is that it is giving us a constitutive explanation of reasons, and constitutive explanations are grounded in property analyses, which tell us what things *have in common*. So if it did turn out to be fundamentally disjunctive, then that would be like saying that there isn't anything, at bottom, that reasons really do have in common. So I think that there is strong pressure, if you think of properties as what things have in common, not to settle for analyses that are fundamentally disjunctive.

---

[8] Of course, pieces of jade have a great deal more in common—they are both minerals, and so on. But these are not things that they have *distinctively* in common, setting them apart from other things—they have nothing to do with what make them pieces of jade. A third mineral might have all of the superficial properties of jade—in fact, might be mid-way between jadeite and nephrite with respect to superficial properties on which they differ—but that wouldn't make it a third kind of jade. Being jade is just being jadeite *or* being nephrite.

Once we understand reductive views in this way, I think it is easy to see why they are important. A reductive theory about shaded squares can not only enable us to give an explanation—a constitutive explanation—of why D is a shaded square. It can also enable us to explain some perfectly general facts about shaded squares. In particular, it can explain *modal* facts about shaded squares—why certain things turn out to be metaphysically impossible. I take it, for example, that it is impossible for anything to be a shaded square but not shaded, or a shaded square but not a square. Given, however, that things are shaded squares *by* being shaded and *by* being squares, it is easy to explain this. It is not possible for there to be a shaded square that is not shaded because in order for it to be a shaded square it must be so by being shaded. So *ipso facto* it is not not shaded. And similarly for squareness. So property analyses look like the right kind of thing to explain metaphysical impossibilities.

This means that property analyses are well suited to play an important theoretical role. Many philosophical domains are characterized by distinctive metaphysical impossibilities. For example, it is widely thought to be uncontroversial, or nearly so, that the set of all normative properties and relations supervenes on the set of all non-normative properties and relations over the set of all possible worlds. If so, that entails that an awful lot of ways of recombining normative with non-normative properties turn out to be metaphysically impossible. But that certainly seems to call out for some kind of explanation! After all, it doesn't take very much for something to be merely *possible*. But if normative properties are all reducible in terms of non-normative properties, then that would explain why the normative supervenes on the non-normative.

On this view, there is a natural connection between supervenience and reduction which falls short of entailment. Authors such as Jaegwon Kim and Frank Jackson have argued, using the view that reduction is property identity and their view that properties are unstructured, that supervenience entails reduction.[9] On the picture that I am offering, there is also a close connection between supervenience and reduction. But it is *explanatory*. Reductive views, on my view, are particularly good candidates to explain metaphysical impossibilities, and supervenience theses commit to huge

---

[9] Kim [1984], Jackson [1997]. Jackson's argument is actually problematic, even given his assumptions. See also Gibbard [2003], whose argument closely resembles Kim's, although he formulates the supervenience thesis in a more metaphysically neutral way, without reference to supervening properties.

numbers of metaphysical impossibilities. So reductive views are well suited to explain them. Since the normative is widely supposed to supervene on the non-normative, it follows that the reducibility of the normative to the non-normative should be an attractive explanatory hypothesis. It would be the right kind of hypothesis to successfully explain the impossibilities that we independently recognize.

Of course, it is not completely uncontroversial that the normative supervenes on the non-normative. But the reducibility of the normative to the non-normative can be motivated on the basis of far weaker assumptions about metaphysical impossibilities. Here is the most uncontroversial metaphysical impossibility about recombining normative and non-normative properties that I've been able to come up with: I think that it is impossible that the entire universe could be exactly like it is actually in all non-normative respects, but the fact that my mother is my mother is a reason for me to torture her. Supervenience is a strong thesis, so I can see room to doubt it. But I can't see any room to doubt that the scenario I've just described is impossible. So it follows that there are at least some impossibilities about how normative and non-normative properties can be recombined, and hence that the reducibility of the normative to the non-normative is an attractive explanatory hypothesis.

On the picture that I've been sketching, there is nothing peculiar or weird about saying that properties have structure. To say that a property has a certain structure is simply to say something about what things that have it have in common. Since reductive views elucidate the structure of properties, therefore, there is an intimate connection between reduction and constitutive explanation, reduction is asymmetric, and it is a metaphysical view, rather than one about how we use our words or how we find out about things. Finally, on the picture I've been sketching, because reductive views elucidate the structure of properties and the structure of properties tells us something about what *explains why* things have the structured property, it follows that reductive views can provide attractive explanations of metaphysical impossibilities. And that, I think, makes reductive hypotheses, particularly about the normative, to be deeply theoretically attractive.

All of this goes some way toward making sense of how it is that Hypotheticalism conceives of reductive explanation, and why reductive views about the normative, of which Hypotheticalism is an example, should be at least initially attractive as theoretical hypotheses. But it does not get around the problem that reductive views about the normative are widely supposed to be quite hopeless. In the remainder of this chapter I will provide a diagnosis of why such views are so often viewed to be hopeless, argue that there are good grounds to think that things are not quite as bad as they seem, and explain how to read the rest of this book as a defense of reductive realism about the normative, just as much as a defense of the Humean Theory of Reasons.

4.3   Reduction and Elimination

Most discussions of whether any reductive view about any normative property could possibly be true focus on one or another version of Moore's Open Question argument. But this is hard to take seriously, once we clarify that reduction is a metaphysical thesis, rather than one about our normative concepts or the meanings of our normative words. Open Question arguments employ tests of cognitive significance—for example, they ask whether someone can believe that Ronnie has a reason without believing anything about Ronnie's desires, or conversely. If concepts are what we use to distinguish between *thoughts*, then this is a good test for whether the concepts are identical. But as I am understanding reduction, it is not a view about our thoughts. Alternatively, Open Question arguments substitute terms in different sentences, and ask whether the two sentences are synonymous. Again, this *may* be the right test for synonymy, but as I am understanding reductive views, they are not views about synonymy.

Solving the Open Question problem is an exercise in philosophical cut-and-paste. All of the Open Question tests for cognitive significance distinguish between Hesperus and Phosphorus and between Superman and Clark Kent. But no one concludes that Hesperus is not Phosphorus, or that Superman is not Clark Kent. On the contrary, philosophers have any number of theories about why we get the results about cognitive significance that we do with respect to co-referring names. There are several Fregean answers to this question, non-descriptive, descriptive, neo-, and otherwise, and several varieties of Millian answers to it, and all of these now come at increasing levels of sophistication. Solving the Open Question problem doesn't even require taking any particular view about any of these questions. All that it takes is borrowing your favorite theory about names and applying it to predicates. So in the absence of some careful, sophisticated reasoning in the philosophy of language to explain why we won't be able to generalize many of these accounts from names to predicates, it seems to me that Open Question arguments are a non-starter; they don't even raise the right issues.

It should be bizarre, then, if the main general argument against reductive views is a non-starter, that reductive views are so often thought to be completely hopeless. It is held to be *obvious* that any reductive theory would be wrong, and even that reductive theories all fail to be realist—reducing the normative, it is thought, amounts to eliminating it. For example, Graham Oddie thinks it goes without saying that '[t]hat which is reducible is less real than that to which it reduces',[10] while in a textbook on metaethics, David McNaughton explicitly categorizes reductive views as irrealist, despite the fact that they satisfy his own definition of 'realism':

While such a reductive account ensures that moral views are true or false in virtue of facts that are independent of the speaker's opinion on the matter, it is nevertheless an irrealist position. For it does not allow that there are *distinctive* moral facts which are independent of our current opinions, waiting to be discovered by our moral inquiries.[11]

I think that this thought cuts closer to the heart of what people find most dissatisfying about reductive views than does the Open Question argument. In this section and the next I'll introduce my diagnosis of what the biggest, hardest challenge is for reductive views about normative properties such as that of being a *reason*, and how I think it needs to be solved.

It is Thomas Nagel, I think, who puts the objection best: 'If values are objective, they must be so in their own right, and not through reducibility to some other kind of objective fact. They have to be objective *values*, not objective anything else.'[12] The problem is that according to typical

---

[10] Oddie [2005: 18]. In a similar vein Derek Parfit writes without argument of Humean theories of reasons: 'Of the writers who give such reductive accounts, some claim to be describing normative reasons. But on such views, I believe, there aren't really any normative reasons. There are only causes of behavior' [forthcoming]; manuscript, July 2006, 45.

[11] McNaughton [1989: 44]. McNaughton's definition of 'realism' comes at [1989: 39]: 'The moral realist denies the existence of that sharp and significant division between fact and value which is the hallmark of his opponent's position. In the realist's view, moral opinions are beliefs which, like other beliefs, are determined true or false by the way things are in the world.' Notice that in the official definition, there is no mention of the need for these facts to be 'distinctive'.

[12] Nagel [1986: 138].

classifications of metaethical views in the literature, including those by virtue of which typical reductive realists classify themselves as 'realist', what it takes to be a realist is to be a cognitivist but not an error-theorist—to hold that normative sentences express beliefs which are sometimes true. But Nagel rightly thinks that this makes realism far too easy to come by. Suppose that I accept the following 'reductive' view about the sentence, 'murder is wrong'. I hold that it means that pigs are mammals. And since it is true that pigs are mammals, I hold that 'murder is wrong' is not only truth-apt, but expresses a truth. So I satisfy the standard definition of 'realism'. But does it follow that I am a realist about wrongness? Intelligibly, the answer is 'no'. If I tell you that this is what I mean by 'murder is wrong', then when I tell you that I believe that murder is wrong, correct principles of charitable interpretation seem to require attributing to me the belief that pigs are mammals, rather than the belief that murder is wrong. After all, that is what I told you that I meant by 'murder is wrong'!

I think this is Nagel's thought, and the thought of many other critics of reductive views about the normative. The thought is simply that it is *not enough* to believe in values to assign 'values' a referent in which you believe. You have to assign *values* as the referent of 'values'. And this is what Nagel, McNaughton, Oddie, Parfit, Shafer–Landau, Hampton, and many others believe that it is not possible for any reductive view to do. Of course, the trick is that they don't think that it will be possible to do this because they think no reductive normative theory is *true*. But that won't do as a premise in a non-question-begging argument against reduction.

Nevertheless, I think that we are on the right track, for I think an analogy can be highly instructive about what Nagel clearly has *right*.[13] Suppose that Lauren, a previously professed atheist, lets you know that she's come around to believing in God. Fortunately, she advises you, this did not require any changes in her world-view, but only a change in her understanding of the referent of 'God'. What she realized was that God is love, and that she already believes in love—it is the relation that she bears toward her family and her friends. It is natural to think that Lauren still does not believe in God. Since she's told you what she means by 'God',

---

[13] I take the analogy from a remark of Alvin Plantinga's, in response to Kit Fine's suggestion that he is engaged in a reductive project about possibilia: 'This strikes me a bit like an effort on the part of a genial atheist to offer a "truth-preserving" translation of theistic discourse into discourse committed to only the sorts of entities acceptable to atheists.' Plantinga [1986: 330–1].

and that it is just love, when Lauren tells you that she believes in God it is natural to interpret her as believing in love. But if she previously believed in love while counting as an atheist, she should not now count as a theist for believing in it.

It is highly plausible that the same would follow *no matter* what referent Lauren assigns to 'God'. As long as it is the sort of thing that is acceptable to atheists, she will not count as believing in God after all, even though given her new uses of her terms, she will be able to mimic the claims of theists, and to sincerely utter such sentences as 'God exists'. She will merely mean something different by such sentences than we do. Traditional theism is plausibly *not* subject to naturalist-friendly reduction, and couldn't be. If that thought makes sense, I take it that non-reductive realists such as McNaughton, Oddie, Nagel, Parfit, Shafer–Landau, Hampton, and Enoch,[14] when they find it obvious that no reduction of the normative would really be sufficiently realist about normativity, are thinking that it is like the theological in this way.

Unfortunately, however, none of these theorists has told us what independent test we can apply that is satisfied by the theological and not by triangles. But this is a crucially important task. For not all reductive views are manifestly eliminativist, in the way of the reduction of the theological. If Lauren tells you that she believes in triangles because she believes in three-sided figures, and thinks that 'triangle' picks out three-sided figures, you will not thereby conclude that Lauren does not believe in triangles after all but only three-sided figures. Since triangles *are* just three-sided figures, you will conclude that that is all that it takes for her to believe in triangles.

The difference between triangles and God, I think, and this is the first prong of my two-prong diagnosis, is that on any acceptable view about God, God has properties that love does not. God is supposed to be omniscient, but love is just a relation—it doesn't know anything. God is supposed to be the creator of the universe, but love didn't do that. And so on. To capture the central claims of theological discourse, it's *not* enough to make sense of the thesis that God exists, by assigning 'God' a referent. You have to assign 'God' a referent which created the universe

---

[14] McNaughton [1989], Oddie [2005], Nagel [1986], Parfit [forthcoming], Shafer–Landau [2003], Hampton [1998], Enoch [2007: ii. 21–50].

and is all-knowing and all-powerful, since these are some of the central claims which theological discourse is supposed to capture. So if you don't really believe that there is a thing such that it created the universe and is all-knowing and all-powerful, then you can't capture the central claims of theological discourse, no matter what referent you assign to 'God'. On the other hand, it is easy to observe that all the properties of triangles are possessed by three-sided plane figures—the proofs can be found in Euclid.

I think that this is the key difference between God and triangles. God has properties that atheists don't believe are satisfied by anything—and that is why they don't count as believing in God, even if they accept a theory on which 'God' has a referent. But triangles don't have any properties that people who believe in three-sided plane figures are skeptical about. On the contrary, what makes the theory that triangles are just three-sided plane figures such a good theory, is simply that three-sided plane figures have all the properties that triangles are supposed to have. There is much more to be said about this, and I have tried to say some of it elsewhere,[15] but when it comes down to it, most interesting objections to reductive normative theories amount to versions of this idea. They pose some feature that normative properties are supposed to have, and argue that no reductive account could possibly explain that feature.

But I said that my diagnosis consists of two prongs. The second prong arises when we consider how a sophisticated reductivist might try to solve these problems, in order to avoid committing to so many local errors about God. For there *is* room to wiggle. You may start by assigning an interpretation to 'God' in the sentence, 'God exists,' and then notice that the thing you assigned to it—love, for example, did not actually create the universe, at least in the ordinary sense of 'create'. But if you're a clever reductive theorist, you have some tricks to pull out of your sleeve. You can provide 'created' a special sense in this context. When theists say that God created the universe, you can posit, what they mean is that God is a relation between creative people and their creations. Assuming that creative people love their creations, 'God created the universe' turns out to be true. So in this way, you can capture the central truths of theistic discourse with your reduction.

---

[15] Schroeder [2005a].

Or can you? You have a theory on which 'God created the universe' comes out to be true, but you haven't got a theory on which it is true that God created the universe. For by hypothesis, you mean something else by 'God created the universe' than that God created the universe. Creation, on your account, is not a unified or interesting phenomenon, as people have always believed, but in fact is fundamentally disjunctive. It can be true that X created Y either if Y did not exist, and then was made to exist through X's efforts, or else if X is love, and is a relation between creative people and their creations. Your account makes the central claims of theological discourse come out sounding true only because it trades on the ambiguity between these two ways of being created. But theists have always wanted the universe to come out created by God in the *same* sense as the half-finished matchstick model of 1879 Hall in my living room comes out created by me. So giving a disjunctive or ambiguous account of 'created' won't help you capture the central claims of traditional Christian theism.

You might try and fix this by holding that your reinterpretation of 'created' is in fact how the word 'created' works *all of the time*. This would make it more plausible that you've captured the central claims of theism, for when you say that God created the universe, you mean that he created it in the same sense that I created the half-finished matchstick model of 1879 Hall in my living room. But just as your revisionary account of 'God' had to capture the central claims about God in order to count as robustly realist, your revisionary account of creation is going to have to capture the central claims about creation, in order to be plausibly an account of *creation*, as opposed to some other thing. It will have to capture, for example, the claims that creation is an *action*, and that before something is created it does not exist, while after it is created it does.[16] If your account can't capture these kinds of truths, then you haven't succeeded in talking about creation. And if you haven't succeeded in talking about creation, you haven't succeeded in giving a reductive account of God.

This is the problem of what I call *propagating implications*, and it is the second prong of my diagnosis of what makes the theological look to be

---

[16] This one by itself might be hard enough for a theist who believes that God created the universe *outside* time, rather than at some point *in* time.

irreducible. Because the central commitments of theological discourse are set out primarily in non-theological terms, anything we tweak in our account of 'creation' or 'omniscience' in order to avoid local errors is going to enmesh us in further errors about creation and knowledge in domains that on the face of it have nothing to do with theology. Since the implications of tweaks in our account of the central theological notions *propagate*, it's highly unpromising to think that there could ever be a way to smooth out the carpet—the bulge is always going to end up someplace else, and likely to grow along the way.

If this is the right diagnosis of what makes it seem like the reductive view about God is hopelessly atheist, then the correct response on behalf of the reductive theorist about the normative should be clear: that the normative is not subject to propagating implications in the same way as the theological. It is not hard to see why this is so. For the central commitments of theological discourse are primarily set out in wholly non-theological terms—creation, knowledge, and so on. But many of the central commitments of normative discourse are primarily set out at least in part in terms of other normative notions.

Claims connecting the normative up with the non-normative are mostly highly tendentious, until the non-normative side is provided some kind of normative qualification. For example, metaethical internalists claim that it is a central commitment of normative discourse that whenever someone makes a normative judgment, she will be motivated to act accordingly. But very few people accept this straightforward version of metaethical internalism anymore. Almost all proponents of internalism allow that when someone makes a normative judgment, it is only if she is *practically rational* that she will be motivated to act accordingly.[17] The principal work, here, in all such views, seems to be done by the notion of practical rationality. Indeed, since Michael Smith takes metaethical internalism to be *the* central commitment about the normative, it is precisely this fact that lets him capture it. He gives a reductive account of practical rationality on which it is essentially the disposition to acquire desires that will motivate one to act in accordance with one's normative judgments. In other words, he gives it precisely the reduction necessary in order to make meta-ethical internalism come out true, no matter what the account of the other normative

---

[17] See especially Korsgaard [1986] and Smith [1994].

phenomena turns out to be—reductive or not.[18] This kind of tweak in order to avoid error suppresses the error locally, instead of spreading it under another part of the carpet. So it avoids the propagating implications of the reductive account of God, while capturing the important truth (if it is a truth) of meta-ethical judgment internalism.

4.4 Capturing Normativity

If meta-ethical internalism is true, however, it is still only one interesting and central claim about the normative that a reduction will have to capture in order not to plausibly count as being eliminative. It used to be said that judgment internalism was one of the features that a reductive realist view could not capture. But in full awareness that reductive theorists have made real progress in accounting for such phenomena as judgment internalism, non-reductivists have raised the stakes. They now say that it is the *normativity* of normative properties and relations for which reductive theorists will not be able to account.[19] But as I'll now show, it is actually easy for reductive views to account for the normativity of normative properties and relations. Their ability to do so follows directly from my observation about what makes for propagating implications and what does not. What makes it so easy to account for normativity is that normativity itself is best explained in terms of *reasons*, another normative relation. So the datum that normative properties must be normative is not one that is cashed out wholly in non-normative terms, in the way that the datum that God created the universe is. And that is precisely what I said made it possible to make the data work out without leading to propagating implications.

So what *does* it take to be normative? Surely for dialectical purposes we can do no better than to look for the *hardest case* for reduction. And for that, I turn to Jean Hampton, who claims to have diagnosed exactly this: precisely what the feature of normative claims is, which could not possibly be acceptable to any reductive theorist. It is that normative claims involve claims about *reasons*: 'At last we have in hand the "queer" element in the

---

[18] Smith [1994]. The details in Smith's view are somewhat more complicated, and Smith himself denies that his overall account is reductive, but this is essentially the picture, and the solution could be adopted by someone who did understand the overall picture as reductive.

[19] See e.g. Parfit [unpublished], Hampton [1998].

objectivists' moral theory that precludes its scientific acceptability... It is the claim that there are moral norms that are "objectively authoritative" *in the sense that they give us normatively necessary reasons* for various human activities.'[20] The distinctively queer thing about the normative, according to Hampton, is that normative claims commit us to the existence of *reasons*. But reasons themselves are a normative category, so we're already doing well with respect to the problem of propagating implications.

Of course, there is a long and troubled tradition of trying to characterize what is distinctive of the normative by means of the *entailments* of normative claims.[21] To cite just one relevant issue, there is intuitively an important distinction between what I call normatively *relevant* claims, and claims which are actually normatively *contentful*. But both of these categories entail the existence of reasons. So, for example, consider the fact that by pulling the trigger of the gun while it is pointed at one's skull, one will ensure one's own death. Plausibly, this truth has as a necessary consequence that there is a reason for one not to pull the trigger of the gun while it is pointed at one's own skull. But that doesn't mean that we should therefore think that facts about guns and death count as normative. These facts are, one might have thought, paradigmatically *non*-normative, even if they might have obvious normative consequences. I call such facts normatively *relevant*, even though they are not normatively *contentful*.

Though this is terminology of art, of course, it is not implausible to think that it strikes near enough to describing what the relevant difference is between the claim that pulling the trigger will result in your death, and the claim that it is better not to pull the trigger. Though the first claim may have a claim about reasons as a *consequence*, it is intuitively not itself *about* reasons, in the way that the second one may be. So on this view, if Hampton's thesis is right, we have to further understand her as saying not merely that normative claims *entail* the existence of reasons, but that they themselves *involve* claims about the existence of reasons.

Now there may be more than one way to understand what this talk of a normative claim's already being *about* reasons, or already *involving*

---

[20] Hampton [1998: 115], italics added for emphasis. But we don't have to settle for Hampton's opinion of the matter. Compare Joseph Raz [1999b: 67] on the same subject: 'The normativity of all that is normative consists in the way that it is, or provides, or is otherwise related to reasons.' Raz is no more friendly to reduction or the Humean Theory of Reasons than Hampton is.

[21] See e.g. Prior [1960].

claims about reasons. But on a natural view, it is the thesis that normative properties and relations have to be partly *analyzed* in terms of reasons:

Reason Basicness   What it is to be normative, is to be analyzed in terms of reasons.

The normative is all about reasons. And I think that this is a broadly attractive thesis about what is distinctive of the normative, something like which is currently accepted or at least found attractive by moral philosophers of extremely different bents. Any view that looks attractive to Jonathan Dancy, Jean Hampton, Michael Smith, Derek Parfit, T. M. Scanlon, and Joseph Raz has to be one with some kind of very broad appeal.[22]

This way of characterizing the normative has a very impressive lineage; for centuries moral philosophers have characterized their subject matter as being everything which ultimately involved claims about what was *good*, or as everything which ultimately involved claims about what was *right*, or as everything which ultimately involved claims about what someone *ought* to do. All of these views claim that what it is for a property or concept to be normative, is for it to be ultimately analyzable in terms of some *basic* normative property or relation or concept. They merely disagree about what this basic property or concept *is*.

But if attractive views about what is distinctive of the normative so often take this *structural* form, then the result that *good*, and *right* and *just* and *reason* and so on are truly *normative* properties, is one that it is actually incredibly *easy* for a reductive theorist to get right. Since being normative is a matter of a *structural* relation to some basic normative property like that of being a *reason*, the reductive theorist can accept this characterization of the normative. Then, she can accept whatever analyses of each *non*-basic normative property in terms of the basic property are accepted by the non-reductive theorists who share this conception of what is distinctive of the normative. And finally, she gives her reductive theory as an analysis of the basic normative property or relation. So it turns out that even the normativity of normative properties is easy for a reductive theory to capture.

---

[22] See Dancy [2004], Hampton [1998], Smith [1994], Parfit [unpublished], Scanlon [1998], and Raz [1999*b*].

It obviously doesn't follow from this that any reductive view is true. At best, what I've succeeded in doing in the last two sections is diagnosing and rebutting the most prominent motivation for thinking that reducing the normative is *hopeless*. So I think it is not hopeless. But I do think that if what I've said here is on the right track, then figuring out whether any reductive view is *true* is not the sort of thing that we can do without getting our hands dirty. In the absence of any particular reductive account, we can point out the theoretical explanatory advantages of reductive accounts, and we can point out the challenges that they must overcome. But in the end, the way to figure out whether triangularity can be analyzed is to propose that triangles are three-sided plane figures, and then do the geometry to see whether this checks out. The way to see whether the notion of a limit can be analyzed is to propose the delta-epsilon definition, and then do the real analysis to see whether it checks out. And similarly, the way to see whether normative properties like that of being a reason can be analyzed, is to propose your analysis, and see whether it checks out.

In addition to being an existence proof of a viable version of the Humean Theory of Reasons, this book also purports to be an existence proof of a viable reductive view about the normative. If we follow the argument of this section, then a reductive account of normative properties and relations can capture their *normativity* only if it accepts Reason Basicness. But this means that any viable version of reductive realism will need an analysis of *reasons* in non-normative terms. And according to sections 4.1 and 4.2, such an analysis would have to underwrite a perfectly general explanation of why things are reasons—an explanation that would have to appeal to only non-normative properties and relations. But notice that this is exactly what the Humean Theory of Reasons is trying to do! So according to Hypotheticalism, desires serve in the explanation of reasons by serving as part of the *analysis* of reasons, and this doesn't only help us explain Ronnie's reason—it also plays a key role in defending a reductive account of the normative more generally, which is, as I argued, an independently attractive explanatory hypothesis.

But the standards for a successful reductive account are high: it must get the right results about all the things that are true about reasons. Yet the Humean Theory of Reasons is generally believed to be hopeless on this score. It is thought to get the wrong results about the most obvious questions, starting with *which* reasons there are. It is both thought to allow for Too Many reasons, and for Too Few. So if Hypotheticalism is going to get anywhere, it will have to deal with these objections to the Humean Theory. Doing so will be the focus of the next three chapters.

5

Too Many Reasons

5.1 Too Many Reasons

We spent Chapters 2 through 4 looking into how it is that Hypotheticalism understands the 'because' clause in the claim that Ronnie has his reason because he desires to dance. A small number of interesting views led to a variety of important challenges to the Humean Theory. In Chapters 5 through 7 we turn to focus on the two most straightforward kinds of objection to the Humean Theory—that it gets extensionally the wrong results, either by allowing for reasons that there aren't, or by not allowing for reasons that there are. The former objection is the focus in Chapter 5; the latter in Chapter 6.

My Aunt Margaret wants to reconstruct the scene depicted on page 78 of the November 2001 *Martha Stewart Living* catalogue on Mars. In order to do this, she needs to construct a Mars-bound spacecraft—for no one is going to give her one. Nevertheless, intuitively, Aunt Margaret still ought not to build her Mars-bound spacecraft. Now the Humean Theory of Reasons is consistent with this verdict. But the Humean theory *is* committed to claiming that there *is some* reason for Aunt Margaret to build her spacecraft. And intuitively, this is also not the right result. According to a very natural intuition, there is simply *no* reason for Aunt Margaret to build her spacecraft. Since the Humean theory says that there is, it must be false. This is the *Too Many Reasons* objection to the Humean Theory of Reasons. It is the accusation that the Humean explanation of Ronnie's reason will overgeneralize.

In order to deal with the Too Many Reasons objection, most Humeans adopt *restrictions* on their Humeanism. They say, for example, that not just any desire is sufficient for the presence of reasons, but only desires that would survive *cognitive psychotherapy*[1] or persist in *reflective equilibrium*.[2] Or they say that it is what we *desire to desire* that matters, or what we *value*, or what our *life projects* are.[3] These are all possible theories about the kind of psychological state that explains the difference between Ronnie and Bradley—about what *desires* are, in my technical sense. The harder it is to get into this kind of psychological state, the fewer cases there will be in which someone is in it, and consequently the fewer the cases in which someone is in it, but intuitively has no corresponding reason.

In contrast, according to Korsgaard, Humeans are committed to saying that someone desires something just in case it is an action that she actually does.[4] And according to Warren Quinn, a Humean must think that any behavioral disposition whatsoever must count as a desire.[5] If either of these views were true, then it would make desires in the sense required by the Humean very easy to come by. And the easier desires are to come by, the more unintuitive results to which the Humean will be committed. But we know from Chapter 1 that all that a Humean needs is that all reasons are explained by the same kind of psychological state—within these bounds a Humean can take many different views about what kind of psychological state this is. And so according to *restricted* versions of the Humean Theory of Reasons, desires in the relevant sense are relatively hard to come by.

The idea, then, is that we get one of two results. Either desires are so hard to come by that Aunt Margaret turns out not to qualify, or once we clarify how she satisfies all the relevant requirements, it is not so unintuitive after all that she has a reason to build a Mars-bound spacecraft. Perhaps, for example, a desire like hers would not survive in reflective equilibrium, or could easily be cleansed by cognitive psychotherapy. Or perhaps, being

---

[1] Brandt [1979].   [2] Smith [1994].

[3] See Frankfurt [1971], Lewis [1989], Watson [1975], and Williams [1973].

[4] Korsgaard [1997: 223]: 'If the instrumental principle is the only principle of practical reason, then to say that something is your end is not to say that you have a reason to pursue it, but at most to say that you are *going* to pursue it (perhaps inspired by a desire). [...] the instrumental principle instructs us to derive a reason from what we are *going* to do.'

[5] Quinn [1993b: 235–6]: 'To say in the intended sense that someone has a pro-attitude toward world peace is to say, among other things, that his psychological setup disposes him to do that which he believes will make world peace more likely [...] How can the fact that we are set up to go in a certain direction make it (even *prima facie*) rational to decide to go in that direction?' Quinn claims, at the beginning of this paper, to be criticizing not the Humean Theory of Reasons, but rather non-cognitivism. But then he conflates non-cognitivism with the Humean Theory of Reasons in a way that no moderately sophisticated non-cognitivist would accept. So I take it as fair to assume that the real target of the central argument in the paper is the Humean theory.

merely a whim, it is not something that she desires to desire, or genuinely values, or sincerely has as one of her central life projects. Then, if our restricted version of the Humean Theory of Reasons requires these things, we won't be committed to saying that she has a reason to build her spacecraft.

This is an excellent tactic to use in confronting the Too Many Reasons objection. But the problem with this tactic is that it appears to be insufficient. For surely it is at least *possible* that Aunt Margaret's desire *would* survive in reflective equilibrium, and really is her central life project. It is true that assuming this to be the case tends to mitigate the unintuitiveness of saying that she has a reason to build her spacecraft. But it does not eliminate it entirely, and pretending otherwise does the Humean theory a disservice. It is very natural to think that there is still no reason for Aunt Margaret to build her spacecraft. Moreover, it seems that there can be a reason for Ronnie to go to the party, even if dancing doesn't exactly qualify as one of his central life projects.[6] Hypotheticalism, therefore, holds that even if we adopt the most restricted version of the Humean Theory of Reasons, we still owe a further response to the Too Many Reasons objection. And once we have this further response in hand, Hypotheticalism holds that our Humeanism no longer need be so restrictive—unlike the most restrictive version, it can be relaxed enough to account for Ronnie's case after all.

The Too Many Reasons objection might be bad enough by itself—it seems to be a general argument that any version of the Humean Theory of Reasons is going to be committed to a wide range of false predictions. In company with my diagnosis of what is most problematic about reductive views from Chapter 4, however, the objection is much more important. For to the extent that a Humean is willing to admit to accepting results that are intuitively false, other philosophers are going to legitimately infer that he has simply changed the subject, and is talking about something else entirely. It is natural to think that if someone holds that there is a reason for Aunt Margaret to build a Mars-bound spacecraft in her backyard, then he simply can't be talking about the honest-to-goodness *objective normative*

---

[6] I'm not suggesting, here, that this ultra-restrictive version of the Humean theory is the best restrictive account. I'm just pointing out that there is a cost to restricting the kinds of thing that can count as desires, for the purposes of the theory. Plausibly, whatever restriction is necessary in order to ensure that counterexamples are *impossible* will be too much of a restriction to allow for the full range of cases like that of Ronnie in the first place.

sense of 'reason', in which reasons count in favor of what they are reasons for, and play a contributory role in determining whether someone ought to do it.

I take it that this is a good reason for Humeans—even those who have always been satisfied with accepting more restricted forms of the Humean Theory as a response to the Too Many Reasons objection—to take the objection more seriously. For these reasons, the Too Many Reasons objection is a legitimate worry, and we need to take more care over it. I believe that a better answer to the objection can be had, and will give it in the second half of this chapter. But first, it is worth surveying four more important objections to the Humean Theory which all assume that the Too Many Reasons objection works. The existence of these arguments, I think, is evidence that *critics* of the Humean Theory, at least, are *very* bothered by the Too Many Reasons objection. And that should be enough to motivate defenders to say more about it, whether they are themselves bothered by it or not.

5.2 Four More Incoherence Arguments

In Chapter 3 we saw that one implication of the Standard Model Theory was that the Humean Theory of Reasons would have to be literally incoherent—committed to the existence of a reason to pursue one's desires that both does, and does not, explain itself. This isn't the only interesting argument, however, that the Humean Theory of Reasons is literally incoherent. In fact, there is a small industry of offering arguments that this is the case. One might have thought that a view which is apparently popular enough to be so often described as 'the favoured view among professional philosophers'[7] should admit of at least one possible interpretation on which it is merely false, rather than actually self-contradictory. But apparently this isn't so.

Fortunately for the sake of taxonomy, most of these arguments can be better understood as posing *dilemmas* for the Humean Theory of Reasons. The dilemma is this: either the Humean must accept that he is committed to Too Many Reasons, or he can accept one or another friendly 'fix' to

---

[7] This is the description of Bond [1983: 3], but it fits the flavor of a great deal of discussion.

his explanation of Ronnie's reason. And the problem with this fork of the dilemma is that each of these 'fixes' results in an incoherent view, once we propose to generalize it to the explanation of *every* reason.

I say that we should think of these arguments as dilemmas. The philosophers who offer them don't see them that way; they treat them as straightforward arguments that the Humean Theory of Reasons must be incoherent. But like all general objections to the Humean Theory of Reasons, they trade on assumptions about how the explanation of Ronnie's reason is supposed to work. In particular, they assume that the account of Ronnie's case has to incorporate one or another of the 'fixes' that I mentioned. The philosophers who offer these arguments don't, with the exception of Quinn and Scanlon, take seriously the idea that a Humean would insist on accepting a view that incorporates none of these 'fixes'. (Or, for that matter, that a Humean would incorporate a different 'fix' than the one they suggest.) But in the case of each incoherence argument, the assumed 'fix' is motivated on the grounds that it would give a way around the *too many reasons* objection. Since in each case that is the key assumption motivating the arguments, I say that we should think of them as dilemmas.[8]

I take it that any version of the Humean Theory of Reasons is going to endorse some reading of this conditional:[9]

1   If doing *A* promotes what Ronnie desires, then there is a reason for Ronnie to do *A*.

The Too Many Reasons objection is simply that no matter what *desires* are and what it takes for an action to *promote* one, this thesis will have intuitive counterexamples. But perhaps that can be fixed. Each of the incoherence arguments offers a putative 'fix' of 1, together with an explanation of why that fix will make the Humean Theory of Reasons incoherent.

Korsgaard's argument is the most straightforward of these. Korsgaard holds that the needed fix to 1 is that in the sense in which 1 is true, we can't think of 'desire' as naming a non-normatively specified merely dispositional

---

[8] And the very fact that any philosopher could think of such an argument as demonstrating a view to be incoherent is ample evidence for how serious critics of the Humean Theory take the Too Many Reasons objection to be.

[9] Humeans will, of course, disagree about what kind of psychological state a desire is, in the required sense (see Chs. 1 and 8), what it takes for an action to *promote* a desire (see Ch. 6), and even what the consideration is, which is the reason for Ronnie to do *A* (see Ch. 2).

psychological state.[10] Her view is that 1 leads to unacceptable consequences whenever we supply a non-normative story about what counts as a desire.[11] But if we supply a *normative* story about what counts as a desire, then the claim that X has a desire whose object is p must appeal to some normative claim or other, and hence (recall the thesis of *Reason-Basicness* from section 4.4) to a *reason*. For example, suppose we say[12] that in the stipulative sense of 'desire' someone's desires are the things that there is a *reason* for her to desire in the colloquial sense, or which there is a reason for her to desire and she actually does desire. If one of *these* is the kind of psychological difference that we think distinguishes Ronnie from Bradley, then 1 can help explain why Ronnie ought to do something only if there are things that there is antecedently a reason for Ronnie to do. But these reasons can't in turn be explained by desires in this same way, on pain of circularity or regress.

An argument due to T. M. Scanlon and Warren Quinn to which we'll return in Chapter 8 is very similar to Korsgaard's in flavor.[13] Quinn and Scanlon propose that 1 is really only plausibly counterexample-proof if we understand desires as a kind of psychological state that involves seeing certain considerations *as reasons* or certain states of affairs *as valuable*. Quinn and Scanlon don't quite say that this would make the Humean theory incoherent; they simply say that it gets things the wrong way

---

[10] She puts it by saying that we can't think that our *ends* are simply given by what we *desire*. But that's because she's using the word 'end' in the stipulative sense, for whatever psychological state it is that the 'instrumental principle' is true about—i.e. which makes a difference in such cases as Ronnie and Bradley's. And she's using the word 'desire' in something more like its colloquial sense. But as I stipulated in Ch. 1, I'm using the word 'desire' for the kind of state that makes the difference in such cases as Ronnie and Bradley's.

[11] Korsgaard's argument on this score is highly questionable—she seems to claim that the only conception of desire available to the Humean Theory of Reasons is that on which someone desires to do A just in case she actually does it [1997: 220–34]. But not even economists interested only in 'revealed preferences' would accept such a view. Fortunately for Korsgaard, I think it is possible to construct a more careful argument that would do the right work for her, and with less (apparent) reliance on the assumption that the merits of the Humean Theory of Reasons can be adequately assessed by critiquing Hume's own views.

[12] Neither of these is the version of the proposal that Korsgaard actually advocates, but her proposal complicates things considerably and in any case I'm not certain that it works. The proposal that she prefers may actually be a version of what I'm calling the Quinn–Scanlon line, but I think that complicates both whether it gives us a good explanation of Ronnie's reason (see Ch. 8) and whether it shows any version of the Humean theory to be incoherent which doesn't purport to provide an *analysis* of reasons (see main text).

[13] Scanlon [1998], Quinn [1993b]. Their arguments bear strong affinities to Anscombe [1957: 70–2].

around. But on one way of pushing their point, we do get an incoherence argument. It isn't the same as Korsgaard's, because someone who accepts the Quinn–Scanlon 'fix' isn't using actual further reasons in order to explain Ronnie's reason, but only psychological states that have something about reasons as part of their *content*. So there is no explanatory circle. But there is a *conceptual* circle for some forms of the Humean Theory of Reasons. Hypotheticalism, for example, claims to explain Ronnie's reason by providing an analysis of reasons in terms of desires. So it can't accept the Quinn–Scanlon fix that desires are really to be further analyzed in terms of reasons, without being incoherent. I'll have considerably more to say about the Quinn–Scanlon line in Ch. 8.

The two remaining incoherence arguments grant the Humean that we are to understand 'desire' to pick out a non-normatively specified psychological state. Still, something must be done in order to avoid the dreadful consequences to which claim 1 commits us. These two arguments assume that what must be done is to understand the plausibility of 1 as deriving from the truth of another principle:

2   There is a reason for Ronnie to *either* do what promotes each of his desires or not have those desires.

The analogue of this view is widely promulgated concerning not what there are *reasons* to do, but what people *ought* to do. On this view, there may be an uncontroversial truth that you ought to do what promotes your desires, but if there is, we have to understand the 'ought' as taking 'wide scope' over the conditional.

This way of putting things derives from the idea of deontic logicians that 'ought' is a sentential operator rather than a relation between an agent and an action.[14] If 'ought' really works this way, then 'if doing A is a means to your ends, then you ought to do A' should be subject to a scope ambiguity. We should be able to understand the 'ought' as taking scope over the whole sentence, or as taking scope over the consequent of the conditional. The 'wide scope' view is that it must take scope over the whole conditional,

---

[14] See Schroeder [2004] for further discussion. In general, the wide-scoping program in the philosophy of practical reason is highly touted as 'obvious' and those who don't accept it are often described as making a 'mistake'. But even putting aside their questionable semantic treatment of 'ought', wide-scope views should actually be quite controversial for a number of other reasons I discuss, ibid.

and it is motivated by cases such as that of the axe murderer and of my Aunt Margaret.[15]

This is only one 'fix' in response to the *too many reasons* objection, but it results in two incoherence arguments, because there are *two* problems that result when we try to explain every reason by appeal to claim 2. Each is structurally similar, moreover, to one of the incoherence arguments that we've already considered. Suppose that we use 2 in order to explain why there is a reason for Ronnie to go to the party. Still, we surely can't use 2 in order to explain why there is a reason for Ronnie to either do what promotes his desires or not have those desires. So if the Humean Theory of Reasons purports to explain Ronnie's case by appeal to 2, then it must be incoherent. (This is another way of reading Hampton's incoherence argument.[16])

But Stephen Darwall is most bothered by a different difficulty along these lines. He notes that unlike 1, we actually *can't* use 2 in combination with the fact that Ronnie desires to dance to explain why there is a reason for Ronnie to go to the party. For by the lights of 2, Ronnie could do just as well by ceasing to desire to dance as by actually going to the party. So Darwall believes that we need to invoke a further reason in order to explain why there is a reason for Ronnie to go to the party. We have to assume that there is a reason for him to desire to dance.[17] Since any explanation of reasons by desires modeled on 2 will have to work in this way, there are going to have to be some reasons that are not explained by desires in order for there to be any reasons at all. Either way, the Humean Theory of Reasons is incoherent.[18]

---

[15] For the sake of the arguments in which I am interested, we don't have to think that there is such an ambiguity. All we have to think is that 2 is true but 1 is not. See also Hill [1973], Greenspan [1975], Gensler [1985], Broome [1999], and Wallace [2001]. Since the Humean Theory of Reasons is not, directly, a theory about what people *ought* to do, wide-scope theories about what people *ought* to do, given their ends, are not strictly speaking relevant. So I've taken the liberty of restating Darwall and Hampton's objections in terms of a wide-scope view about *reasons*, as in 2.

[16] So far as I can tell, there is absolutely nothing in the text of Hampton's *The Authority of Reason* that clearly decides which of these two arguments she was trying to offer—the one that depends on the Standard Model Theory, or the one that depends on wide-scoping. Both are good candidates, however, for the argument that she meant to have offered. See Hampton [1998], Joyce [2001: 115–23].

[17] Or at least, a reason for him to not *cease* desiring to dance. This isn't what Darwall says, but the difference is important for some further difficulties that arise for the wide-scope account of Ronnie and Bradley's case. I briefly discuss the issues at the end of Schroeder [2004]. See also Greenspan [1975].

[18] Darwall [1983: ch. 1].

The first of these worries has the same structure as the argument I attributed to Hampton in section 3.1. It claims that the Humean Theory of Reasons is incoherent because in its explanation of Ronnie's case, it appeals to some general, high-level thing which everyone *antecedently* ought to do. The second of these worries has the same structure as Korsgaard's argument. It claims that the Humean Theory of Reasons is incoherent because in order to succeed in explaining Ronnie's case, it is going to have to appeal to some *particular* thing that Ronnie antecedently ought to do—namely, to desire to dance.[19]

Each of these arguments offers an interesting theory about how Ronnie's case is to be explained. And each of these theories is, as advertised, incompatible with the Humean Theory of Reasons. But that only makes the Humean Theory of Reasons problematic if there is good independent reason to accept one of these theories. And whether that is the case depends entirely upon whether there is a good general answer to the Too Many Reasons objection. For each of these theories about what is going on in Ronnie's case is motivated as a way of evading this problem.[20]

5.3 Negative Reason Existentials

The Too Many Reasons objection rests on our intuitions about cases that pose putative counterexamples to 1. In each case it is observed that the Humean Theory is committed to holding that *there is* a reason for X to do A, for some specified X and A. But our intuitions are supposed to make clear that for this choice of X and A, *there is no* reason for X to do A. So the Too Many Reasons objection turns on our negative existential intuitions about reasons. But this is a problem. For negative existential intuitions about reasons are not to be trusted. They are demonstrably unreliable, in

---

[19] Explanations of Ronnie's case like those of Korsgaard and Darwall, which appeal not only to a desire of Ronnie's, but to a reason for him to have that desire, are what I call *trickle-down* theories about how Ronnie's reason must be explained. I discuss trickle-down theories in Ch. 10.

[20] Here I depart from my advertised agenda of demonstrating that for each theory about Ronnie's case that Hypotheticalism rejects, rejecting this theory gives us a better account of Ronnie's case. But I do so only for expositional simplicity, not because I think these 'fixes' actually lead to good accounts of Ronnie's case. I *will* explain why *trickle-down* theories such as those of Korsgaard and Darwall give worse accounts of Ronnie's case (Ch. 10), and against the Quinn–Scarlon account of desire (ch. 8). I've argued against wide-scope views at length elsewhere (Schroeder [2004], [2005b], [2005c]).

systematic ways that can be explained on the basis of ordinary pragmatic principles.

Consider a simple, familiar, case involving epistemic reasons. In a first version of the case, you see Tom Grabit come out of the library, pull a book from beneath his shirt, cackle gleefully, and scurry off. Intuitively, you have a reason to believe that Tom just stole a book from the library. But in a revised version of the case, Tom has an identical twin, Tim, from whom you cannot visually distinguish him. If you're aware of this, then it turns out that you don't have any reason to believe that Tom stole a book after all. Right? Of course that's right. This, after all, is a classic case of an *undercutting defeater*, and as everyone knows, undercutting defeaters make it the case that things that would otherwise have been reasons for you, instead are not.[21]

This is a natural thought about the case, but your intuitions mislead you. That you still do have some reason to believe that Tom stole a book can be observed by comparison with yet a third version of the case. In the third version, Tom and Tim have a third identical sibling, Tam. In this case, you have even less reason to believe that Tom stole a book than in the second, and so in the second it can't have gone away entirely. By similar reasoning, you still have a reason to believe that Tom stole a book even in the third case, because there is a fourth case in which there are four identical siblings and your reason to believe that Tom stole a book is still worse.

A different case can be constructed for desire-based practical reasons like Ronnie's. Suppose that there are three routes that you can take home from work—Timely, Compromise, and Scenic. If you take Timely, you will get home by six. If you take Compromise, you have even odds of getting home by six, but the scenery will be much more pleasant. And if you take Scenic, you will not get home by six, and the scenery will be exactly as pleasant as if you take Compromise. Suppose, further, that you want to get home by six, but are indifferent to scenery. Is there any reason for you to take Compromise? Intuitively, no—it doesn't get you anything that you want that you can't get better of by taking Timely.

But again, I think that this intuition is wrong. There *is* a reason for you to take Compromise, but simply not as good a reason as there is for you to take Timely. And this can be observed by counterfactually changing

---

[21] Pollock and Cruz [1999: 37].

your other desires. Suppose that you *do* care about scenery—quite a lot. If your desire to get home by six only gave you a reason to take Timely, then you should be indifferent between Compromise and Scenic. But no matter how much you care about scenery and little you care about getting home by six, so long as you care at least a *little* about getting home by six, you ought to take Compromise instead of Scenic. Your reason to take Compromise derives from your desire to get home by six. So desiring to get home by six *does* seem to give you a reason to take Compromise, even though it will turn out to be important only if you have other kinds of reason. Similarly, your reason to believe that Tom stole a book in the Tim case will only turn out to matter if you have some other evidence.

It is easy to see what is going on, here. Sometimes when there are reasons to do things, but those reasons are not particularly weighty, or even simply not as weighty as the reasons that are obviously sufficient to decide what we should do, it seems to us that there is no reason to do those things. The less weighty the reason, the more compelling the intuition that there is no such reason. But in these cases it is easy to see that we really should allow that there are such reasons. They can make a difference, after all, when other reasons counterfactually come into play.

Moreover, I think that this is a phenomenon of which we can give a natural explanation, merely by appeal to straightforward features of talk about reasons and pretty uncontroversial principles of conversational pragmatics. What I will now do is *explain* why our negative existential intuitions about reasons are prone to be misleading in this way. The explanation comes in two steps, each of which yields a testable empirical prediction. So I'll then proceed to test these predictions.

The first step is to observe what we already have noted—that reasons can have more or less weight. The reasoning in our two examples suggests that they can actually have quite little weight. But we are interested in reasons mostly for practical purposes—because we want to know what we ought to do. Weighty reasons have a great bearing on what we ought to do, but reasons of little weight have very little bearing on what we ought to do. Understanding this is sufficient to understand why there should be a standard presumption in discussions of reasons that reasons of very little weight have very little relevance. In fact, if there are very many reasons of very low weight, knowing what they are will quickly become impracticable.

The second step of my explanation is to note that standard Gricean principles predict that this standing presumption should be reinforced in the case of merely existential claims about reasons. In addition to such claims as 'the fact that there is coffee in the lounge is a reason for Susan to go there', which tell us what Susan's reason is, we also often make merely existential claims about reasons, such as 'there is a reason for Susan to go to the lounge'. But merely existential claims are less informative. In fact, if most actions have at least *some* poor reason in favor of them, true bare existential claims about reasons will be hardly informative at all. So Grice's maxim of quantity[22] predicts that if this is the case, then I can convey to you that there is a relatively *weighty* reason for you to do *A*, by telling you that there is a reason for you to do *A* but not telling you what it is. For if I do not tell you what the reason is, but I mean to convey only that it is a bad reason, then I should, in order to be informative, have at least told you what the reason *is*. But if I have a relatively weighty reason in mind, then what I say can be informative, even if I don't tell you what the reason is. So we can predict that existential assertions about reasons will reinforce the standing presumption that the speaker has a relatively weighty reason in mind.

And so we have our two-step pragmatic explanation of why we often find it unintuitive or inappropriate to say that there is a reason for someone to do something even when, in fact, there is a reason for her to do it. It yields two predictions. If I tell you that there is a reason for you to do something that there are only poor reasons for you to do, what I say will sound wrong. But—first prediction—it will sound *less* wrong if I tell you *what* the reason is, because doing so will remove the pragmatic reinforcement of the standing presumption that I have only relatively good reasons in mind. And second, if I then tell you that I *don't* think it is a particularly weighty reason, I should be able to cancel the presumption, and so the unintuitiveness of what I say should go down a second time.

These predictions are testable, so let me tell you about such a reason: you have a reason to eat your car.[23] That sounds crazy, right? Surely there is no

---

[22] 'Make your contribution as informative as is required' Grice [1967: 26].

[23] This case is simply an illustration. For my purposes here, it doesn't matter whether or not you actually have a reason to eat your car. Whether you do depends, on my view, on whether you have some desire that your doing so promotes. If you desire to get at least the recommended daily allowance of iron, then you do. Other desires may also be capable of explaining this reason; whether they do or

reason for you to eat your car. But let me say what I think that it is. The reason for you to eat your car is that it contains the recommended daily allowance of iron. Now what I've said still sounds false. But it sounds *less* crazy, confirming our first prediction. After all, the fact that it has the recommended daily allowance of iron is certainly at least the right kind of thing *to be* a reason for you to eat your car, if anything is. But now let me emphasize that I do not think that this is a particularly weighty reason for you to eat your car. In fact, I think it is of about as little weight as any reason could possibly be. Not only do I think that you would be crazy to actually eat your car, I think that something would already be going wrong if you even considered it. You may still think that what I've said sounds false, but its unintuitiveness has gone down a second time, confirming our second prediction. Conclusion: negative existential intuitions about reasons really are misleading, and basic pragmatic principles suffice to predict and explain this.

I conclude from this that intuitively overgenerating existential predictions about reasons is not in and of itself a bad problem for the Humean Theory. So long as the Humean can get the right results about what those reasons would be, if there *were* such reasons, and allow that they are not particularly weighty, she can explain our negative existential intuitions about reasons just as well as views that deny that there are any such reasons. Provided the Humean Theory satisfies these two constraints, therefore, we can't rely on negative existential intuitions about reasons to decide between our theories.

So in a sense, I'm advocating a bullet-biting response on behalf of the Humean. Humean views really do intuitively overgenerate, but that is not, by itself, I'm suggesting, *all that bad*. But the argument that it is not that bad is, I think, perfectly general. It is not that I think the Humean view gets some bad results that I'm willing to learn to live with. On the contrary, I think that using negative existential intuitions about reasons to evaluate ethical theories is a pervasive mistake in moral philosophy, suspect on the same methodological grounds wherever it arises.

Consider, for example, the following argument against egalitarianism—a version of the 'leveling down' objection. It is a commitment of egalitarianism that if society A is perfectly equal and society B is not, then there

---

not will depend on complications about how the *promotion* relation works. I discuss this question at length in section 6.2.

is a reason to prefer society A to society B. But the following example is supposed to be an intuitive counterexample. In society A everyone has an income of 9, while in society B half have an income of 100 and half have an income of 99. Intuitively, the argument goes, in such a case there is no reason to prefer society A to society B. But recall that the cases in which negative existential intuitions about reasons are likely to lead us astray are just those cases in which the reason is relatively weak. But this case is deliberately designed to be such a case. The difference in equality between A and B is *very small*, and the benefit to the well-being of all in B is *very great*. So even egalitarians, I think, can easily explain our intuitions about the case. And the same goes for many other arguments in moral philosophy.

These same predictions apply in the case of Aunt Margaret. Suppose that it really is true that Aunt Margaret has a reason to build her spacecraft, but only a very weak or poor one. Our two predictions show that it would still be particularly odd to say that there is a reason for her to build her spacecraft—the commitment expressed by claim 4, and the one that is supposed to constitute the basis for the *too many reasons* objection. For in saying this, we don't say what her reason *is*. Her reason, according to Hypotheticalism, is that no one is going to give her a Mars-bound spacecraft. It still may not seem as though this is a reason for her to build her own Mars-bound spacecraft, but at least it is the kind of thing that would be a reason for her to do so, if anything were.[24] And now, if we make clear that Aunt Margaret's reason is only a particularly weak or poor one, it also becomes much less unintuitive to say that it is a reason for her.

5.4 Proportionalism

In order to deal with the Too Many Reasons objection in this way, Hypotheticalism has to claim that in fact, the unintuitive reasons such as that of my Aunt Margaret are actually not particularly weighty reasons. But

---

[24] To my ear, for the kind of consideration discussed in Ch. 2, this sounds better than to say that her reason is that she desires to replicate the scene depicted on page 78 of the November 2001 *Martha Stewart Living* catalogue on Mars. So I think that having dealt with those issues already puts Hypotheticalism in a better position with regard to the Too Many Reasons objection.

this clashes with a thesis that is universally thought to go along with the Humean Theory of Reasons—a thesis that I call *Proportionalism*. For our purposes, we can understand Proportionalism as yet another theory about *how* Ronnie's reason is explained by his psychology. Proportionalism gets started with two simple observations about Ronnie's case. Suppose that we vary Ronnie's case by making his desire to go dancing stronger. Then the fact that there will be dancing at the party becomes a better reason for him to go there. How *weighty* a reason this is for Ronnie to go to the party seems to be proportional to how much Ronnie cares about dancing. If he cares about nothing more than dancing, then it's a particularly weighty reason, but if wanting to dance is only a whim, then it should carry hardly any weight at all.

We can also vary Ronnie's case in another dimension. Suppose that we alter how likely it is that he will have a chance to dance at the party, by supposing that there will be more or fewer other distractions at the party. If Isabelle, Ronnie's ex-girlfriend, is going to be there hogging the dance-floor with her new fiancé, then perhaps Ronnie won't dance anyway, even if he goes. Or suppose that we vary what other places there are where Ronnie can go dancing. Perhaps there are going to be several other parties tonight, and there will be dancing at all of them. These ways of varying Ronnie's case change how *well* it is that going to the party promotes Ronnie's desire to dance. And it seems that when going to the party *better* promotes Ronnie's desire to dance, Ronnie's reason to go to the party is also better—of greater weight.

These cases suggest that the weight of Ronnie's reason is in two ways proportional. It is proportional to the strength of his desire, and it is proportional to the degree to which going to the party promotes that desire. *Proportionalism* is the thesis that when a reason is explained by a desire, as in Ronnie's case, its weight varies in proportion to the strength of that desire, and to how well the action promotes that desire. Many versions of the Humean Theory of Reasons accept Proportionalism. Since Ronnie's reason is proportional, and they hold that all reasons are at bottom like Ronnie's, they hold that all reasons are proportional.

Adding Proportionalism to the Humean Theory of Reasons yields the thesis that you always ought to do that action which best promotes your desires on balance. For what you ought to do is a matter of the weights of your reasons in favor of each option. And for each option, the total weight of the reasons in favor of it is a matter of how well it promotes each of your desires, and how strong those desires are. So versions of the Humean Theory of Reasons which accept Proportionalism are far from minimal—they commit directly to claims about what Ronnie *ought* to do, as in claim 3.

But—no surprise here—I hold that like the *self-interest* theory, Proportionalism overgeneralizes from Ronnie's case. We don't have to hold that all reasons are like Ronnie's in being proportional, in order to accept that all reasons are explained in the same way as Ronnie's. After all, as should already have been clear from the statement of Hypotheticalism in Chapter 2, it is not the *strength* of Ronnie's desire, or how *well* going to the party promotes that desire, that explain his reason. It is the fact that he *has* the desire, and that going to the party promotes it to *some* degree, that explains it. So despite the natural appeal of broadening the generalization from Ronnie's case, Hypotheticalism holds that this is simply overgeneralization.

But there is something else that motivates some real-to-life Humeans to accept Proportionalism. Sarah Broadie puts it this way:

> If desire is to carry the burden of explaining practicality, we should expect the degree of the agent's *practical* endorsement to be reflected in the desire: in its degree. If I think something well worth going out of my way for and that something else merits little effort or none, surely I feel *more* strongly about the first and desire it *more*? To deny this is to incur the obligation of explaining what, besides degree of desire, makes the difference between levels of practical commitment.[25]

The problem, it appears, is this: if it is not degrees of desire (together with degrees of promotion) that constitute degrees of the strength of reasons, then in what does the strength or weight of reasons consist?

On the face of it, this is a thought that should worry a view like Hypotheticalism in particular. For I claimed in Chapters 3 and 4 that Hypotheticalism purports to provide an *analysis* of what objective normative reasons *are*. And by accepting Subjective[26] and Motivating, it thereby purports ultimately to offer a reductive account of all talk about reasons in

[25] Broadie [1990: 275]. Here Broadie is writing about *judgments* about reasons, rather than about reasons themselves, but the thought is essentially the same.

[26] Or a suitably qualified version thereof.

terms of desires, promotion, and explanation. Is a view like this supposed to be comfortable accepting an unexplained notion of the *weight* of reasons? The fact that Ronnie's reasons seem to be proportional seems to cry out: pick me! I'm a natural story about where the strength of reasons comes from—what it consists in. Like Hypotheticalism's analysis of reasons, I'm a naturalistic story! If you like Hypotheticalism, you should like me! I take it that this is the real reason why most Humeans accept Proportionalism—not simply by overgeneralizing from Ronnie's case, but because they feel the pressure to offer *some* account of the weight of reasons. The argument is this: the Humean needs some account of the weight of reasons, and this one would be closely connected to her view, so she is under pressure to accept it.

But I think that this pressure is illusory. For distinguish two senses in which we might understand Proportionalism. It might be merely a claim about which reasons happen to be weighty ones. It might, that is, only aspire to be extensionally or necessarily extensionally correct. I've been taking it that Aunt Margaret's case is a reason to think that if the Humean Theory of Reasons is true, then Proportionalism is not even extensionally correct. But Proportionalism might purport to do *more* than this. It might purport to provide an analysis of *what it is* for a reason to be weighty—for it to be closely related to a strong desire. We've just been looking at an argument that Hypotheticalism should be committed to accepting that Proportionalism is extensionally correct, because it needs an analysis of *what it is* for a reason to be weighty, and Proportionalism is—how does Heidegger put it?—*ready to hand.*

But in order for this to be a good argument, Proportionalism has to be more than extensionally correct (which Aunt Margaret's case already should give us reason to doubt). Proportionalism has to also look like a good analysis of what it is for a reason to be weighty. But Proportionalism has all the wrong earmarks to be a good analysis of what it is for a reason to be weighty. For one thing, the *weight* of reasons is a *normative* matter, and it is commonly claimed—and I argued in Chapter 4 that Hypotheticalism, insofar as it is a reductive view, should agree—that all normative properties and relations are analyzable in terms of reasons, for that is what makes them normative. If that is right, then claims about the weight of reasons need to themselves be analyzed in terms of reasons. And Proportionalism understood as an analysis attempts to reduce the weight of reasons directly in non-normative terms.[27]

More generally, we already *know something* about what it is for a reason to be weighty. This doesn't have to do with whether people *actually* place weight on the reason, but it certainly has something to do with whether it is *correct* to place weight on it. Proportionalism, as an *analysis*, is ill-suited to explain the truism that it is always *correct* to place more weight on a reason that is weightier. If Proportionalism is the right analysis of the weight of reasons, then this truism is completely mysterious. Why should it be that it is always correct to place more weight on a reason that is more closely related to a stronger desire? On the other hand, some more natural analyses of the strength of reasons make this truism as obvious as it should be. For example, one Attractive View is that what it is for one reason to be weightier than another is just *for* it to be correct to place more weight on it. The truism falls out trivially from this analysis.

As we'll see in Chapter 7, there are also problems with this truistic analysis. But it obviously looks like a better candidate for an analysis of the weight of reasons than Proportionalism. Since I hold that Proportionalism is ill-suited to be an analysis of the weight of reasons, I don't see why even a Humean should be under such great pressure to believe that it is even extensionally correct. But this doesn't mean that Hypotheticalism doesn't *owe* us an analysis of the weight of reasons. It *does* owe us at least enough of an account of the weight of reasons in order to make good on the crucial claim necessary for my response to the *too many reasons* objection to work. It owes us an explanation of *why* it is that Aunt Margaret's reason to build her Mars-bound spacecraft is not a very weighty one, even if it is necessary

---

[27] Of course, a committed Proportionalist could accept these points and be unfazed. One way to adopt the strategy of Ch. 4 *and* Proportionalism, would be to argue that the basic normative relation is not the three-place *reason* relation, but rather a *four*-place relation, involving not just a consideration, an agent, and an action, but a *weight*, as well. Compare e.g. Skorupski [1997]. But I hold that we should be strongly hesitant about reifying weights of reasons. What are these weights? Are they numbers? As far as I can tell, our practice of weighing reasons only supports the view that reasons can sometimes weigh more or less than one another—I see little evidence that they have numerical weights, and much evidence that they don't. It seems at least *conceivable*, for example, that there are pairs of conflicting reasons, neither of which weighs more than the other. See Ch. 7. Another problem with making a number one of the *relata* of the *reason* relation is that even if we *can* successfully *model* the weights of reasons using numbers, it is natural to think that any scalar multiple of the numbers we use would do just as well, corresponding only to a difference in scale. But if numbers are actually one of the *relata* of the basic *reason* relation, then only one of these assignments will be the *correct* one. But it is bizarre to think that the fundamental *reason* relation could have units built into it in this way.

to the thing she most desires—reconstructing the scene depicted on page 78 of the November 2001 *Martha Stewart Living* catalogue on Mars.

This debt will have to wait for Chapter 7 to be discharged; for rejecting Proportionalism is also an essential part of the response that I advocate to the Too Few Reasons objection, to which we now turn.

6

Too Few Reasons

6.1 Too Few Reasons

Larry left his wife and infant daughter several years ago, and has never once looked back. He couldn't care less how either of them is doing. But Anne is his daughter. So he does have some reason to support her. The fact that she is his daughter is a reason for him to support her. And it is a reason for him to support her, even if he could not care less how she is doing. It is a reason for him *to* care how she is doing. Katie needs help. That is a reason for Ryan to help her, but it is also a reason for you to help her and a reason for me to help her. Indeed, it is a reason for anyone to help her. It is a reason to help her, *simpliciter.* These are supposed to be hard cases for the Humean Theory of Reasons. They are hard cases because it looks as though the Humean Theory is committed to saying that there are no such reasons. And that, intuitively, is simply false. So the Humean Theory of Reasons is committed to Too Few Reasons.

Larry's reason is one that is special to him—although you may have some reasons to support Anne, the fact that she is Larry's daughter is not among them.[1] Ryan's reason to help Katie, however, is not special to him. There is a reason for anyone to help Katie. Reasons like this present extra problems for the Humean. But many reasons seem to be like this, and in particular, conventional morality seems to presuppose that they are ubiquitous. If murder is genuinely wrong, then there must be some reason for anyone not to murder people. If giving money to world hunger relief is genuinely *required*, then there must be some reason for anyone to do it. In Chapter 1 we called such reasons *agent-neutral.*

---

[1] The fact that Anne is Larry's daughter may be a reason for others besides Larry to support her—for example, for his mother or his brother. But it isn't a reason for *everyone* to support her.

The Humean Theory of Reasons holds that whether the fact that Katie needs help is a reason for you to help Katie is held hostage to whether you, in fact, have some desire that could explain such a reason in the very same way as Ronnie's desire explains *his* reason. Since such a reason is hostage to your desires, it seems to follow that whether it is a reason for you depends on what you desire. And so it seems that the fact that Katie needs help cannot be a reason for *anyone* to help her after all—but only for those who have some appropriate desire.

So on the face of it, explaining Larry's case and explaining the reason to help Katie are different problems for the Humean Theory of Reasons. But they needn't be. We can *subsume* Larry's case under the problem of accounting for reasons like the one to help Katie. An explanatory model that we encountered in section 1.4 and again in Chapter 3 tells us how to do this. It is the *Standard Model*. According to the Standard Model, though Larry's reason is merely agent-relative, it *derives* from an agent-*neutral* reason. This is the reason to do one's best to make sure that whatever children one brings into the world have good lives. Larry's merely agent-relational reason seems not to depend on his desires because it derives from this agent-neutral reason, which, like all agent-neutral reasons, is a reason for everyone, no matter what their desires.[2]

Rachel ought to write about pillows on Monday and about Phil's smile on Thursday. This is because on both days she ought to write about what she is thinking about, and on Monday, because she is thinking about pillows, writing about pillows is the way to do it, while on Thursday, because she is thinking about Phil's smile, writing about Phil's smile is the way to do it. Likewise, there is something that you and Larry both have a reason to do—to do your best to make sure that whatever children you bring into the world have good lives. For Larry, because Anne is his daughter, supporting Anne is necessary for this. But since Anne isn't your daughter, supporting her has nothing to do with this reason of yours.

---

[2] In section 1.4 and again in Ch. 3, I noted that Hypotheticalism does not accept that the Standard Model tells us the truth about the relationship between agent-relational and agent-neutral reasons. But what is at issue over the Standard Model is not whether it is *ever* the right way to explain the differences in what someone ought to do or what there is a reason for them to do. Rachel's case is definitely a case in which the Standard Model applies. The issue over the Standard Model is whether it *always* applies, or always *has* to apply, because it gives the proper *analysis* of the agent-relational reason relation in terms of the agent-neutral reason relation. In section 3.3 I argued that the Standard Model explanation of Ronnie's reason can't work. But that doesn't show that it can't work for Larry's reason.

In Rachel's case, we could say *two* things about what reason she had to write about pillows on Monday. First, we could say that the fact that her homework assignment was to write about what she was thinking about was a reason for her to do this. This is the reason that she had on both days. But second, we could also say that the fact that she was thinking about pillows was a reason for her to write about pillows. This is the reason that she had only on Monday. Similarly, in Larry's case, one reason for him to support Anne is the same reason that you have to support whatever children you might have—say, that parents are causally responsible for their children's lives. But another reason for Larry to support Anne is that she is his daughter. This isn't a reason that you have, either to support Anne, or to support your own children.

But because this further fact is needed in order to complete the explanation of why supporting Anne is a way for Larry to do his best to make sure that his children have good lives, it must also be needed in order to complete the explanation of why supporting Anne promotes the object of one of Larry's desires. So if Hypotheticalism manages to explain the agent-neutral reason to do one's best to make sure that whatever children one has have good lives, then it can also deal with Larry's reason. This account successfully subsumes cases such as Larry's under the problem of explaining agent-neutral reasons such as the reason to help Katie. So it reduces the Too Many Reasons objection to the problem of accounting for agent-neutral reasons. And it is therefore the version of the Too Few Reasons objection involving agent-neutral reasons that I will concern myself with from here forward.

Before we can see how Hypotheticalism deals with Katie's case, it is important to distinguish several different features of that case. First, there is the fact that it makes sense to say, 'the fact that Katie needs help is a reason to help her', without saying for whom it is a reason. Call this the agent-neutrality of the *ascription*. Second, there is the fact that, unlike typical utterances of, 'the fact that there will be dancing at the party is a reason to go there', this claim about Katie seems to imply that it is a reason for *anyone* to help her. Call this the *universality* of the reason to help Katie. Third, there is the fact that the universality of the reason to help Katie does not seem to be *contingent*—for example, on the fact that the only people around happen to value Katie's welfare. Call this the *weak modal status* of the reason to help Katie. And fourth, there is the fact that it seems that for any desire, an agent would have a reason to help Katie even if he did not have that desire. Call this the *strong modal status* of the reason to help Katie.[3] Now let us say that the reason to help Katie is *genuinely agent-neutral* because it is universal and has both the weak and the strong modal statuses. In order to account adequately for the agent-neutrality in Katie's case, the Humean Theory of Reasons needs to explain not only the agent-neutrality of this reason ascription, but also the universality of the reason, and how it could have both the weak and the strong modal statuses. Indeed, it needs to explain yet one more thing: how a reason could be an *equally weighty* reason for everyone for whom it is a reason.

Some of these phenomena are easy to explain. In section 1.4 I explained how to deal with agent-neutral reason ascriptions. According to Hypotheticalism, to say that there is a reason to help Katie is to say that there is a reason for all of *us* to help Katie, where the scope of who *we* are is contextually determined, and in some contexts includes *everyone*. It follows from this account that a particular agent-neutral reason ascription could entail that the reason ascribed is universal and has the weak modal status. For if, in the context, the scope of 'us' includes everyone, the reason must be universal. And if, in the context, the scope of 'us' includes *everyone*—everyone there might be—then the reason must have the weak modal status.[4]

It also does not follow from the Humean Theory of Reasons that there are no reasons that are universal. Suppose, for example, that there is some desire that everyone shares. Then it is easy to imagine how there could be reasons that everyone shares—they would all be explained in the same way by this desire. In fact, there are good psychological and evolutionary reasons to suspect that there very well might be desires that everyone shares, even if most desires are not shared by everyone.[5] So it is easy to imagine how a Humean could account for the universality of reasons.

---

[3] Actually, as the example of Susan in the main text will shortly illustrate, the 'strong' modal status is not strictly stronger than the weak modal status. The two cross-cut one another, as a matter of logic. But this categorization is really harmless, and makes clear the advantages of the account of agent-neutral reasons that I will eventually defend on behalf of Hypotheticalism, because it draws attention to the fact that it is the strong modal status that is hard to account for.

[4] This account does not yield the result that an agent-neutral reason ascription could *semantically* entail that the reason ascribed has the *strong* modal status. But it is easy to see how this could be a pragmatic concomitant of the agent-neutral ascription. And though the reason to help Katie does seem to have the strong modal status, it is not obvious that this is entailed by the agent-neutral ascription.

[5] See e.g. Sober and Wilson [1998].

The real trick for the Humean Theory is not to account for the agent-neutrality of reason ascriptions, or the universality of reasons. It is to account for the *modal* statuses of reasons. So in the same vein that we have been considering, suppose that there is a desire that every agent *necessarily* has. David Velleman has defended a view of broadly this kind. He claims that there are 'aims' that are constitutive of agency—no one could count as someone who was capable of *acting* unless she had them.[6] Call this the *Velleman hypothesis*. If the Velleman hypothesis is true, then it is easy to see how there could be universal reasons that also have the weak modal status. No matter what agents there were, holding fixed that it is a reason, it would be a reason for all of them. Such reasons would be explained in the same way for everyone by the desire that everyone shares. Since there couldn't be an agent who didn't have this desire, there couldn't be an agent who didn't have this reason.

The Velleman hypothesis suffers from two structural flaws, as a possible defense for the Humean theory. First, it is extraordinarily difficult to defend the view that there is some desire that you have to have in order to count as an agent. Velleman's own defense of this kind of view is extremely creative and resourceful, but his positive arguments are something less than compelling.[7] But there is a second worry that we might have about this approach. For though it would account for the universality of the reason to help Katie, and its weak modal status, it would not account for its strong modal status. It would not be true, on this view, that even if you didn't have the desire that all agents necessarily have, there would still be a reason for you to help Katie. So even if the Velleman hypothesis turns out to be true, an explanation of agent-neutrality grounded on it would still fail the test of the strong modal status.[8]

---

[6] See Velleman [1989], [1996], [2000a], [2000b].

[7] See Railton [1997] for an excellent general discussion of some of the relevant issues.

[8] This latest worry need not be conclusive. For if the Velleman hypothesis is correct, then someone who didn't have the desire that all agents necessarily have wouldn't be an agent. And if she weren't an agent, it would be no surprise that she didn't have that reason—for then she wouldn't have *any* reasons. But I don't think that failing to account for the strong modal status has to be a *fatal* defect of the Velleman hypothesis in order for a view which accounted for it to have an advantage. That is what Hypotheticalism aspires to do. Either way, I'm indifferent to whether the Velleman Hypothesis turns out to be true. I'm merely trying to show what doesn't follow from the Humean Theory as a matter of logic. My point is that it does not logically follow from the Humean Theory even that no reasons have the strong modal status.

I take it that this is the state of the art, with respect to the project of explaining agent-neutral reasons by desires. Agent-neutrality of ascription, universality, and the weak modal status are relatively straightforward to account for, at least logically speaking, but what needs to be understood is how desire-dependent reasons could have the *strong* modal status or be of equal *weight* for everyone. In the remainder of this chapter I explain how to account for the strong modal status, and in Chapter 7 I deal with considerations about weight.

6.2 The Strong Modal Status

On the face of it, it seems to be inconsistent with the Humean Theory of Reasons that any reason has the strong modal status. Indeed, nearly all philosophical discussions have taken this for granted. For the Humean Theory says that every reason needs to be explained by a desire. So it seems to say that your reasons depend on what you desire, and this suggests that if your desires were different, then your reasons would be different. But this is a mistake. The Humean Theory of Reasons only says that every time someone has a reason, she must have some desire that explains why. It does not say that for every reason, there must be some single desire that explains why each person who has that reason has it. For all that the Humean Theory says, each of the people who has a reason has it in virtue of a different desire.

Hypotheticalism makes this feature of the Humean Theory explicit. According to Hypotheticalism, for R to be a reason for X to do A requires X to have *some* desire whose object her doing A promotes. If one action can promote the object of more than one desire, therefore, then the same reason might be explained by more than one desire. Take, for example, the case of Susan. Susan wants some coffee. So the fact that there is coffee in the lounge is a reason for her to go there. But perhaps this is doubly determined. For example, perhaps philosophers tend to congregate and talk shop where there is coffee. And perhaps Susan wants to talk shop about some idea she's recently had. This could also explain why the fact that there is coffee in the lounge is a reason for Susan to go there. If this is so, then this is a reason for Susan twice over. The fact that there is coffee in the lounge would be a reason for Susan to go there even if she didn't want a cup of coffee, and it would be a reason for her to go there even if she didn't want to talk shop. So there is no single desire on which it depends.[9]

But this does not show that Susan's reason is not explained by her desires. It just allows that it is *overdetermined* that the fact that there is coffee in the lounge is a reason for Susan to go there. The Humean Theory of Reasons claims that all reasons have to be explained by desires. It says nothing about whether reasons can be explained by more than one desire. For all that it says, there might be reasons that can be explained by *any* possible desire.

Hypotheticalism's favored proposal for how there could be genuinely agent-neutral reasons is therefore that genuinely agent-neutral reasons are *massively* overdetermined. They are reasons for anyone, no matter what she desires, simply because they can be explained by any (or virtually any) possible desire.[10] Suppose that some reason is like this—it can be explained by any possible desire. Then anyone who has any desires whatsoever will have this reason. So if to count as an agent, you must at least have *some* desire or other—a much weaker constraint on agency than that postulated by the Velleman hypothesis—then any possible agent would have this reason. And there would be no desire such that if you did not have that desire, then it would not be a reason for you. So such a reason would not only be universal, but have both the weak and strong modal statuses. It would be *genuinely agent-neutral*, in our sense.

Like the Velleman hypothesis, so far this is only a formal proposal for how there *could*, consistently with Hypotheticalism, be such genuinely agent-neutral reasons. It would take some explaining, in order to show why some given reason could be explained by *any* possible desire. And if no such explanation can be given, then there must not be any reason

---

[9] Notice that this move hinges on the distinction between reasons and background conditions. If we thought that the desire that explained a reason was really part of the reason, then two different desires could not explain the same reason—by virtue of being different desires, they would make the reason different. And then no reason could be overdetermined by different desires.

[10] Compare John Rawls [1971: 92] on primary goods: 'Now primary goods, as I have already remarked, are things which it is supposed a rational man wants whatever else he wants. Regardless of what an individual's rational plans are in detail, it is assumed that there are various things which he would prefer more of, rather than less. With more of these goods men can generally be assured of greater success in carrying out their intentions and in advancing their ends, whatever these ends may be.' One of the problems Rawls is supposed to have, is in determining how the basket of primary goods is to be *balanced*—how the primary goods weigh against one another. So the overdetermination hypothesis needs *less* than Rawls's assumption of the existence of primary goods. Rawls needs to be able to say how these goods balance against one another, but the overdermination hypothesis only needs that there are such things, in the first place.

that could be explained by any possible desire. If it turns out that, given Hypotheticalism's explanation of Ronnie's reason, there is no reason that could be explained in this way by any possible desire, then the formal proposal is empty. So Hypotheticalism needs more than such a formal proposal. It needs, at the very least, a story about why it should be possible to explain some reasons, starting with any possible desire.

So my answer to the problem of accounting for the strong modal status of reasons has three prongs. The first is the logical point just made—that the strong modal status of a reason is not *inconsistent* with the Humean Theory of Reasons, provided that the reason is overdetermined. The second prong is a diagnosis of how views about how likely the overdetermination hypothesis is to be true turn on a kind of assumption about how Ronnie's reason is explained by his desire. In particular, they turn on what view we take about the *promotion* relation that an action must bear to the object of Ronnie's desire. And the third prong of my account of the strong modal status is to illustrate by means of a model how an explanation of the overdetermination of some reason would work. We've had the first prong; now we need the second.

As I see it, how hard it is to explain genuinely agent-neutral reasons has everything to do with how hard it is to explain the existence of reasons in the first place. So if you want genuinely agent-neutral reasons to be easy to come by, you should make *reasons* easy to come by. And indeed, this is probably not such a bad thing to do. For remember that we do not have to adopt a highly restricted form of Humeanism in order to deal with the Too Many Reasons objection, but can deal with that objection perfectly well as long as the unintuitive reasons we commit to are not very good ones. So it is the strategy of Hypotheticalism, in meeting the Too Few Reasons objection, to make reasons easy to explain in general. And we've already dealt, in Chapter 5, with the obvious problems that this might otherwise raise or at least exacerbate. An explanation of our intuitions about Too Many Reasons is easy to come by, so we shouldn't be overly shy about intuitively erring in this direction, subject to the qualifications in section 5.4.

Most of the work to be done in making agent-neutral reasons sufficiently easy to explain comes in filling in a sufficiently weak account of the *promotion* relation. Until this point, I have said virtually nothing about how Hypotheticalism conceives of the promotion relation. But obviously a great deal turns on it. If very few actions promote the object of any given desire, then it seems rather unlikely that there is some interesting action that promotes the object of any desire whatsoever. But if any given desire has an object promoted by many different actions, then the hypothesis that there is some action that promotes any—or virtually any—desire becomes correspondingly more reasonable. Hypotheticalism advocates a view on which the promotion relation is surprisingly weak. But the surprise about the weakness of the promotion relation derives only from the fact that philosophers have always assumed it to be much stronger—not from the fact that it is *reasonable* to assume it to be much stronger.[11] For the Hypotheticalist view about the promotion relation, like each view that it takes, deals better with cases like that of Ronnie and Bradley.

Let's begin with a theory about the promotion relation commonly attributed to the Humean.[12] According to this view, the Humean holds that there is a reason for you to do A only if you desire *to do A*. So on this view, the promotion relation is *identity*. An action counts as promoting a desire just in case it is the *object* of the desire. This is a very strict view to take about promotion. In our case, we didn't explain Ronnie's reason by a desire to go to the party—we explained it by a desire to go dancing. So promotion can't be this strict. At least, if it were, that would give us a worse account of Ronnie's case.

Consider, then, a slightly weaker theory suggested by one reading of Kant.[13] On this view, an action promotes a desire just in case it is a *necessary means* to the object of that desire. On Kant's view, hypothetical imperatives tell us to do what are necessary means to our ends. This would be a very nice view, if we were only worried about what Ronnie *ought* to do. For so long as some action is not necessary for the object of one of Ronnie's desires, perhaps Ronnie can still accomplish that desire even if he doesn't do it. So in a natural sense, he doesn't *have* to do it. The Kant-inspired view is a good view about what, in this sense, Ronnie has to do. But it is a

---

[11] In fact, it derives wholly from the fact that earlier discussions of cases like that of Ronnie and Bradley have nearly always been framed in terms of what Ronnie *ought* to do, rather than in terms of what there are *reasons* for him to do.

[12] This seems to be assumed by Korsgaard [1997: 223], for example, in what purports to be a perfectly general refutation of the Humean theory: 'the instrumental principle instructs us to derive a reason from what we are *going* to do'.

[13] Strictly speaking, Kant isn't offering a view about reasons, so the following points don't bear on whether this account is adequate for his purposes.

terrible view about what there are reasons for Ronnie to do. There may be dancing in several different places. But that doesn't mean that the fact that there will be dancing at the party is not a reason for Ronnie to go *there*.[14]

Consider, again, the case in which you desire to get home from work before six, and could take any of routes Timely, Compromise, or Scenic.[15] The Kant-inspired account of the promotion relation predicts that there is no reason *at all* for you to take Timely, and no reason *at all* for you to take Compromise. It predicts that there is only a reason for you to either-take-Timely-or-take-Compromise. But this is wrong. In that case, besides this reason, there are also reasons for you to take Timely and for you to take Compromise. As noted before, we know that there is *some* reason for you to take Compromise, because even if you care much more about scenery than about getting home by six, you should not be indifferent between Compromise and Scenic. You should choose Compromise over Scenic. So your desire does give you some reason to choose Compromise.

Now vary the case by gradually decreasing the chance that Compromise will get you home on time. So long as there is *some* chance that Compromise will get you home on time, there is a reason for you to take Compromise. It is not a reason to choose Compromise *over Timely*. But it is nevertheless a reason to choose Compromise. For if you cared enough about scenery, Compromise would be the way that you ought to take. If, as stipulated, Compromise and Scenic are *equally* eye-friendly, then the chance that you will get home by six taking Compromise could become vanishingly small, but there would still be at least some reason for you to take it.

On Hypotheticalism's view, therefore, we need a *very* weak understanding of the promotion relation, simply in order to account for the straightforward cases like Ronnie's and Bradley's, in which there are reasons which should obviously be explained by desires. So on this view it is not at all unmotivated to claim that reasons are relatively easy to come by, when we are trying to explain genuinely agent-neutral reasons.

---

[14] It is easy to verify this observation. Assume that Ronnie also doesn't want to go very far from home, and that the party is not very far from home, and Joe's Tavern (where you wouldn't dare be caught dancing) is the only other place to go that is not very far from home. Plausibly in such a case, the thing for Ronnie to do is to go to the party, even if there are other places where there will be dancing. Surely what explains this is that the fact that there will be dancing there is a reason to go there—for this is what makes the difference between going to the party and going to Joe's Tavern.

[15] I hope you're a quick reader, or you're likely to be quite late by now.

So the view to take about the promotion relation is this: X's doing A promotes p just in case it increases the likelihood of p relative to some baseline. And the baseline, I suggest, is fixed by the likelihood of p conditional on X's doing nothing—conditional on the status quo. This is how weak the promotion relation seems to have to be in order to successfully deal with the full range of versions of the Compromise case.

6.3 Explanations of Agent-Neutral Reasons

So we have seen how (prong one) the overdetermination hypothesis makes the strong modal status of reasons consistent with the Humean Theory. And we have seen how (prong two) a view about the promotion relation which better fits cases like Ronnie's and Bradley's makes room to think that the overdetermination hypothesis is not obviously false. But it remains to figure out (prong three) why anyone might think that the overdetermination hypothesis is *true*. So it is to this task that we now turn. Of course, it is far too big a task to try to argue, for each and every intuitively agent-neutral reason, that it is overdetermined in the right way. So what I'll do instead is to provide a model for how such explanations might go, and adduce some general considerations in favor of restrained optimism that the obvious moral reasons can be explained in this way.

My model is this: consider whether there is some reason for anyone to believe an arbitrary proposition only if it is true.[16] And take some arbitrary agent, Mary, with an arbitrary desire—say, to have a new pair of shoes. There is nothing that Mary *has* to believe the truth about, in order to succeed at acquiring a new pair of shoes. If all her beliefs are false in an

---

[16] In principle, I hold the view that a good account of reasons should apply equally well to both epistemic reasons for belief and to practical reasons for action. And I do think that something in the neighborhood of the following explanation may be the right way for Hypotheticalism to account for epistemic reasons. But the relationship between talk about epistemic reasons and practical reasons is subject to some distracting complications. For example, the word 'reason' in epistemology is typically understood to pick out its subjective normative sense, whereas in ethics it is usually objective reasons that are picked out with the word 'reason'. In this book, I'm considering only whether Hypotheticalism can provide an adequate account of reasons for action. So the explanation is offered merely in the spirit of the *kind* of explanation that Hypotheticalism can offer for genuinely agent-neutral reasons. I'm remaining uncommitted on whether this particular argument actually shows what it is purported to show, and whether if it *does*, that should be understood as explaining *epistemic* reasons for belief, or merely *practical* ones.

interesting enough way, she could happily succeed at buying a new pair of shoes from a local strip mall, all the while believing that she is in the process of turning cartwheels down Broadway. But on the other hand, there are a lot of things that it is useful to know—or at least, not to have false beliefs about—in order to acquire a pair of shoes. For example, it is useful to know what sorts of places sell shoes, what size one wears, how to try shoes on, how to pay for them, and so forth. So not being in error about these subjects promotes the object of Mary's desire to at least some degree, though it is not necessary for it.

Now, there are plenty of topics which don't bear directly on how to succeed at acquiring a new pair of shoes. For example, it is hard to see the connection between buying a pair of shoes and knowing that my brother lives in Los Angeles, or knowing how many moons circle Jupiter. But of those topics which don't bear directly on buying shoes, *some* do bear directly on questions that are quite relevant to buying shoes. Being in error about them could lead one to form the wrong beliefs about matters that it is important to be right about, in order for one's shoe-acquiring to go smoothly. And now consider the class of propositions, being in error about which can affect whether one is right about one of *these* questions. And then the class of propositions, being in error about which can affect whether one is right about one of *these* questions. And so on. A relatively weak hypothesis about the holism of belief formation says that the closure of this process will include any proposition.

Suppose that that is right. Then being in error about any proposition is ultimately relevant to Mary's desire to get a new pair of shoes. Being in error about it might lead to being in error about other things, such that being in error about them might lead to being in error about other things, and so on until something might lead to Mary having trouble getting new shoes. If this is right, then for any proposition, Mary's desire to get a new pair of shoes will serve to explain why there is a reason for Mary to believe it only if it is true.

Nothing about the structure of this explanation turned on the assumption about what Mary's desire was *for*. So if this is a good explanation, then by parity of reasoning *any* desire of Mary's could explain why Mary has such a reason. So by this account, such reasons can be explained by Mary's desires, but they would be reasons for Mary no matter what she desired. More: there is no desire of Mary's, such that if she didn't have that desire, then she wouldn't have such a reason. So if this kind of argument can work, then Mary's reasons are *genuinely agent-neutral*, in our sense. And they are not *empty*—they are reasons to do relatively concrete things: to believe some given proposition only if it is true.[17]

Hypotheticalism holds that it is reasonable to hope that all genuinely agent-neutral reasons—including those accepted by conventional morality—can be explained in this way. But I am not going to offer such explanations of particular moral reasons here. There is no particular such explanation that I happen to favor, and this broad-brush defense of Hypotheticalism is in any case not the place to become bogged down in the details of such an explanation.

I think about it this way: many philosophers have attempted to provide explanations of the content of moral requirements within the bounds allowed by some or another version of the Humean Theory of Reasons.[18] And by any reasonable standard, all have failed. But these philosophers have all been working with an impoverished conception of how the *promotes* relation might work. In particular, they have all assumed that it is too strong—too strong not only to account for the agent-neutral reasons of morality, but too strong even to account for all the reasons, like Ronnie's and Bradley's, that obviously should be explained by desires. So I don't see why inductive evidence that they have all failed should undermine our confidence that Hypotheticalism can succeed.

I am optimistic for several reasons. First, I think that it is reasonable to accept a very weak thesis about the unity of the virtues: that someone who has one of the central moral virtues cares about something that gives her a reason to acquire each of the other central moral virtues. If that is right, then there should be *many* ways in to explaining the agent-neutrality of the moral reasons. For such explanations could work by first explaining reasons to have any one of the virtues, and then we may be able to use the reasons

---

[17] On one natural reading, Kant recognizes the possibility that an imperative applying to everyone, no matter her ends, might nevertheless be hypothetical, because for each person, it is explained by her ends. On a natural reading, the imperative of prudence is supposed to be like this. But he thinks that any such imperative would be 'empty': there wouldn't be any concrete advice that it could give to everyone to whom it applied. At best, the only concrete actions that it would recommend would be recommended only by 'counsels', since they would have exceptions. See Kant [1997: 4: 415–20].

[18] Hobbes is one obvious historical example. Foot [1959] and Gauthier [1986] are relatively well-known recent attempts in this vein. The instances are certainly numerous enough to support Prichard's view that the very question, 'why should I be moral?' is asking for self-interested reasons to behave morally. See Prichard [1912].

given by the virtues to have each of the other virtues, in order to explain those other reasons.

This is akin to the thought that when some philosopher tries to give us an account of why we ought to be moral, he usually gets at least *something* right. Scanlon, for example, tells us that he can justify much of morality on the basis of reasons to be able to justify ourselves to one another, and Korsgaard tells us that she can do so on the basis of some kind of personal integrity.[19] I think that properly understood, they both might be right. I don't see why we should think that there must be a paucity of explanations of why we all have the standard moral reasons. On the contrary, I think that these explanations can complement each other perfectly well, when appropriately interpreted. Indeed, the whole idea of the overdetermination hypothesis is that none of the deep and illuminating attempts to explain why we should be moral or to justify moral requirements has to be the whole story. Which is a good thing, because such stories as Scanlon's and Korsgaard's, even while they seem to get something importantly and interestingly right, also seem as though they couldn't be the whole story.

Another reason to be optimistic about the prospects for Hypotheticalism is optimism about the possibility of genuine moral education. It would be nice to think that it is at least in principle possible to educate someone about morality without conditioning or indoctrination—by providing her with reasons for acting as she ought. Such a process is necessarily slow, because at the beginning the person being educated may not accept or recognize most of the reasons for her to try to change her attitudes and behavior, and may be insufficiently motivated by those she does accept. But it would be nice to think that at least in principle, it is possible to give her *some* reasons that she *can* accept. Then, later, once she has further changed, she will care about more of the things that a virtuous person cares about. And in doing so, she will gradually come to be sensitive to more of the moral reasons. But it would be nice to think that, even if we can't actually motivate someone to change her behavior now, we could at least get her to see *some* reason in favor of becoming more virtuous. And if that is possible, then she really must now already have the right kind of desires to sustain these explanations.

---

[19] See Scanlon [1998] and Korsgaard [1996].

It would obviously be an enormous project to try to explain each and every intuitively agent-neutral reason in this way. It is, I think, one of the most interesting and illuminating projects of moral theory. All I hope to have done, is to have given an attractive model for how such explanations can go, and lowered the constraints that are typically thought to accompany such an enterprise. And I take encouragement from the fact that it looks as though even Kantian thinkers such as Scanlon and Korsgaard can be understood as having made significant contributions to this project, whether they would describe their aims that way or not.

6.4 A Spectrum of Views

If, given my account, explanations of the overdetermination of reasons by desires turn out to be easy *enough* to give, then Hypotheticalism can succeed at giving the kind of account that I've offered here. Such an account is, in a certain respect, *Kantian*, in that it fully respects the intuition that some reasons are genuinely agent-neutral—reasons for any possible agent, and not just because there is some desire that all agents share. What I've shown in this chapter is that the Humean Theory of Reasons is not inconsistent with this kind of Kantian ambition for the objectivity of morality, and what I've further argued is that the prospects for Hypotheticalism of being able to accomplish this ambition are reasonably good.[20]

But perhaps, nevertheless, the explanatory burden of accomplishing this Kantian aim can't quite be fulfilled. Perhaps there simply aren't enough actions that would promote the object of some desire of any possible agent, no matter what her desires are. But perhaps there *are* plenty of actions that promote the object of some desire of any possible *human* agent, no matter what her desires are. And that would still be a fairly remarkable thing. Reasons that any human agent would share would have a certain kind of robust universality, even though it would fall short of the Kantian ambition of genuine agent-neutrality. And in a certain sense, this kind of objectivity is an *Aristotelian* goal.[21] So even if the Kantian account of

---

[20] The account I'm offering obviously isn't genuinely Kantian, in the fullest sense. It merely respects some of the Kantian's most important *pre-theoretical* aspirations.

[21] Compare Anscombe [1958] and Foot [2001].

agent-neutral reasons ultimately fails to discharge its explanatory burdens, those sympathetic to Hypotheticalism can still resort to the comfort of this Aristotelian strategy.

Nevertheless, even this is some kind of explanatory burden. Perhaps there are not even any desires that all human agents share, nor any interesting constraints on what *kinds* of desires human agents can have. In that case, someone who accepted Hypotheticalism would have to admit that genuine agent-neutrality is simply too hard to come by. In this eventuality, agent-neutral reason ascriptions will have to be understood either as false, or as having restricted scope—implying only that the reason is a reason for all of *us*, around *here*, to perform the action. Accepting this view amounts to restricting our ambitions for the universality of morality. Such ambitions are less than Kantian or Aristotelian: they are more familiarly 'Humean'.

The latter of these two options would naturally lead to a view on which moral talk is, to a certain extent, context-sensitive. If, properly speaking, there isn't an interesting class of things that *everyone* has a reason to do, then claims of the form, 'there is a reason to do *A*' will best be understood as being restricted to apply to less than *everyone*. This can be done merely by imposing a restriction on the scope of who counts as one of *us* in the statement of Agent-Neutral, from section 1.3. We would then expect that if moral concepts such as *wrongness* were to be analyzed in terms of agent-neutral reasons, these would also inherit this context-dependent element.[22]

The first of the options facing this more familiar 'Humean' strategy was to agree that some agent-neutral ascriptions really *do* purport to entail that the reason ascribed is *genuinely* agent-neutral. If we accept this move, then we reject any restrictions on who can count as one of *us* in the statement of Agent-Neutral from section 1.3. This allows that sometimes when we say that there is a reason to help Katie, what we mean is that there is a genuinely agent-neutral reason to help Katie. But if that is right, and there are no such reasons, then all claims of this form are false. There are no genuinely agent-neutral reasons, and so moral claims implying that there

---

[22] This view, although differently motivated, would be quite close to that advocated in Dreier [1990] and [1999]. There are standard objections to such views, but since this one would be a fallback position motivated by an error theory about it turning out that there are any genuinely agent-neutral reasons, I think it could be more comfortable accepting the unintuitive results.

are genuinely agent-neutral reasons are also false. This leads to an error theory.[23]

This motivation doesn't by itself result in a *global* error theory about reasons or about the normative. It only leads to an error theory about genuinely agent-neutral reasons. But in Chapter 5 we considered the account that one reason is weightier than another only if it is correct to place more weight on it. And it is plausible that if correctness can be understood in terms of reasons, it will involve agent-neutral reasons. In fact, this is the view that I will defend in Chapter 7. So on that view, if there are no genuinely agent-neutral reasons, then even though there may still be reasons, there won't be any *weighty* reasons. And since when we talk about reasons, we are mostly only interested in relatively weighty reasons, it follows that what we are interested in even when we say, 'there is a reason for Ronnie to go to the party' could on this view come out to be false. So in the extreme case, a failure to fulfill the explanatory burden still remaining for Hypotheticalism *could* still lead to a *global* error theory about the normative.[24]

This is a spectrum of views that are all compatible with the Humean Theory of Reasons and with Hypotheticalism's particular view about how Ronnie's reason is to be explained. Nothing about the view forces us to accept any of the results at the Humean end of this spectrum. But it is still the right *kind* of view to motivate the theories at the Humean end of the spectrum. As I see it, I've shown how Hypotheticalism makes genuinely agent-neutral reasons easy enough to explain that if we start with a very high credence that there actually are genuinely agent-neutral reasons, then we should be very confident that the central agent-neutral reasons of

---

[23] See Mackie [1977]. Mackie's argument from queerness can be understood in several different ways, but the argument from the Humean Theory of Reasons is the one that I find most interesting. I suspect that he is most often interpreted as offering an argument based on motivational considerations simply because the argument based on the Humean Theory has not always been carefully enough distinguished from the motivational argument. Joyce [2001] also offers this argument for an error theory.

[24] Such a global error theory could also serve to motivate a revisionary semantics for normative terms. On one reading, this is what Mackie is doing in the second part of his [1977], since he continues to theorize about morality, even after having claimed to establish that moral claims are systematically false. Indeed, this might be one of the better ways of motivating expressivism. A *revisionary* expressivism wouldn't have to accept the general semantic commitments necessary to defend expressivism against the Frege–Geach problem and other problems. It could accept unintuitive consequences, on the grounds that such an account is the best way to proceed, if we want to cling to ways of speaking that understood in any other way would simply be systematically false.

morality can be successfully explained on this model. But it leaves them sufficiently hard to explain that if we start with a low enough credence that there actually are agent-neutral reasons, then this should be enough to make us give up on them entirely.

That, I think, is the best that we can hope for. The general view of Hypotheticalism can be accepted by anyone with any in this spectrum of views. Disagreement about what this entails about the objectivity of morality can be converted simply into disagreement about how well explanations of genuinely agent-neutral reasons actually work. If we think that such explanations *can* work, then the mere fact that we have to give them shouldn't make us uneasy. Compare, for example, Humean puzzlement about the objectivity of moral reasons to Humean puzzlement about the objectivity of *epistemic* reasons. Many have argued[25] that since epistemic reasons have the same *kind* of objectivity as moral reasons, it is incoherent for a Humean to be puzzled about the objectivity of moral reasons but not about the objectivity of epistemic reasons. Yet this asymmetry in Humean puzzlement is something that we can now explain. For suppose that (as I have not committed either way) the Humean Theory is offered as an account both of moral *and* of epistemic reasons. Still, it is plausible to assume that more optimism is warranted about the success of explanations of epistemic reasons on the model of my explanation of Mary's reasons, than about the explanation of moral reasons such as the reason to help Katie. If so, then it makes sense to think that the explanation of epistemic reasons *works*, even though the explanation of the reason to help Katie does not. Hypotheticalism therefore actually *predicts* this kind of asymmetric reaction which is so common, and which other views actually make out to be literally incoherent.

I hold that this allows us to make sense of Hypotheticalism as the kind of view that *has* motivated 'Humean' worries about the objectivity of morality.[26] I'm offering a defense of a version of the Humean Theory of Reasons against critics who were worried about 'Humean' conclusions about the objectivity of morality. But if I do too *well* at showing that these 'Humean' conclusions don't follow, then the critics will say that this just goes to show they never meant to be arguing against Hypotheticalism in

---

[25] See e.g. Putnam [1990], Parfit [forthcoming], and Jackson [1999].
[26] See e.g. Foot [1959], [1975], Harman [1975], [1978], [1985], and Mackie [1977].

the first place. In the face of this possible objection, I think that this defense of Hypotheticalism does just well enough. If Hypotheticalism is true, that creates real pressure to explain why it is that the agent-neutral reasons that we intuitively think there are are overdetermined by desires. I've shown how such explanations are possible, and I hope why it is even reasonable to hope that they can be given. And I've explained how this actually leads us to predict the existence of a wide range of views, simply as reactions to the question of whether it is plausible that the reason to help Katie can be explained on the model of Katie's case. But the explanations still need to be given.

Finally, I think that leaving open the possibility that these explanations of agent-neutral reasons will fail is not leaving open too much, in order to plausibly count as having given a successful account of *reasons*, as opposed to an account of some other things, as discussed in Chapter 4. Surely one thing that a successful account of reasons *does* need to explain is the existence of such widespread disagreement about the range of views discussed in this section. And Hypotheticalism explains this disagreement well, by converting it into disagreement about whether the philosophical program of explaining the overdetermination hypothesis will pan out. The fact that disagreement about this is warranted, I think, makes Hypotheticalism a better account of the full range of data a theory about reasons needs to deal with.

6.5 Weighting for an Alternative to Proportionalism

The Hypotheticalist account of agent-neutral reasons is as follows: there are some actions that promote any possible desire. So the reasons to perform these actions are reasons for anyone, no matter what she desires. But they are, nevertheless, explained by desires. This accounts for the strong *and* weak modal statuses of agent-neutral reasons.

Still, one might think this: Mary's reason to believe p only if p is true may be a reason that she would have, no matter what she desired. But my explanation of that looks as though it makes her reasons differ in strength, for different propositions p. For propositions that are closely related to the task of acquiring new shoes, it sounds as if Mary has a pretty good reason to believe them only if they are true. But for propositions only remotely related, such as propositions about the number of moons of Jupiter, the argument seems to allow only that they are relatively poor reasons. I suspect that this objection has now been bothering you for several pages, even if you can predict the essentials of my response.

The response is easy in essentials, but tricky in detail. The objection assumes that we are accepting *Proportionalism*. For Proportionalism is the thesis that tells us that the weight of a reason varies in proportion to how well the action that it is in favor of promotes the desire which explains it. But in Chapter 5 I explained that Hypotheticalism rejects Proportionalism. We now have yet another reason for Hypotheticalism to reject Proportionalism. Still, Hypotheticalism does face a certain challenge: it needs to get the result that the agent-neutral reasons of morality are *equally good* reasons for everyone. This is a further challenge of accounting for agent-neutrality, over and above all those discussed in this chapter.

We are now in need, then, of an account of the *weight* of reasons which does three things. First, it must account for reasons' weight in terms of reasons, in order to preserve Reason Basicness, from section 4.4, and to get around Broadie's point in section 5.4. Second, it must yield the result that Aunt Margaret's reason to build her spacecraft is not a good one, in order to allow my response to the Too Many Reasons objection to work. And third, it must yield the result that the agent-neutral reason to help Katie is equally good for everyone, in order to capture the final and crucially important feature of genuinely agent-neutral reasons. And besides all these, we might *also* like, as noted in section 5.4, to be able to explain why it is a truism that if one reason is weightier than another, it is *correct* to place more weight on it in deliberation. This is what I claimed Proportionalism fails to explain, if understood as an analysis of reasons' weight.

7

Weighting for Reasons

7.1 Where We Are

Recall that this book is a study of the viability of the Humean Theory of Reasons. The structure is simple: I'm arguing that each of a wide range of apparently quite deep and general objections to the Humean Theory of Reasons turns on one or more assumptions about how that theory works that are really shared only by particular *versions* of the Humean Theory. These assumptions can all be understood as views about *how* Ronnie's reason is explained by his psychology. So in Chapters 2 through 4 we considered some very general theories about how to understand the 'because' clauses of answers to the question, 'Why is the fact that there will be dancing at the party a reason for Ronnie to go there?'

And now, in Chapters 5 through 7, we've been focusing on specific objections to the effect that the Humean theory is extensionally incorrect, and our attention has turned to many other questions on which we might disagree about what is necessary in order to explain Ronnie's reason. In Chapter 5 we considered whether *desires*—the psychological states that can explain reasons such as Ronnie's—have to be themselves understood in terms of reasons, and whether the explanation of Ronnie's case has to be *wide-scope* in character. In Chapter 6, we considered how strong the *promotion* relation has to be in order for Ronnie's going to the party promoting his dancing to explain a reason for him to go to the party. And in both chapters, the view about the explanation of Ronnie's reason that really facilitated the objections was the view called *Proportionalism*, which says that just as Ronnie's desire explains the existence of a reason for him, so its strength and how well the action promotes it explain the *weight* of Ronnie's reason.

If Humeans must accept Proportionalism, then neither of my chief arguments in the last two chapters goes through, or at least achieves very much. In Chapter 5, I explained away intuitions to the effect that the Humean Theory allows for Too Many Reasons, but only on the assumption that Aunt Margaret's reason is a poor or not very weighty one. And in Chapter 6, I used a weak account of the *promotion* relation and a model for explanations of reasons as in cases such as Mary's, in order to show how the Humean Theory can even allow for reasons with the strong modal status. But this is small progress if we must admit that moral reasons are lousy reasons for some people. Moreover, just as in Chapters 2 and 3, it is one thing to reject plausible-sounding and widespread views, it is quite another to provide an alternative positive view to step in and take their place.

So just as Chapter 4 concerned itself with a positive alternative to the views rejected in Chapters 2 and 3, the burden of this chapter is to present a positive account of the weight of reasons which serves as a viable alternative to Proportionalism. This account, moreover, must yield the right results about the weights of Aunt Margaret's reason to build her Mars-bound spacecraft, and of the agent-neutral reason to help Katie, when combined with Hypotheticalism. And although this isn't *necessary* to respond to the objections posed in the last two chapters, ideally it should be independently motivated and be broadly appealing in its own right as an account of reasons' weight. Then, as on other points, Hypotheticalism can maintain that its account is actually superior to Proportionalism as an account of what is going on in such cases as Ronnie and Bradley's. I'll begin, in the remainder of section 7.1, to articulate a framework for thinking about the weight of reasons. Then in sections 7.2 and 7.3 I'll give an independently motivated account of what it is for one reason to be weightier than another. Finally, in section 7.4 I'll argue that this account yields the predictions that Hypotheticalism requires of it.

Philosophers often write as if when a reason has a certain weight, what it has is a certain *amount* of something—weight. In my view, this is a mistake, for it raises several unfortunate puzzles. For one thing, many philosophers believe that reasons can be incomparable in weight—one reason can be neither weightier than, less weighty than, nor equally weighty to some other reason. But if what makes one reason weightier than, less weighty than, or equally weighty to another reason is simply whether its *amount* of weight is greater than, less than, or equal to the amount of weight of the second, then explaining how it is even intelligible that reasons could be incomparable in weight in this way would commit us to explaining how these *amounts* could be incomparable in the requisite ways. But this, I think, is a puzzle better avoided. Other things being equal, I think a framework for thinking about the weights of reasons should leave open at least the intelligibility of the idea that reasons might have incomparable weights, in as uncommitting a way as possible.

Two more puzzles arise with respect to the question of how reasons' weights 'add up'. If there will be both dancing and good food at the party, then these might both be reasons for Ronnie to go there. Together, they might count more in favor of Ronnie's going there than either separately. For example, the fact that Isabelle, Ronnie's ex-girlfriend, is going to be there, might be a weightier reason for him to stay away than the fact that there will be dancing there is for him to go, so that if only those two reasons were in play, the thing for him to do would be to stay away. And the fact that Isabelle will be there might be a weightier reason for him to stay away than the fact that there will be good food is for him to go, so that if only *those* two reasons were in play, the thing for him to do would be to stay away. But nevertheless, it might still be the case that since all *three* of these reasons are in play, the thing for Ronnie to do is to *go*—for together, the fact that there will be dancing and the fact that there will be good food outweigh the fact that Isabelle will be there, even though neither does, separately. So any adequate account of reasons' weight will have to make sense of how the weights of separate reasons can 'add up', in this way.

But unfortunately, the idea that reasons' weights are just *amounts* of something raises two puzzles in connection with this idea. For if reasons' weights are just amounts of something, then it is all too easy to see how to add up the weights of reasons. You just add the amounts of weight of the two reasons. But this, I think, both wrongly prejudges what goes on in certain cases and overgeneralizes.

The cases that it wrongly prejudges include cases in which two things are both reasons, but since they are not *independent* in the right way, intuitively their weights should not add up. For example, in Chapter 2 I argued that the existential fact that there is a reason for Nate to go into the living room is itself a reason for Nate to go into the living room. It is a reason, moreover, of non-zero weight. But in order for it to be a reason, it must be true, and in order for it to be true, there must be some other consideration that is a reason for Nate to go into the living room—for example, that a surprise party awaits him. However, though on the view that I offered, each of these reasons has non-zero weight, they should not add up, in the way that Ronnie's reasons to go to the party can add up. Now certainly this view is controversial, to say the least. But it is a view that I think should be attractive, so long as we can get the facts about reasons' weights to play out correctly. So whether or not you were convinced by my argument for this view, I think it ought to be more attractive to have a framework for thinking about the weight of reasons that does not prejudge the issue.

And finally, this idea, that 'adding up' is simply adding amounts of weight, overgeneralizes in a bad way, for it makes some questions turn out to be intelligible which I do not think ought to turn out to be intelligible. Though it makes sense to ask how Ronnie's two reasons to go to the party add up, I do not think that it makes sense to ask how Ronnie's reason to go to the party adds up with Susan's reason to go to the lounge. Ronnie's two reasons to go to the party need to be able to add up in order to outweigh his reason to stay away. That makes sense. But it is simply bizarre to think that Ronnie's reason to go to the party and Susan's reason to go to the lounge can add up in some way, for there is nothing that they would need to outweigh. Yet on the view on which the way that reasons add up is simply by adding up the amounts of each reason, it *is* intelligible to ask how the weights of Ronnie's reason and Susan's reason add up. Since I don't think this makes sense, I think it should be a constraint on an adequate account of the weight of reasons that it rule this out.

So a general account of the weight of reasons, I propose, should be general enough to make sense of the possibility that some reasons are of incomparable weight, and to make sense of how reasons can add up, without ruling out the view that Nate's reasons do not add up, and without overgeneralizing so as to make it intelligible that Ronnie's and Susan's reasons might add up. The framework that I propose is simple, and accommodates these simple constraints. Strictly speaking, I will say, it is not reasons that have weights, but only *sets* of reasons. Not any old set of reasons has a weight, however. Only sets of reasons for the same agent to do the same thing count. And finally, I will define the weight of a set of reasons not by establishing a correspondence between sets of reasons and some further thing—amounts of weight—but by defining a partial ordering on sets of reasons: the *weightier-than* ordering.

So formally, we can represent[1] reasons by ordered triples $< R, X, A >$, where R is a reason, X is an agent, and A is an action-type. Let us say that $< R, X, A >$ is *proper* if R is a reason for X to do A, and let S be the set of all such proper triples. So S represents the set of all reasons. Now we can define a new set, S^S, of 'addable' subsets of S. The members of S^S are subsets of S that are invariant with respect to x and a. Intuitively, they are sets of reasons that it makes sense to add up.[2] And then we define a relation on $S^S \times S^S$, $\succ$, which represents the weightier-than relation. $\succ$ is irreflexive, antisymmetric, and transitive, and holds between two sets when the reasons in the first set add up to more than the reasons in the second set.[3]

So to take a simple case, suppose that Q is the fact that there will be dancing at the party, R is the fact that there will be good food there, and S is the fact that Isabelle will be there. Also, let X be Ronnie, A be the action of going to the party, and $\sim A$ be the action of staying away from the party. This gives us three reasons, represented by the proper triples $< Q, X, A >$, $< R, X, A >$, and $< S, X, \sim A >$ (I'll now abbreviate these 'Q', 'R', and 'S', to avoid clutter). So $\{Q\}$, $\{R\}$, $\{S\}$, and $\{Q, R\}$ are all in S^S, but $\{Q, S\}$, $\{R, S\}$, and $\{Q, R, S\}$ are not. $\{Q\} \succ \{S\}$ just in case the fact that there will be dancing at the party is a weightier reason for Ronnie to go there than the fact that Isabelle will be there is for him to stay away. Similarly for $\{R\} \succ \{S\}$, and so on. $\{Q, R\} \succ \{S\}$ just in case together the two reasons for Ronnie to go outweigh the reason for him to stay away. And so, for example, the following scenario is coherent and interesting: $\{S\} \succ \{Q\}$, $\{S\} \succ \{R\}$, and $\{Q, R\} \succ \{S\}$. This is the scenario described earlier. In this case, Ronnie's reason to stay away from the party is collectively outweighed by his reasons to go, even though neither

---

[1] Reasons, of course, are not actually ordered triples; nor is the weightier-than relation a relation among sets of ordered triples: it is an ordering on sets of reasons. Here I frame things in terms of these triples simply in order to state clearly and simply the formal properties of the ordering and make visible where they come from.

[2] Again, strictly speaking, they only represent such sets, because strictly speaking reasons are not ordered triples, but the point is immaterial for understanding how the framework works.

[3] Jeff Horty [2007] has shown how to formalize several of the ideas in this chapter in the framework of default logic. He doesn't use sets to model the adding up of reasons, but his treatments of weight and of undercutting defeat (see sect. 7.2) are very similar.

outweighs it separately. If these are all of his reasons, then as things are he should go, but were either the food or the dancing to be cancelled, the thing for him to do would be to stay away.

The framework therefore captures exactly as much as we need in order to make sense of the idea that reasons' weights can add up, without building in unnecessary theory. Facts about adding up, as I've formalized them, are merely facts about which things stand in the $\succ$ relation—the same kinds of facts as those about whether one reason is weightier than another. So let the fact that there is a surprise party waiting in the living room be U, and the fact that there is a reason for Nate to go into the living room be V. I argued in Chapter 2 for the view that V is itself a reason for Nate to go into the living room, but that U and V should not add up to weigh more than either does separately. The second part of this claim can be captured by saying that it should not turn out that $\{U, \ V\} \succ \{U\}$ or $\{U, \ V\} \succ \{V\}$. Since this is merely a fact about what stands in $\succ$ to what, the framework that I've articulated leaves it open whether this is so. So within the framework, it is possible to formulate views according to which if $\{U\}$ and $\{V\}$ are both in S^S, then $\{U, \ V\} \succ \{U\}$. But it is also possible to formulate views according to which this is not the case. If I became convinced that there were such a constraint on how reasons add up, then I would give up on the view that existential facts about reasons are themselves reasons. But I know of no good argument for such a constraint, so I am happy to accept the view about existential facts about reasons.

So just to recap: how does this framework for thinking about the weight of reasons fare by the lights of the criteria that I distinguished to begin with? First, I said that a good account should leave open whether there can be reasons of incomparable weight. So far, this account leaves this open, because the only claim made is that $\succ$ is an (at least) partial ordering on members of S^S. Second, I said that an adequate account should make sense of how reasons' weights can add up, and not prejudge whether two things can both be reasons without their weights adding up. Treating $\succ$ as an ordering on sets of reasons allows us to do this in an elegant way, on which all questions boil down to questions of what stands in $\succ$ to what. And finally, I claimed that an adequate account must not overgeneralize, making some questions turn out to be intelligible which otherwise seem not to be, such as how Ronnie's reason to go to the party adds up with

Susan's reason to go to the lounge. The treatment that I've given rules this out, because those sets are not in S^S, on which $\succ$ is defined.[4]

7.2 Toward a Positive Account

So far, I've sketched a framework for thinking about the weight of reasons. The framework is designed to accommodate many different views about which reasons are weightier than which, and is compatible with many different accounts of *what it is* for one set of reasons to be weightier than another. So it remains to actually offer a positive analysis of the weightier-than relation—the relation that is modeled by $\succ$. In this section I'll motivate the shape of the analysis of the weightier-than relation that I advocate, and I'll spell it out in section 7.3. The motivation for the shape of my analysis consists in five simple ideas.

1. The first idea I have is that to say that one reason is weightier than another is to make a normative claim akin to the claim that one person is more admirable than another. One person is not more admirable than another because she is more widely admired, or because it is easier for people to admire her, but because it is *appropriate* or *correct* to admire her more. Similarly, one reason is not weightier than another because it carries more weight in deliberation, but because it is *correct* for it to carry more weight in deliberation.

I think this is a very natural and attractive idea. When agents deliberate, various factors come to light, and the agent places more weight on some of these factors than on others. The weight of a reason surely has something to do with this process. But what? Surely not with how any agents actually weight that consideration. The weight of a reason, it seems, must be how it is *correct* to weight that consideration in deliberation. So on this picture, the weight of reasons is like admirableness, disgustingness, funniness, and blameworthiness, a member of a wide class of normative properties which can attractively be understood in terms of the correctness of a certain kind of response. So to recap, my first idea about the weight of reasons is that the following kind of analysis looks very attractive:

---

[4] This last move may seem ad hoc so far, but it drops out of the positive analysis that I'll give of the *weightier than* relation in section 7.2.

Attractive Idea For R to be a weightier set of reasons to do A than S ($R \succ S$) is for it to be correct to place more weight on R than on S in deliberation about whether to do A.[5]

This is the same Attractive Idea that I considered at the end of Chapter 5, in explaining why I think that using Proportionalism as an analysis of the weight of reasons would be on the wrong track. Ultimately, I will allow that the Attractive Idea is not exactly right, and should not be understood as an analysis of the weightier-than relation, but for now I simply want to emphasize that it is attractive.

2. The second idea which I want to bring out in motivating the shape of my positive analysis of the weight of reasons is an idea about the relationship between an agent's reasons and what she ought to do. In the example of the last section, we considered two reasons for Ronnie to go to the party and one reason for him to stay away. We needed to be able to make sense of how his two reasons to go could 'add up' in order to outweigh his reason to stay away, because it could turn out that he ought to go, even though the reason for him to stay away is weightier than any individual reason for him to go. The idea which informed that discussion was that there is a close connection between what Ronnie ought to do and the weight of Ronnie's reasons, when added up. The idea was that if the set of all of the reasons for Ronnie to go outweighed the set of all of the reasons for Ronnie to stay away, then Ronnie ought to go.

Let $S_{X,\,A}$ be the set of all of the reasons for X to do A and $S_{X,\,\sim A}$ be the set of all of the reasons for X not to do A. Then we can capture this idea in the following account:

Ought For it to be the case that X ought to do A is for it to be the case that $S_{X,\,A} \succ S_{X,\,\sim A}$.[6]

---

[5] Let me immediately head off a distracting but easily discharged objection. You might worry that there are sometimes weighty reasons in cases in which it would be a mistake to deliberate. It would be a mistake to deliberate about whether to torture your nephew, for example, but that doesn't mean that there aren't weighty reasons not to do so. But the sense in which it is natural to think that the weight of reasons corresponds to correct deliberation is not that of whether it is correct *to deliberate*; it is a matter *within deliberation*. If you do find yourself deliberating about whether to torture your nephew, things are going badly if you are not treating the fact that it would cause him extreme pain as counting against.

[6] 1. This analysis is compatible with—in fact, even suggests—the idea that there might be related senses of 'ought' in which the set of relevant reasons is restricted in some way—for example, to

This thesis contrasts with another thesis about the connection between reasons and *ought* that I considered in section 2.3. According to Toulmin's view considered there, reasons were to be analyzed in terms of *ought*, rather than conversely. Similarly, according to Broome, reasons were to be analyzed in terms of what plays the right role in an explanation of what someone ought to do. Here I am proposing the reverse idea. First there are reasons, which weigh in favor of and against a given action. Then, if the reasons on one side outweigh those on the other, that is what the agent ought to do. Again, I think this is an incredibly natural idea.

(3) The third idea that I want to bring out follows from the first two. If what an agent ought to do is a matter of what the totality of her reasons weigh in favor of, and one set of reasons is weightier than another just in case it is correct to place more weight on it in deliberation, then it follows that what an agent ought to do would also be the result of correct deliberation from full information. For if an agent were fully informed, then she would be aware of all of her reasons. By Ought, she ought to do A just in case the complete set of reasons for her to do A is weightier than the complete set of reasons for her not to do A. But since she is fully informed, she is aware of all of these reasons on both sides. So by the Attractive Idea, correct deliberation will require her to place more weight on the set of reasons to do A than on the set of reasons not to do A. And so if the result of

epistemic reasons, moral reasons, prudential reasons, or otherwise. On this view, obvious analyses of 'morally ought', 'prudentially ought', and so on would follow from the same account, given a restriction on the sets of reasons involved that results from intersecting each of $S_{X, A}$ and $S_{X, \sim A}$ with the set of moral reasons, or with the set of prudential reasons, etc.

2. Gilbert Harman [2002] agrees that this seems to be extensionally right about reasons for action, but claims that one of the important differences between reasons for action and reasons for belief is that it fails for reasons for belief. Harman's idea is that the mere fact that one's evidence for p outweighs one's evidence against p is insufficient to guarantee that one ought to believe p. If the evidence for p only *barely* outweighs the evidence against p, perhaps what the agent ought to do is to withhold belief with respect to p.

In this book, I don't mean to be committing myself to any claims about reasons for belief. But in principle, I am strongly tempted to think that what is going on with epistemic reasons will be very much like what is going on with practical reasons. So am I worried that this account of *ought* seems not to generalize to the belief case? No, because although I agree with Harman's observation, I think he has misdescribed it. It is true that it doesn't follow from the fact that one's evidence for p outweighs one's evidence against p that one ought to believe p. But evidence against p is only one kind of reason not to believe p—it is reason to believe $\sim p$. But in addition to believing p and believing $\sim p$, an agent has a third option—withholding with respect to p. So the complete set of reasons not to believe p includes not only the evidence against p, but the reasons to withhold with respect to p. When the evidence for p outweighs both the evidence against p and the reasons to withhold with respect to p put together, then I think it *does* follow that she ought to believe p. So I do think that this kind of analysis can plausibly be generalized to the case of beliefs.

deliberation is a result of how much weight she places on the considerations on each side, then the result of her deliberation will be to do *A*. So she ought to do *A* just in case correct deliberation from full information would have that result. And that, I think, is a very nice prediction. It is puzzling to think that correct deliberation from complete information could lead us astray from what we ought to do. So I think that this prediction suggests that something about idea (1) and idea (2) have put us on the right track.

(4) My fourth idea pointing in the direction of a positive analysis of the weight of reasons is an observation based on cases of undercutting defeat. The example that I'll use is a case of an epistemic reason, but I think the phenomenon is perfectly general, and works for practical reasons as well. Undercutting defeat is well-illustrated by the case of Tom Grabit, familiar from Chapter 5, who you see come out of the library, pull a book from beneath his shirt, cackle gleefully, and then scurry off.[7] When you see this, you have some reason to believe that Tom has just stolen a book from the library. But if Tom has a twin brother Tim, from whom you cannot visually distinguish him, then the case is more complicated. At first it seems that in this modified version of the case, you no longer have a reason to believe that Tom stole a book. But as we saw in Chapter 5, this can be observed to be incorrect by considering a third version of the case, in which Tom and Tim have a third identical sibling, Tam. In that case, your reason for believing that Tom stole a book is even worse than in the second case, so it can't have gone away entirely in the second case.

What the Tam case shows is that undercutting defeaters like the fact that Tom has a twin brother from whom you can't visually distinguish him somehow affect the weight of your reason to believe that Tom stole a book. If Tom has no identical siblings, your visual experience is excellent evidence that Tom stole a book, if he has one sibling, Tim, then your visual experience is not such good evidence, and if he has two or more, your visual experience becomes progressively worse evidence about who stole the book. The fact that Tom has a twin is not itself evidence that he did *not* steal the book, however. What it does is to somehow lower the weight of your original reason.[8]

---

[7] Lehrer and Paxson [1969].

[8] Jonathan Dancy calls partial undercutters like this one 'attenuators' [2005: 38–43]. But it is an important part of the suggestion that I am advancing, that attenuation is not a *sui generis* relation.

How does it do that? I think the right answer is a natural one. It does it because it is itself a reason to place less weight on your initial visual experience, in favor of the conclusion that Tom stole a book. If Tom has an identical twin, then you should take your visual evidence about Tom very cautiously when forming beliefs about what Tom has done, and if Tom has two identical siblings, you should take it even more cautiously. So the fact that Tom has such a twin is a reason for you to place less weight on your visual evidence about Tom. So the close to uncontroversial observation was that the weight of reasons depends on the existence of partial undercutting defeaters like the fact that Tom has a twin brother. And the natural idea that was my positive suggestion, was that partial undercutting defeaters are reasons to place less weight on the reason that they undercut. It follows from these two ideas that the weight of a reason depends on the existence or not of reasons to place less weight on it.

(5) This doesn't *explain* why reasons to place less weight on a reason can have an effect on how weighty it is. But we *can* explain this, if we put the Attractive Idea together with the proposal that what it is correct to do gets analyzed in terms of reasons, in a way similar to the analysis of *ought* in terms of reasons above. Of course, what it is correct to do is not a matter of just *any* old reasons—many reasons are of the wrong kind. For example, as Justin D'Arms and Dan Jacobson have argued, moral reasons not to laugh at some joke have nothing essentially to do with how funny it is.[9] And Wlodek Rabinowicz and Toni Rønnow-Rasmussen have reminded us that prudential reasons to admire someone do not contribute to making her more admirable.[10] This is the justly famous 'wrong kind of reasons' problem.[11] With respect to any activity *A*, if correctness in *A* is to be accounted for in terms of reasons at all, it can only be accounted for in

Rather, I will be suggesting that attenuators are reasons of the right kind to place less weight on another reason.

   [9] D'Arms and Jacobson [2000].   [10] Rabinowicz and Rønnow-Rasmussen [2004].

   [11] Others who have worried extensively about the wrong kind of reasons problem include Parfit [2001], Piller [2001], [2006], Olson [2004], and Hieronymi [2005]. Most discussions of the problem, however, construe it too narrowly. According to Parfit and Piller, the problem is confined to reasons to be in certain kinds of mental states that have contents. They call it the 'attitude/content' or 'state-given/object-given' distinction. According to Hieronymi, it is more general, but still confined to reasons to have certain kinds of mental states. But importantly, the distinction arises in every domain governed by some standard of correctness. There are right and wrong kinds of reasons to make moves in chess, for example. But moves in chess are not mental states, and they don't have contents. So whatever the fundamental distinction between the right and wrong kinds of reasons is, views on which it is ultimately to be explained by something about attitudes or contents simply have to be on the

terms of the *right kind* of reasons. Nevertheless, if we only had the right way of restricting to the right kind of reasons, then if we analyzed correctness in terms of the right kind of reasons, it would fall out of that analysis and the Attractive Idea that the weight of a reason can be affected by reasons to place less weight on it—provided that they are of the right kind. And so in that way, we would be able to account for the data I pointed out under idea (4).

There are two reasons why I think this is a very attractive way to go. First, correctness is clearly a normative property, and for independent reasons I believe that all normative properties should be analyzable in terms of reasons in some way or other. In fact, I followed many other authors in suggesting in section 4.4 that being analyzable in terms of reasons is precisely what it is for a property to be normative. But second, I think that some solution to the wrong kind of reasons problem must be forthcoming anyway, because there is such a wide class of normative properties that seem to have the same kind of structure. The wrong kind of reasons problem comes up for 'admirable' and 'desirable', but it is compelling to think that to be admirable is to be correctly admired and that to be desirable is to be correctly desired. So that gives us grounds for optimism that some solution must be forthcoming.

So at a first pass, the account of correctness might be constructible in a similar way to Ought, above. Let S_A be the set of all reasons of the right kind to do A and $S_{\sim A}$ be the set of all reasons of the right kind not to do A. Then the account can be simple:

Correct   For it to be correct to do A is for it to be the case that $S_A \succ S_{\sim A}$.

It only remains to provide an account of which are the right kinds of reasons. My suggestion is simple. I don't know if it is right, but it seems to me to be on the right track. Correctness, I think, is always relative to some activity. There are correct and incorrect cases of blaming, correct and incorrect levels of admiration, correct and incorrect moves in chess, and correct and incorrect ways of weighting reasons. In order to see what is in common across these cases, I think that we must factor out the activities

wrong track. In what follows I give my best attempt to try to set out a more general approach to understanding the nature of the distinction.

of blaming, admiring, playing chess, and deliberating. Correctness is always correctness *within some activity*. The right kind of reasons, I think, need to be understood by reference to the relevant activity.

So how do we do this? I think that the answer is simple. The right kind of reasons involved in any activity are the ones that the people involved in that activity have, *because* they are engaged in that activity. So, for example, there are correct and incorrect moves to make in chess. The incorrect moves are ruled out, I think, by reasons to follow the rules of the game. Who has those reasons? Anyone who is playing chess. No one is playing chess, I think, unless she has some minimal level of desire to be following the rules of the game. And so anyone who is playing chess is guaranteed to have some reason not to, for example, castle out of check, because that is against the rules. People who are not playing chess do not have such reasons, but that does not matter.

There are also reasons that everyone who is playing chess shares but are of the wrong kind. For example, everyone who is playing chess has moral reasons. But moral reasons are of the wrong kind, because it is not the fact that they are *playing chess* that explains why they have those reasons. Finally, we might imagine a fantastic case in which an all-powerful demon pledges to grant wealth beyond imagining to any chess player who castles out of check (but not to a non–chess-player). This case is harder, because then there would be a reason any chess player had to castle out of check—and had because of being a chess player (that is the content of the demon's pledge). But again, I think that we can rule these cases out if we are careful enough. The fact that someone is a chess player is not *sufficient* to explain the existence of these reasons—that requires the existence of the demon's pledge, as well. So I think we can rule out the wrong kinds of reasons as reasons that accrue to those engaged in an activity for some other cause than simply that they are engaged in that activity. So, roughly:

Right Kind of Reasons   The right kind of reasons to do A are reasons that are shared by everyone engaged in the activity of doing A, such that the fact that they are engaged in doing A is sufficient to explain why these are reasons for them.

That was five ideas. Together, the Attractive Idea (1) and Ought (2) predict (3) that what you ought to do is what would be the result of correct deliberation from full information, which I think is evidence that the Attractive Idea and Ought are on the right track. And together, the Attractive Idea (1) and Correct (5) predict that the weight of reasons can be affected by reasons to place less weight on them (4)—provided that the reasons to place less weight are of the right kind. And this, I've suggested, is a true prediction—reasons' weight *can* be affected in this way, and the combination of the Attractive Idea with Correct can explain this. That it can do so again constitutes, I think, evidence that we are on the right track. Moreover, if Right Kind of Reasons is anywhere near on the right track, then it should not be obvious that the famous wrong kind of reasons problem constitutes an insuperable obstacle to this approach.

7.3 A Recursive Account

The foregoing ideas are, I think, highly attractive, and they fit together in a very natural way. But unfortunately, I think, they cannot all be right. For if the Attractive Idea is our analysis of the weight of reasons, then the weightier-than relation is analyzed in terms of correctness. But if Correct is our analysis of correctness, then correctness is analyzed in terms of the weightier-than relation. But that looks like a circle, and circular analyses should be objectionable, on the conception of analysis that I sketched in Chapter 4. So the Attractive Idea and Correct cannot both, I think, be correct analyses.

There also appears, on the face of it, to be an explanatory regress. If R is weightier than S only if and because it is correct to place more weight on R than on S, then by Correct this can be so only if and because the set of all the right kind of reasons to place more weight on R than on S is weightier than the set of all of the right kind of reasons to place more weight on S than on R. But then by the Attractive Idea, this can be so only if and because it is correct to place more weight on the former than on the latter, and so by Correct that can be so only if and because the reasons to place more weight on the former outweigh the reasons to place more weight on the latter, and so on, tortoises all of the way down.

My way out of the circular analyses is motivated by observing a natural reason to think that this explanatory regress may not, in principle, turn out to be all that bad a problem. So return to the case of undercutting defeaters, and the Grabit family. The fact that Tom has a twin, Tim, is an undercutter for your visual evidence that Tom stole a book. But this undercutter can also be undercut. Suppose, for example, that this morning Mrs Grabit, the twins' mother, said that Tim is in Thailand this week (supposing, for clarity, that the library is not in Thailand). The fact that Mrs Grabit said this is not a reason for you to believe that Tom stole a book. What it does, is to make it turn out that the fact that Tom has a twin is not such a great reason, after all, to be cautious about your visual experiences of Tom (at least this week). So when your undercutter is undercut, by having its weight lowered, your original reason's weight turns out to be higher after all. So just as in the original case, the weight of the undercutting reason seems to *depend* on whether it is undercut or not. So it seems to depend on the existence or not of reasons to place less weight on it.

In principle, this can go on for a long time. Add to the case that Mrs Grabit is a notorious liar. But then add that this morning she was given a truth serum. Then add that she only believes that Tim is in Thailand because Tim deliberately misled her about his whereabouts. Then add that Tim misled her because he was really planning to visit Mr Grabit, Mrs Grabit's estranged ex-husband, in Estonia (assume that the library is also not in Estonia). And then add that Tim never made it to Estonia, because his flight was cancelled. And so on. Each of these further considerations is an undercutter for the last. So the weight of your original reason depends on whether these things turn out to be the case. The weight of reasons *does* depend on the weight of reasons to place less weight on them, and their weight depends on the existence of reasons to place less weight on them, and so on. I think it should be uncontroversial that this happens—it is the important phenomenon of undercutting defeat.

The reason that this does not make us worry that an explanatory regress threatens, is that we think that undercutters *eventually run out*. At some point, there is an undercutter that is not undercut, and once that happens, we can go back through the chain and determine the weight of your original visual evidence that Tom stole a book. My positive account of reasons' weight builds on this simple idea. I propose to resolve the tension between the Attractive Idea and Correct by replacing the Attractive Idea with a *recursive* analysis of the weight of reasons. The base case of the recursive analysis begins with, intuitively, the point at which undercutters 'eventually run out'. And the recursion clause takes things from there.

Once I've laid out the account and shown how it works, I'll provide an argument that the Attractive Idea is still true, so long as we understand it as a necessary equivalence rather than an analysis. And so the account will be able to preserve the nice picture set up in section 7.2.

To see how the account is supposed to work, start by taking the Attractive Idea, and substituting in the analysis provided by Correct, in order to make the circularity explicit:

Better   For set of reasons A to be weightier than set of reasons B is for the set of all the (right kind of) reasons to place more weight on A to be weightier than the set of all the (right kind of) reasons to place more weight on B.

Appealing to the idea that the *explanatory* regress can be stopped if reasons to place weight on one side eventually run out, let's improve on Better by making it *recursive*:

Weight Base   One way for set of reasons A to be weightier than set of reasons B is for set B to be empty, but A non-empty.

Weight Recursion   The other way for set of reasons A to be weightier than set of reasons B is for the set of all the (right kind of) reasons to place more weight on A to be weightier than the set of all the (right kind of) reasons to place more weight on B.

Weight Recursion is basically just Better. Weight Base gives us an independent way for one set of reasons to count as weightier than another, getting us out of the imminent conceptual and explanatory regress.

The idea behind Weight Base is simply the one lying behind our reaction to the epistemic defeaters in the case of Tom and Tim Grabit. In that case, it seemed that part of what made it the case that your visual evidence was better or worse was whether there were other *defeaters*. But how important or weighty these defeaters were depended on whether they had defeaters themselves, and on how weighty those defeater-defeaters were. And in principle, this seemed as if it could go on indefinitely. But that didn't make us worry, so long as we could be confident that in any actual case, it eventually *does* stop, *someplace*. The place where it stops is where there is no further defeater. Weight Base simply tries to characterize what it takes for things to stop, in this way—or rather, for an explanation of the weight of some reason ultimately to get *started*. Weight Recursion tells us how, once it is started, it continues to proceed.

This, I think, should be an account of the weight of reasons with broad appeal. It makes sense of all of the ideas that I assembled in section 7.2. I haven't offered a knockdown argument for this account; I've only tried to situate it in an attractive context, and to fill in just enough details to make it plausible that they can be further filled in. But I didn't need to provide a knockdown argument for the view, and I don't think that knockdown arguments can be had for detailed positive proposals like this one. We're interested in the viability of the Humean Theory of Reasons, and from my arguments in Chapters 5 and 6 it follows that its viability turns on whether there is an *available* viable view to take about the weight of reasons. So my burden in this chapter is to show that this view can be made to work, and to do the things that the Humean wants of it. I'm also trying to show that the account is far from an ad hoc device to save the Humean, but it is a separate issue whether you find it possible to resist the account's appeal, and one I haven't tried to address. Certainly nothing I've said so far in favor of the account presupposes commitment to any particular theory of reasons.

7.4 Capturing the Attractive Idea

Together, then, Weight Base and Weight Recursion give us an account of the weight of reasons. And it is indisputably a thoroughly disjunctive account. There is no way to restate Weight Base and Weight Recursion that gets around the fact that it is ultimately disjunctive. Moreover, I myself am prone to think that disjunctive accounts are rather problematic.[12] So this, it seems to me, is a drawback in the account. Yet I am less worried about the disjunctive nature of the Weight Base/Weight Recursion account than I might be. The main reason why I am less worried, is that together with Ought and Correct, the Weight Base/Weight Recursion account yields the result that there *is* something interesting and unified that we can say about the weights of reasons. And it is simply that:

---

[12] As discussed in Ch. 4, and in sect. 3.4 with regard to the Revived Chauvinism Objection.

Still Attractive   Set of reasons A is weightier than set of reasons B just in case it is *correct* to place more weight on A than on B.

And that is just the Attractive Idea with which we began, stated now merely as an extensional thesis, rather than as an analysis. It therefore not only tells us something interesting about what weighty reasons all have in common, but allows us to preserve the predictions outlined in section 7.2. Given Still Attractive, it still turns out that what you ought to do is what would be the result of correct deliberation from full information. And we still get an explanation of why undercutting defeaters work in the way that they do. So let me now explain why the account yields the right result.

Suppose that set of reasons A is weightier than set of reasons B. Then there are two cases. Either this is because set B is empty and A is not, or it is because the set of all the reasons to place more weight on A is weightier than the set of all the reasons to place more weight on B. Take the second case first. It follows from Correct that it is *correct* to place more weight on A than on B. Now take the first case. So set B is empty, but A is not. Is it correct to place more weight on A? This doesn't follow directly from Correct. But it does follow, if we make an assumption that I think is eminently plausible—that there is a general reason to place more weight on reasons than on non-reasons in deliberating about what to do, and that there is no such reason the other way around. If we make this assumption, then it follows from Weight Base that the reasons to place more weight on A are weightier than the reasons to place more weight on B. And from this and Correct it follows that it is *correct* to weight the reasons in A more heavily than the reasons in B. So either way, if the set of reasons A is weightier than the set of reasons B, it is correct to place more weight on it than on B.

So now suppose that it is correct to place more weight on A than on B. From Correct it follows that the set of all reasons to place more weight on A is weightier than the set of all reasons to place more weight on B. And so it follows from Weight Recursion that A is weightier than B. So both directions go through. Even though the Attractive Idea didn't succeed at giving us an account of *what it is* for one reason to weigh more than another, it still succeeds at telling us something that is true of, and only true of, cases in which one reason is weightier than another. Indeed, on the view that I've articulated, it doesn't just give us *any old* necessary and sufficient conditions, either. It explains for us *why* the disjunctive account provided by Weight Base and Weight Recursion is nevertheless in a certain way *unified*.

Of course, the way in which this account is unified is somewhat odd. After all, in *unifying* Weight Base and Weight Recursion, it appeals to a notion—correctness—that is itself analyzed in terms of the very relation—weight—of which Weight Base and Weight Recursion give us a disjunctive account. Yet I don't think that the unification provided by Still Attractive is merely *trivial*. Compare: I might have said that for an action to be correct is either for it to be commanded by God or else to conduce to overall happiness, and then claimed that though my account is disjunctive, at least there is this much to be said for the disjuncts—they are both correct. That sort of unification, I think, is no unification at all. I place my hopes to have provided a more substantive explanation of why though disjunctive, *weight* is nevertheless a unified category, in the following observation. My deduction of Still Attractive from Correct, Weight Base, and Weight Recursion needed an *additional, substantive* premise. I had to assume that there is an agent-neutral reason to place more weight on reasons than on non-reasons. As I see it, this is about the most plausible agent-neutral reason that it is possible to imagine, and just about the easiest to be explained along the model explored in Chapter 6. But since it is nevertheless a *substantive* assumption that there is such a reason, my unification of Weight Base and Weight Recursion by means of Still Attractive is certainly not trivial, in the way that the 'unification' of God's commands with the actions which conduce to overall happiness was.

7.5 Ryan and Aunt Margaret

So much for the account. What Hypotheticalism needs from this account, if it is to help it take advantage of my arguments of the last two chapters, is for it to turn out that Aunt Margaret's reason to build her spacecraft is plausibly not a very weighty one, and that Ryan's reason to help Katie *is* a weighty one, even if helping Katie only promotes the objects of his desires in a remote way. In particular, we want the reason to help Katie to be equally weighty for everyone.

Keep in mind that the objection that we still haven't explained how the reason to help Katie is equally good for everyone is a *conditional* objection. It is supposed to arise *conditionally* on the success of our explanation of this reason's strong modal status. If we can't even explain the strong modal status of this reason, then there is no puzzle about how it gets to be equally weighty for everyone. So let's grant that some explanation of the reason to help Katie along the lines of the model proposed in Chapter 6 *works*. I'll now argue that conditional on this assumption, it is quite plausible that the reason to help Katie should be of equal weight for everyone.

To see how weighty the reason for Ryan to help Katie is, our account of the weight of reasons tells us that we have to look, roughly, at reasons of the right kind to place *more* weight on it, and at reasons to place *less* weight on it. What matters, of course, is not simply what *Ryan's* reasons are, to place more or less weight on it. If Ryan can't stand Katie, for example, Ryan may have abundant reasons to place less weight on this reason. But those reasons aren't relevant to its *weight*, because they won't be of the right kind. A reason has a certain weight just in case it is *correct* to place that much weight on it. And correctness is determined by reasons of the right kind. According to Right Kind of Reasons, that means that they must be reasons that everyone who is placing weight on reasons has, in virtue of being someone who is placing weight on reasons. But the activity of placing weight on reasons is just the activity of deciding what to do. So it is simply the activity that every agent is engaged in. So the right kind of reasons with respect to the correctness of placing weight on reasons are precisely the class of *agent-neutral* reasons. It follows that Ryan's idiosyncratic reasons to place less weight on his reason to help Katie are irrelevant, the wrong kind of reason to determine its weight. They are like your reasons not to laugh, when you are the one who is laughable.

So where might agent-neutral reasons to place more weight on Ryan's reason to help Katie come from? I think it is easy to see. Consider, for example, the fact that it is an agent-neutral reason to help Katie. Is this fact an agent-neutral reason to place weight on it in deliberation? Well, for any agent X, this fact helps to explain why helping Katie is a way of doing something that there is a reason for X to do. And since placing weight on this reason promotes actually helping Katie, it helps to explain why placing weight on this reason promotes doing something that there is a reason for X to do. And according to Hypotheticalism, doing something that there is a reason for X to do *has* to promote the object of at least one of X's desires. So it follows that for any agent X, the fact that the reason to help Katie is agent-neutral helps to explain why X's placing weight on this reason promotes the object of one of X's desires. So by Hypotheticalism and Agent-Neutral, there is an agent-neutral reason to place weight on it.

If any argument something like this one can be made out, then Hypotheticalism will successfully yield agent-neutral reasons to place more weight on the reason to help Katie, but the reasons for various agents to place less weight on this reason will generally be idiosyncratic, like Ryan's, and consequently irrelevant to what weight it is correct to place on this reason. So applying Weight Base, the agent-neutral reason to help Katie will turn out to be relatively weighty. And by parity of reasoning, agent-neutral reasons will *generally* turn out to be relatively weighty. So that completes my account of agent-neutrality.

But what about Aunt Margaret's reason? Does it turn out to be relatively poor? Again, I think roughly the same considerations apply. It is relatively easy to imagine that if it is possible to explain *any* agent-neutral reasons, it will be possible to explain an agent-neutral reason not to place weight on merely agent-relational reasons in favor of actions that merely promote enormously costly, fantastically frivolous ends. Even Aunt Margaret has such a reason—for consider anything else that Aunt Margaret desires. Placing inordinate weight on idiosyncratic reasons to take enormously costly means to fantastically frivolous ends is a great way to undertake too many costs in order to accomplish the other things that she wants. Of course, it may be that *on balance* what Aunt Margaret wants most is simply to reconstruct her catalogue scene on Mars, even at the cost of everything else that she wants. But so long as there are some things which she desires to at least some degree, and which are at least put in *jeopardy* by the action of placing great weight on reasons to take enormously costly means to fantastically frivolous ends, then we should be able to successfully run this explanation even in Aunt Margaret's case.

Moreover, we can run this explanation in her case without being committed to explaining away the weight of Ronnie's reason to go to the party. For going to the party is not an enormously costly means to a fantastically frivolous end. In fact, that is precisely what makes Ronnie's reason seem uncontroversial and Aunt Margaret's seem so controversial. I've now claimed that this difference plausibly falls out, once we start seeing what agent-neutral reasons to place weight on reasons it will be possible to explain.

And to complete our explanation, the agent-neutral reason to place less weight on reasons like Aunt Margaret's is not similarly balanced out by agent-neutral reasons to place more weight on it. Of course, Aunt Margaret has reasons to place more weight on it—but these reasons are idiosyncratic to her, and have to do with the fact that she—bizarrely—is obsessed about reconstructing the scene depicted on page 78 of the November, 2001 *Martha Stewart Living* catalogue on Mars. So they are of the wrong kind to play a part in determining her reason's weight. And that completes my answer to the Too Many Reasons objection.

So here is where we now find ourselves: we are investigating the viability of the Humean Theory of Reasons, which is the parity thesis that all reasons are, like Ronnie's, explained by some feature of their agent's psychology, which we are stipulatively calling a *desire*. Since this parity thesis leaves open what view we take about how Ronnie's reason *is* explained by his desires, we've been looking at how different views about this question affect the liability of the resulting version of the Humean Theory of Reasons to a wide class of objections.

Chapters 2 through 4 looked at three very general theories about the function of the 'because' clause when we say that the fact that there will be dancing at the party is a reason for Ronnie to go there *because* he desires to dance. We saw in Chapters 2 and 3 that two of these theories led to a variety of problems, and so in Chapter 4 I provided an alternative theory which avoids those problems. Then in Chapters 5 through 7 we switched from focusing on different views about the explanation of Ronnie's reason to focusing on two very general objections to the Humean theory—that it both allows for too many reasons, and for too few. I argued in Chapters 5 and 6 for the conditional view that if Proportionalism is false, then a good solution to both these objections can be had, and now in Chapter 7 I have offered an account of the weight of reasons to serve as an alternative to Proportionalism.

Now in Chapters 8 through 10 we again shift our focus. So far, I've taken no view about what kind of psychological state *does* explain Ronnie's reason, so that is the question in Chapter 8. Then in Chapter 9 I'll use the accounts of the weight of reasons from Chapter 7 and of desire from

Chapter 8 in order to construct the beginnings of a surprisingly Aristotelian moral epistemology and moral psychology, which I'll argue is on the right track to solving several important and outstanding problems in those domains. I also have not anywhere treated the large class of arguments that the Humean Theory of Reasons is committed to one or another of a wide variety of 'instrumentalist' conclusions, which we will know enough about Hypotheticalism in order to address in Chapter 10. And finally, in Chapter 11 I'll take stock and lay out what I take to be the positive motivation for Hypotheticalism.

8

Desire

8.1 What Are Desires?

I have throughout been using 'desire' as a technical term, stipulated to pick out that psychological state, whatever it is, which most fundamentally explains the difference between Ronnie's and Bradley's reasons. For it is only in this stipulative sense that it can be at all uncontroversial that there even *are* cases in which a reason is explained by a desire. As soon as we settle on a more precise view about what desires in the stipulative sense are, it will cease to be uncontroversial that *any* reasons are explained by that kind of psychological state. Although some hold that some reasons are explained by what people take pleasure in, others hold that this is not so. Although some hold that some reasons are explained by desires in a more conventional sense, others hold that this is not so. And although some hold that some reasons are explained by what agents take themselves to have reasons to do, others hold that this is not so. These disputes are facilitated by the fact that in ordinary cases like that of Ronnie and Bradley, Ronnie and Bradley differ psychologically in *more than one way*, and it is hard to keep track of which of these psychological differences is doing the explanatory work.

The conventional way to resolve such disputes and adjudicate what kind of psychological state it is that most fundamentally explains the difference between Ronnie and Bradley, is to construct hypothetical cases which try to isolate a single psychological difference between Ronnie and Bradley, and to test our intuitions on these cases. So we try to construct a case in which Ronnie would take pleasure in dancing, if he did, but does not know this, does not want to dance any more than Bradley does, and so on. Do we think that there is intuitively a reason for Ronnie to go to the party in this case? Or, imagine a case in which Ronnie wants to dance, but does not enjoy dancing, does not see value in dancing, does not intend to dance, and so on, and Bradley exactly the same as Ronnie except that he does not want to dance. What are our intuitions about Ronnie's reasons, in this case?[1]

I hold that this methodology is unpromising. It is hard to be certain enough about our intuitions in the bizarrely abstracted cases, which really manage to isolate a single psychological feature. It is hard both because it is difficult to construct cases which really isolate only one psychological feature, and because our intuitions even in these cases are not completely clear. But more importantly, given my treatment of the Too Few Reasons objection, we have to take great care in trying to construct such control cases. It is not enough to stipulate, for example, that Ronnie does not desire to dance, in the ordinary sense. Perhaps, though Ronnie does not desire to dance, he *does* have some *other* desire which would explain his reason to go to the party. For example, perhaps Ronnie desires to enjoy himself. In order to control for this, our test cases would have to stipulate that Ronnie has *no* desire that would explain a reason for him to do what he enjoys. But given my strategy for explaining why some reasons might have the strong modal status, this might turn out to be stipulating the impossible. For it might be that there is a reason for Ronnie to do what he enjoys that is explained by some desire, but would be explained by any desire. If that were the case, then we couldn't set up the cases that we need in order to evaluate whether it is facts about desires or facts about enjoyment that explain reasons like Ronnie's.

So it seems more promising, to me, to try and triangulate the psychological state that does the real explanatory work by taking a closer look at what kind of psychological state is most *suited* to explain the existence of reasons, subject to some of the constraints on a good account of Ronnie and Bradley's case that we have encountered in earlier chapters. Indeed, I think that we can use some general observations about how Ronnie's psychological state is supposed to explain his reason, in order to draw some very specific conclusions about the kind of psychological state which explains it.

In this chapter I will argue that these general observations support the view that Ronnie's reason is explained by one of his desires in

---

[1] E. J. Bond is one who saliently tries to construct cases with some of the right kinds of controls. See Bond [1983].

the more common philosophical usage—a psychological state that is (1) motivationally efficacious, and motivation by which is (2) capable of making you count as having acted *for* a reason. I take it that these are two of the features ordinarily ascribed to a common Humean conception of desires, and I will argue for them in this first section. Then in the rest of the chapter I will try to defend a more concrete characterization of what desires are, that they have these two characteristics.

The chief feature of the explanation of Ronnie's reason on which I want to focus, is the idea that the psychological state which explains it does so by being part of its *background condition*. In favor of this view I offered a generalization of the sophisticated version of the Objectionably Self-Regarding objection to the Humean Theory. This objection was that if the psychological state which ultimately explains Ronnie's reason has to count as part of the reason itself, then Ronnie's reasoning is merely enthymematic, if he does not think about his own psychology when deliberating about what to do. If Ronnie is really reasoning carefully and completely, the objection goes, then he would have to pay attention to what his reasons are, and on this view his reasons are, at least in part, facts about his own psychology. So if he is reasoning fully and completely, then he is thinking about his own psychology. But this seems to be an objectionably self-regarding way for Ronnie to proceed, even when the only reasons in play are ones that Bradley doesn't share. Surely if Ronnie likes to dance, it is good and complete reasoning for him to note that there will be dancing at the party, in deciding to go there.[2] So the advantage of rejecting the No Background Conditions view is that it lets us say that Ronnie is taking all of his reasons into account when he reasons in this way.

So now suppose that Ronnie *does* reason in this way. He likes to dance, he's wondering what to do tonight, it occurs to him that there will be dancing at the party, and so he goes to the party. Intuitively, Ronnie can count as having gone to the party *for* this reason—that there will be dancing there. But in order to obtain the advantages of maintaining the distinction between reasons and background conditions, it has to be possible for Ronnie to do this *without* thinking about the background

---

[2] As Darwall, an anti-Humean, puts it, '[u]sually when we act as we desire we are not moved to act by our awareness of the fact that we desire. Rather, a desire itself partly consists in a disposition to be moved by certain facts connected with its *object*' [1983: 37].

conditions on his reason. So this has to be possible: that Ronnie acts *for* a reason, without knowing that the sufficient conditions for it to be a reason for him are satisfied.

This is puzzling. How can it be that someone can act for a reason, without knowing that the conditions on it being a reason are satisfied? For if Ronnie does not know that the conditions for the fact that there will be dancing at the party to be a reason for him to go there are satisfied, then how can he know that it *is* a reason for him to go there? And if he can't know that it is a reason for him to go there, then how can he count as acting *for* this reason? For all that he knows, it is not a reason at all, so how, in such a situation, could he be responding to it in the particular way that reasons require? Yet we can't gain the advantages of maintaining a distinction between reasons and background conditions, unless we have something to say about this puzzle. Perhaps, in fact, this puzzle is the right way to set up the *most* sophisticated version of the Objectionably Self-Regarding objection.

Yet I think that it is not hard to see how to solve this puzzle. For it is not as if we know nothing about what kind of things figure in the background conditions of Ronnie's reason. By hypothesis, the chief element of the background conditions of Ronnie's reason is one of Ronnie's psychological states. What if (1) that psychological state were itself motivationally efficacious? And what if (2) being motivated in the right way by this state counted as acting for a reason, even if one has no explicit beliefs about what reasons one has? That would solve all our problems. For then it could be the background condition *itself* that explains how Ronnie could act for a reason, without appeal to Ronnie being aware either of the background condition, or that he actually had a reason. All that we have to say in order to dispel our puzzle in this way, are two things: (1) that the psychological state that explains the difference between Ronnie and Bradley is *motivationally efficacious*, and (2) that being motivated in the right way by this state counts as acting *for* a reason.

These, moreover, are two of the chief characteristics of the more ordinary philosophical usage of 'desire', employed by Humeans about motivation. If that is right, then I have just reversed the usual order of argument. As we noted in Chapter 1, it is usually thought that the Humean Theory of Reasons is motivated by the Classical Argument that reasons require motivation and motivation requires a desire. The Classical Argument starts by positing a crucial link between desires and motivation, and uses that to find a link between reasons and desires. But I've argued the other way around. I've started by supposing a link between reasons and desires—in the stipulative sense. And I've used this to argue that we should think of desires in the stipulative sense as having a crucial link to motivation.

Of course, this leaves as much puzzle as it dissolves. We still need to say a lot more about what kind of psychological state desires are, that they can both be motivationally efficacious and sufficient to make you count as having acted for a reason. For according to common non-Humean views, the kinds of motivating states to which the Humean Theory is allowed to appeal could at best explain motivation, but could not explain why someone so motivated would count as having acted for a reason. And so in order to explain this, we will have to look not only at what desires are, but at the theory of motivating reasons. We need to address an important argument that I think is best articulated by T. M. Scanlon, but which has also been offered by other authors, including Warren Quinn.[3]

8.2   Scanlon's Argument and Acting for Reasons

We first encountered the essentials of Scanlon's objection in section 5.2. There I introduced it as a possible version of the incoherence arguments by dilemma, of which Korsgaard, Hampton, and Darwall also offered versions. Each of these arguments posed a dilemma to the Humean theory: either admit to allowing for Too Many Reasons, or else accept a 'fix' in order to avoid this—but this fix rules out the possibility that *all* reasons are explained in this way, so it is incoherent for the Humean to accept it. I argued in section 5.2 that it is better to think of these arguments as bringing out the importance of the Too Many Reasons objection, than as being arguments for incoherence outright.[4] For allowing for Too Many Reasons is clearly not as bad as being internally inconsistent. And indeed, I went on to offer a further response to that objection.

The suggested 'fix' that I have attributed to Scanlon was that we think of Ronnie's desiring to dance as involving seeing certain considerations

---

[3] Scanlon [1998], Quinn [1993*b*].

[4] Indeed, this is really how Quinn and Scanlon *do* put their version of the objection, which I merely put with the others for the sake of taxonomy.

as reasons—either as reasons to dance, or as reasons to do things which would promote Ronnie's dancing.[5] There is something appealing and, I think, right about the idea that a psychological state that involves seeing certain considerations *as reasons* is better suited to explain reasons than other psychological states might be. But it is important to understand *why* this thought is appealing and *what* seems right about it, and to distinguish this from a possible interpretation of Scanlon that is definitely wrong.

Start with the interpretation that is definitely wrong. On this interpretation of Scanlon's idea, the mere fact that Ronnie *takes* there to be a reason for him to go to the party can be sufficient in order to explain a reason for him to go to the party. Scanlon himself suggests that Ronnie's taking something to be a reason can explain why there is a reason for him to act,[6] and this is what we need in order for this 'fix' to help us out of the Too Many Reasons problem. But this idea would be a mistake. Surely Ronnie can be fallible about what he takes his reasons to be. He might simply be *wrong* about them. As long as that is possible, restricting Ronnie's desires to those things which involve things *seeming* to him to be reasons isn't going to be enough to escape the Too Many Reasons objection. And so if Scanlon's 'fix' to the explanation of Ronnie's reason by his psychology is to do what it is supposed to do, that can't be simply because it is impossible to take oneself to have a reason to do something that one does not have a reason to do. So we need to look somewhere else, in order to see where the force of Scanlon's idea comes from.

But if we look more closely at Scanlon's arguments, and those of Warren Quinn, we can see that these derive their real force not from the idea that desires in any other sense are insufficient to ground the existence of objective normative reasons, but from the idea that desires in any other sense are insufficient to enable an agent to count as having acted *for* reasons.[7]

---

[5] 'What I am claiming…[is] rather that having what is generally called a desire involves having a tendency to see something as a reason,' Scanlon [1998: 39].

[6] 'A third possibility is that when we say that someone has a reason to look for coffee ice cream because he has a desire for some, what we mean is…that he thinks this pleasure actually is a good reason for acting now or in the near future,' [ibid. 45]. Here the suggestion seems to be that someone's taking something to be a reason can serve to explain why it is a reason. But we shouldn't take this suggestion.

[7] True, Quinn says that he 'cannot see how this bizarre functional state in itself gives me even a *prima facie* reason to turn on radios, even those I can see to be available for cost-free on-turning' [1993b: 237]. But when it comes to saying what is the key feature of his argument, he claims that it is the '*power to rationalize choice*' [239, his italics] which he is after, and which 'subjectivist' views are unable to provide.

After all, I drew two conclusions in section 8.1. First, that if desires figure in the background conditions of reasons, they need to be motivationally efficacious. And second, that if desires figure in the background conditions of reasons, motivation by them has to be able to make one count as having acted for a reason. For what we needed an explanation of, is how it could be possible to act for a reason without acting in knowledge of that reason's background conditions. So when Ronnie desires to dance, and this makes the fact that there will be dancing at the party tonight a reason for him to go there, this desire has to be able to make Ronnie go to the party, in connection with his belief that there will be dancing there. And if Ronnie is motivated in this way by this belief and this desire, he needs to count as having gone to the party *for* the reason that there will be dancing there.

Importantly, as we noted in section 1.3, not just any way of being motivated to go to the party by his belief that there will be dancing there will make Ronnie count as having gone there *for* that reason. To take an uncontroversial case, suppose that Ronnie has a bizarre virus which makes him compulsively start heading toward Liz's house whenever he mentally tokens the word 'party'. So sometimes he thinks, 'George's party was fun last week,' and finds himself compulsively heading toward Liz's house, and sometimes he thinks, 'there will be dancing at the party tonight,' and finds himself compulsively heading toward Liz's house. If the latter happens, and Liz's house is where the party is tonight, then Ronnie will have gone to the party because he believed that there would be dancing there. But surely in this bizarre case Ronnie doesn't count as having gone to the party *for the reason* that there will be dancing there. He is motivated by his belief in what happens to be a reason for him to go there, but this motivation is, importantly, not the right kind of motivation to count as having acted *for* that reason. Acting for that reason requires something else. The challenge, if we think that being motivated by a desire is sufficient to count as having acted for a reason, is to explain how being motivated by a desire is different from being motivated by a bizarre virus, in the way that Ronnie is in this unusual example.

Philosophers have developed a now more-or-less standard way of referring to the extra condition that an agent must satisfy in order to count as having acted for a reason, in addition to simply having been motivated by a belief in that reason. They say that Ronnie must *take-the-consideration-to-be-a-reason*. I hyphenate, in order to highlight the fact that we have to be careful, since this suggestive terminology is only the result of stipulation.

What is uncontroversial is that there is *something different* about the causal etiology of Ronnie's behavior in the cases in which he acts for a reason, and the cases in which he is merely caused to act—for example, by a bizarre virus. But no conclusions about *what* has to be different follow from this simple observation. So in particular, it is not uncontroversial that the required difference involves Ronnie's having any kind of attitude, *taking*, toward the proposition that the fact that there will be dancing at the party is a reason for him to go there. So if we are really after a theory-neutral stipulative term to characterize the difference between action for reasons and merely caused behavior, we can *call* it *taking-the-consideration-to-be-a-reason*, but we can't let ourselves be fooled by our clever use of terminology into thinking that this involves actually having an attitude—*taking*—toward the proposition that something is a reason.[8]

So let's call this further thesis—that *taking-a-consideration-to-be-a-reason*, in the stipulative sense, factors into an attitude, *taking*, and a content about reasons, the *Attitude-Content* view. Philosophers commonly assume the Attitude-Content view merely on the basis of distinguishing between acting for reasons and merely being caused to act. But to do so is simply to be misled by our stipulative terminology. Motivational Humeans of all stripes typically hold that the required difference in causal etiology is simply a matter of being caused *in the right way* to act, and that being caused *in the right way* is simply a matter of being caused to act by a *desire*, and not something bizarre, like Ronnie's unusual virus.[9] This view does distinguish between the required cases, and it does not commit to the Attitude-Content view. So it is possible to make the required distinction without inferring that acting for a reason involves *taking* something *to be a reason*, in any other than the stipulative sense.

---

[8] Arguments which make this mistake are ubiquitous, I think. Compare Korsgaard, 'It is because of the reflective character of the mind that we must act, as Kant put it, under the idea of freedom. [...] the point is that the reflective mind must endorse the desire before we can act on it, it must *say to itself that the desire is a reason*' [1996: 94], italics added for emphasis. It is clear that Korsgaard needs to be understood as committed to this strong claim, because she is trying to offer a transcendental argument for the existence of reasons. Compare also Brandom [1994: 4–6].

[9] This, for example, is Michael Smith's view [1994]. Smith, of course, though a Humean about motivation, is not a Humean about reasons. Smith advocates a Standard Model explanation of reasons like Ronnie's. See Smith [1994: 170–1]. Obviously, even such a view still requires a further proviso, in order to deal with cases of deviant causation, as in Davidson's [1973] mountain-climber example. But then, such a view as Korsgaard's will need to deal with deviant causation as well, so I simply leave it to the side.

Scanlon's idea, and Quinn's, however, is that acting for a reason *does* involve having the *taking* attitude toward the proposition that something is a reason for you to act.[10] If they are right, and this attitude is required in order to act for a reason, and *we* are right that being motivated by a desire is sufficient to count as having acted for a reason, then it follows that being motivated by a desire must be sufficient to count as having *taken* something to be a reason. And then it would follow, as Scanlon claims, that desires involve *taking* things to be reasons—the thesis that Hypotheticalism is not supposed to be able to accept, since it claims to analyze reasons in terms of desires, rather than conversely.

So as I understand the sophisticated version of the Quinn–Scanlon objection, it is based on the Attitude-Content view, which is in turn based on the observation that acting *for* a reason requires *something* more than simply being caused to act in light of a belief in that reason. The first hole in this argument is that the Attitude-Content view simply does not follow from this observation. It is easy to jump to this conclusion, particularly since it is suggested by the (stipulative) terminology that is usually used to pick out the required difference between acting for a reason and merely being caused to act. But it doesn't follow.

I think, however, that we can remedy this first hole in the Quinn–Scanlon argument without threatening Hypotheticalism. After all, it's all well and good for a Humean to insist that the required difference in causal etiology is just a matter of whether someone is motivated to act in the right way *by a desire*, as opposed to by some other state, like having a bizarre virus. That might *draw the line* successfully between actions done for reasons and behavior that is merely caused. But it wouldn't *explain* why behavior caused in the right way by desires should count as action for reasons, and no other behavior. Or at least, it is not obvious how it would provide us with such an explanation.

The Attitude-Content view, on the other hand, makes it very easy to see how we could explain this. The Attitude-Content view, after all, holds that acting for a reason requires taking there to be a reason for which one is acting. So it makes sense in an obvious way of why acting for a reason is a matter of *responding* to reasons. So in this respect, those who accept

---

[10] In Quinn's case, toward the proposition that there is something good or valuable about what you are doing [1993b].

the Attitude-Content view have a leg up on those who deny it. Those who accept it explain why action for reasons is responsiveness to reasons, but those who reject it have no such explanation. So although I think rejecting the Attitude-Content view is perfectly respectable, and hardly ruled out by the mere distinction between being caused to act and acting for a reason, it does seem like the Attitude-Content view is worth taking on board.

But is it really inconsistent with the Humean Theory of Reasons? The next step of the Quinn–Scanlon argument says so. After all, according to the Humean Theory, we have just concluded, motivation by desire is sufficient to count as acting for a reason. But according to the Attitude-Content view, acting for a reason requires taking it to be a reason. So it follows that desire must involve taking things to be reasons. But if that is part of the analysis of desire, then the Humean Theory would be circular! For I've claimed that Hypotheticalism, at least, explains reasons by making desires part of the analysis of reasons. But Quinn and Scanlon claim for these reasons that things have to go the other way around. We can't have both, on pain of circularity.

But as I'll show in the remainder of the chapter, there is still a big hole in this argument. In section 8.3 I'll show how to give an analysis of desire that mirrors Scanlon's own very closely, but does not analyze desires in terms of reasons. And then in section 8.4 I'll show how to use that analysis in order to show that desires have the property of involving taking things to be reasons, even though this is not part of their analysis. Together, this will show that we can obtain all the advantages of the Quinn–Scanlon view without being committed to the conclusion of their argument which is supposed to create trouble for the Humean Theory.

8.3 Directed-Attention Desires

So suppose that like Susan, you want a cup of coffee. You are likely to find yourself thinking about certain topics that are related, in obvious ways, to getting a cup of coffee. For example, you might find yourself wondering whose turn it is to make a new pot of coffee, and trying to remember which coffee shop it was, where you had that great cup of coffee last week. In the evening, when you'd rather drink something stiffer, you don't think about these same things. Instead, you think about who owes you a drink, or which kind of wine goes better with the fish you're preparing for dinner. When you're thinking about these things, and even when you are not, answers to these questions strike you in ways that other kinds of things do not. For example, if you recall that it is Karen's turn to make a new pot of coffee, or that Small World has the best coffee around here, these strike you in a way that noticing that there is a sprinkler valve in your office ceiling does not. They have a certain kind of *salience* that facts which are irrelevant to what you want lack.

When it occurs to you that there is coffee in the lounge, and it is *salient* in this way, that is the kind of thing to prompt you to get up and head to the lounge. You might think better of it—for example, if the thought occurs to you saliently that you've already had three cups today. And you might do something else—for example, if you remind yourself that you made the last pot, and it is now Karen's turn to make the next, you may head over to Karen's office, instead. But if you do find yourself heading to the lounge when the thought occurs to you that there is coffee there, this isn't *alienating*. You don't find yourself puzzled about this behavior, or wondering what made you do it. It seems *natural*.

So when you want a cup of coffee, you find yourself thinking about a wide range of topics, and considerations having to do with these topics strike you in a special, *salient*, way, and when they do, this is the kind of thing to prompt you to act in a way that is non-alienating. These are the kinds of thing that are involved in having a *desire* for a cup of coffee, on my account. Moreover, I can say *which* topics your attention will be directed to, which considerations you will find salient, and which actions they will prompt you to do. You will be prompted to do actions which obviously, given your beliefs, promote P, the object of your desire. The salient considerations that prompt some such action, A, are the things you believe which, given your beliefs, would obviously help to explain why your doing A would help to bring about P. And the topics to which your attention is turned are the topics to which these salient considerations would provide answers.

This gives us Hypotheticalism's *analysis* of desire:

Desire For X to have a desire whose object is P is for X to be in a psychological state grounding the following disposition: when for some action a and proposition r believed by X, given X's beliefs *r* obviously helps to explain why *X*'s doing *a* promotes *P*, *X* finds *r* salient, and this tends to prompt *X* to do *a*, and *X*'s attention is directed toward considerations like *r*.

Notice that Desire does not invoke reasons in its analysis of desires. So it leaves open the possibility that reasons can be analyzed in terms of desires.

Desire gives us a picture of desires that is very much like that of Scanlon. Scanlon depicts our ordinary notion of desires as what he calls 'desires in the directed-attention sense'. When you have a directed-attention desire, you find your attention directed to certain topics that are related to the object of the desire, and considerations related to these topics strike you in a certain way. And when you act, you act in the light of these further considerations, and because they strike you in this way—the way that I've called their *salience*.[11]

Of course, Scanlon has a theory about what this salience consists in. He says that it consists in these considerations striking us *as reasons*. When you want a cup of coffee and the fact that there is coffee in the lounge strikes you in the *salient* way, what is happening, according to Scanlon, is that you are *taking* this consideration to be a reason *to go to the lounge*. This is the view that I proposed to grant at the end of section 8.2. But as I'll now demonstrate, granting this does not force us to say, as Scanlon's objection would require, that desires involve taking things to be reasons as a matter of the correct *analysis* of desires.

---

[11] Scanlon, of course, goes on to say *which* things one sees as reasons, and seems to disagree with my characterization: 'A person has a desire in the directed-attention sense whose object is P if the thought of P keeps occurring to him or her in a favorable light, that is to say, if the person's attention is insistently directed toward *considerations that present themselves as counting in favor of P*' (italics added) [1998: 39]. So if Ronnie has a directed-attention desire to dance, his attention is not directed to such considerations as the fact that there will be dancing at the party, but rather to such considerations as the exhilaration that he feels when dancing. I'm agreeing with Scanlon that desires involve seeing certain considerations as reasons. But I've taken the *other* view—that when Ronnie desires to dance, the things which strike him as reasons are such considerations as the fact that there will be dancing at the party. So according to Scanlon's official definition, I don't think that desires are directed-attention desires. But note that my account *is* consistent with his examples. For example, when he desires to have a new computer [43], the considerations he cites which strike him as reasons are not reasons in favor of having a new computer *as such*, but reasons to get *this* model rather than that. Or when he desires some group to approve of him, against his better judgment [40], it is not reasons *to* care about what the group thinks that he finds himself paying attention to, but whether or not they would approve of *this* action, or *that*. Such considerations are ones which would explain why some way of acting would make the group approve of him—they would be reasons to do things that would promote this desire, not reasons to have the desire in the first place. So I take it that my account of desires, at this level of characterization, is really not so different from Scanlon's.

After all, I've just given a characterization of desires in the directed-attention sense which does *not* appeal to the notion of a reason. I've characterized desires phenomenologically-cum-dispositionally. And I've offered this characterization as my *analysis* of desire. So it follows that we don't *have* to appeal to reasons in order to pick out this particular kind of psychological state. The question that remains is *why* the salient way that considerations strike you when you have a desire counts as having the *content* that those considerations are reasons for you to do the action that they prompt you to do.

But in section 8.4 I'll argue that Hypotheticalism's analysis of desires, together with its analysis of reasons, provide us with the tools that we need in order to understand why, when a desire leads some consideration to strike us in the salient way that is characteristic of desire, that counts as the consideration seeming to us to be a reason. What this will allow Hypotheticalism to do, is to maintain the Attitude-Content view. So far from being a premise in a valid argument against Hypotheticalism, therefore, the Attitude-Content view is a thesis that Hypotheticalism accepts. Moreover, unlike the views held by Quinn, Scanlon, and others, it is something that Hypotheticalism can actually *explain*.

8.4 The Acquisition of Content

Quinn and Scanlon think that desires involve seeing things as reasons (Quinn talks about values). They hold that this gives the best (they think the only) explanation of why acting on a desire is acting for—responding to—reasons. I argued in section 8.2 that this is resistible, but I suggested that we should agree with it anyway. Quinn and Scanlon think that Humeans can't do this, because they think that from this view it follows that desires are to be analyzed in terms of reasons, whereas on the Humean view reasons need to be analyzed in terms of desires. But I'm claiming that this is a mistake. Desires, according to Hypotheticalism, involve seeing things as reasons, but not as a matter of their *analysis*. In section 8.3 I showed how to give an analysis of the very kind of state that Scanlon thinks involves seeing things as reasons—directed-attention desires—without appealing to reasons. What I now want to show, is how we can use Hypotheticalism, together with this analysis of desires, in order to explain why desires do turn out to involve seeing things as reasons.

The situation is this: when you desire to have some coffee, certain considerations strike you in a certain phenomenologically familiar way. They are what I've called 'salient'. And these salience-strikings play a certain functional role: they tend to prompt motivation to act in a way that is non-alienating. And they are the objects of our directed attention. Scanlon claims that we have to understand these strikings in terms of our taking things to be reasons. I think that this isn't so. I think I've given an independent characterization of them in terms of their phenomenology and functional role, both in prompting action and directing our attention. But I want to agree with Scanlon that when a consideration strikes you as salient in this way and tends to prompt you to do A, it *is* striking you as a reason to do A. That is what we want to explain.

Fortunately, we have some obvious tools with which to explain this. For there is an obvious parallel between which considerations strike you as salient in this way, when you desire that p, and which considerations are *reasons* for you, given that desire. When you desire that p, according to Reason, your reasons are the things that help to explain why your doing A would promote p. And according to Desire, the things that strike you as salient are the considerations that obviously, given your beliefs, explain why your doing A would promote p. So there is a very intimate structural connection between your actual reasons and your salience-strikings.

I think that this structural connection is close enough to support the hypothesis that an adequate theory of mental content would yield the result that the salience-strikings associated with desires turn out to have the content that the consideration so striking you is a reason for you to act. This hypothesis would provide a strong answer to Scanlon and Quinn, because it would allow us to say everything that is supposed to be an advantage of their views plus, moreover, to *explain* it. That is what Hypotheticalism would ultimately like to do. Unfortunately, however, we would need a fully worked-out theory of mental content in order to completely defend such a hypothesis. So I'll settle again, here, for grounds for reasonable optimism. What I'll actually argue is that Hypotheticalism is in a better position to maintain the Attitude-Content view than either Quinn or Scanlon. Insofar as the Attitude-Content view should persuade us, therefore, I think we should see that as evidence *for* Hypotheticalism rather than evidence against it.

Let's start with an observation about the resources that a theory of content—of any kind—must appeal to, in order to explain ordinary visual content. Certain events in your visual perceptual system count as having the content that there is something red in front of you. When these events happen but there is nothing red in front of you, you are subject to some kind of visual illusion. The explanation of why these events have this content must appeal both to facts about these events and to facts about the thing they have as their content—*red*. One relevant fact about these events is that they are part of a visual system in which they are triggered by light waves of a certain frequency profile entering your eyes. And one relevant fact about red things is that their surfaces reflect light of those frequency profiles.

Any adequate account of why these events have this content will therefore appeal to facts like these. It is because of the right kind of *match* between the events and red things that they come to have that content. Covariation theories hold that the match is a matter of covariation, and so they need to appeal to them in order to explain why there is covariation.[12] Inferential and causal role accounts need to appeal to them in order to explain why there is the right kind of match between the content and the inferential role of the mental state.[13] And even teleological accounts must appeal to facts like these, though they require, in addition, that the visual system in which the events figure also has a certain kind of function.[14] All these kinds of accounts of content require that there is *some* important connection of *some* kind between the events in your visual perceptual system and red things. The only account of content that can do without simple facts like these is that reference happens by pure magic.

Now I hold that if it does turn out that desires involve certain states—salience-strikings—which have perception-like contents, because they involve 'seeing things as reasons', then this is the kind of thing that requires explanation. We would not be happy with an account of why the events in your visual perceptual system have the content that there is something red in front of you but that this is not the right kind of thing

---

[12] See e.g. Dretske [1981], Fodor [1987], [1990a].
[13] e.g. Harman [1982], [1987], and Peacocke [1992].
[14] e.g. Millikan [1984], Papineau [1987], and Neander [1991].

to admit of any explanation. So we should not be happy with any view on which salience-strikings come to have their contents by pure magic, either. And as with the case of visual perception, any explanation of why they do will have to appeal to *some* kind of facts about these states—when they happen and what kind of mechanism produces them—and to *some* kind of facts about reasons—under what circumstances there are reasons. In the case of red visual experiences, I suggested that the key explanatory factor on any view is that both are connected in a certain way with light frequencies. What I'll now argue is that salience-strikings are intimately connected with desires. They occur only in the presence of desires. So I'll conclude from this that the best prospects for an explanation of how they come to have a content about reasons, lie in the hypothesis that reasons are themselves intimately connected with desires, as Hypotheticalism claims.

We know from Scanlon and Quinn that salience-strikings are *sometimes* connected with desires. But I think that we can conclude more—we can conclude that salience-strikings are *always* connected with desires. This is illustrated by the case of Jack. In one case, when Jack thinks about the fact that there is water at the top of the hill, that strikes him as salient and tends to prompt motivation to go there to fetch some. Similarly, when he thinks about the fact that there is water by the beach, that strikes him as salient and tends to motivate him to go there in order to fetch some. These two salience-strikings will come together, for Jack, if his aim is to get Jill's hair wet. But in this case, the fact that there is coke in the fridge will not similarly strike him. Jack is a bit juvenile, but not malicious—the coke would only make Jill's hair sticky.

In another case, the fact about the coke in the fridge strikes Jack as salient and so does the fact about the water at the top of the hill. This makes sense, if what Jack desires it to quench his thirst. But in this case, the fact that there is water by the beach will not so strike him. He is well aware of how little salt water will do for quenching his thirst. In these two cases, Jack's salience-strikings come *clumped*. When he wants to get Jill's hair wet, more than one consideration strikes him in the salient way, and they are clumped around the end of getting Jill's hair wet. Similarly, when he wants to quench his thirst, more than one consideration strikes him in the salient way, and they are clumped around the end of quenching his thirst.

Salience-strikings, I think, *always* come clumped. And they always come clumped in very specific kinds of ways. It is very hard to imagine what could be going on with Jack, if the fact that there is water at the beach strikes him as salient, but *no* related consideration does so. And it is very hard to imagine what could be going on with Jack, if the fact that there is water at the beach strikes him as salient, and the fact that there is coke in the fridge strikes him as salient, but the fact that there is water at the top of the hill does not. I don't mean to say that it is *impossible* for only one consideration to strike Jack as salient. But I certainly mean to be saying that that is not how things work in normal, well-functioning human psychologies. In normal psychologies, salience-strikings always come clumped, and in clumps that correspond to aims. Similarly, the relevant fact about the events in your visual perception system is not that they are *always* triggered by light of certain frequencies; in a malfunctioning psychology they can certainly occur under other circumstances. The relevant claim is that this is how they work in normal, well-functioning human psychologies.

So I conclude that salience-strikings always occur as part of some desire. But if they always occur as part of some desire, then that is a central feature which will have to play some role or other in any adequate explanation of how they come to have the contents that they do. Indeed, besides the thesis that salience-strikings have contents that are about reasons, we know very little at all about them which could form the basis for an explanation of how they come to be associated with their contents. So any explanation of their contents would do better, I think, if it turns out that there is some relevant connection between reasons and desires. Hypotheticalism is the view that makes this connection exactly as tight as it could be. So I think that Hypotheticalism gives us the best prospects to be able to explain the Attitude-Content view.

This falls short of an explanation of why, given Reason and Desire, salience-strikings turn out to have contents about reasons. All that I have given is a sketch of how such an explanation would go, and going in for a more complete explanation would require opting for a general theory about the foundations of mental content. I simply claim that it shows that Hypotheticalism is in a better position than Quinn or Scanlon to account for the truth of the Attitude-Content view. So to the extent that we are persuaded by them that it is true, we should *like* Hypotheticalism.

So far we've uncovered a number of surprises in the course of our investigation. I started off saying that I was going to defend a Humean theory, but since then I've started saying some surprisingly un-Humean-sounding things. First, I claimed along with Kant that there are some reasons that are reasons for anyone, no matter what her desires. Now I've been saying along with the scholastics that desire involves the perception of reasons. The commitments of the overall view are starting to sound less and less Humean. You may even be starting to wonder whether you've been had—will I next defend central views of Aristotle's?

In the important sense, you haven't been had. Hypotheticalism is still very much a version of the Humean Theory of Reasons that I set out in Chapter 1 to explore and defend. The important lesson, I think, is that commitments of typical Humeans need not be commitments of any given central Humean thesis. To find out whether they are, we can't just take a survey of the kinds of thing that people say; we have to go out and do some philosophy. But of course, in another sense, you have been HAD. In Chapter 9 we'll explore Hypotheticalism's Aristotelian Doctrine. The project, now that we have an account of desire, is to put it to work to solve important problems about moral motivation and moral epistemology. A solution to these problems drops out of Hypotheticalism, and this solution vindicates and explains some of Aristotle's central ideas about virtue in a way that I think is both attractive and illuminating.

9

Motivation, Knowledge, and Virtue

9.1 The Right Connection to Motivation

The conclusions of Chapter 8 put us in a position to draw important conclusions about the kinds of views that Hypotheticalism can take about moral motivation, about moral knowledge, and about virtue. In this section I'll explain why I think that Hypotheticalism leads to an attractive, moderate position with respect to the capacity of reasons to motivate, which I'll elaborate further in section 9.2 and connect to the virtues. Then in sections 9.3 and 9.4 I'll switch to consider moral epistemology, explain what I think are two hard problems in moral epistemology, and show why I think Hypotheticalism has the right kinds of resources in order to address those problems. None of the positive views in this chapter will be developed in any great detail; the point is to illustrate some of the attractive directions in which Hypotheticalism can go.

One of the perennially discussed questions in contemporary metaethics is just what the connection is between reasons and motivation. On some views—paradigmatic internalist views[1]—this connection is very strong. On others—paradigmatic externalist views[2]—it is extremely weak or entirely coincidental. It is natural to think that everyone is a little bit right—that there is *some* connection between reasons and motivation, but that it is simply not as strong as internalists have made it out to be. I have this thought, at any rate, and I am now going to try to explain why. Then I'll go on to explain why Hypotheticalism leads to a moderate or intermediate position.

---

[1] e.g. Hare [1952], Williams [1981a], Korsgaard [1986], and Smith [1994].
[2] e.g. Brink [1989] and Svavarsdottir [1999].

Typical proponents of the Humean Theory, of course,[3] endorse the Classical Argument, and so are committed to Existence Internalism about Reasons, and many critics of the Humean Theory are committed to it as well.[4] Existence Internalism about Reasons is a theory about the connection between the existence of reasons and motivation. When someone has a reason, it says, it must be possible to motivate her to act for it. The thesis is usually underspecified, but a fully specified version should tell us what we are allowed to do to someone in order to motivate her. It would trivialize the thesis, of course, if we were allowed to do *anything* to someone in order to get her to act. For quite plausibly everyone has the property of being motivatable to do *anything*, under *some* conditions or other. Plausible but substantive versions of the thesis require that not just any motivation to do the action counts, but only motivation *for that reason*, and typically say that we are allowed to provide the agent with relevant true information, but not with false information. It is widely thought that there is some such set of circumstances that we can specify, such that in every case of a reason, there will be a non-trivially true subjunctive conditional about the agent's motivation to act for that reason. Internalists hold that reasons are sufficient for facts about motivation of this kind.

I'm highly suspicious about whether plausible, non-trivial, subjunctive conditionals of the right kind can actually be formulated. For example, consider the case of Nate, introduced in section 2.2. Nate loves successful surprise parties thrown in his honor, but can't stand unsuccessful surprise parties. If there is an unsuspected surprise party waiting for Nate in the living room, then plausibly there is a reason for Nate to go into the living room. There is certainly something that God would put in the 'pros' column in listing pros and cons of Nate's going into the living room. But it is simply impossible to motivate Nate to go into the living room for this reason—for as soon as you tell him about it, it will go away. Nate's case looks to me like a counterexample to many strong theses about the connection between reasons and motivation.

Of course, one way to respond to Nate's case is to say that it doesn't count, for some reason—perhaps because the fact that there is an unsuspected surprise party waiting in the living room is not really, after all, a reason for Nate to go there. But this seems to me to be ad hoc. If what Nate enjoyed

---

[3] Compare Williams [1981a] and Hubin [1999].   [4] Compare Korsgaard [1986].

immensely was playing poker, then the fact that there is poker being played in the living room would be a reason for Nate to go in. If what Nate really enjoyed was watching TV, then the fact that there is a TV in the living room would be a reason for him to go in. So I see no obvious reason to insist that Nate's enjoyment of successful surprise parties must be different. I see no reason other than an attachment to some theory to think that there can't be reasons that no one could ever act on. It is not as if such reasons don't matter, after all—they still play a role in determining what Nate ought to do—they still show up on God's list of pros and cons.

Nate's case is one reason why I think Existence Internalism about Reasons is problematic. I also think that it is easy to construct cases in which someone fails to be motivated at all to do some action that she has reason to do, in virtue of massive and decisive contrary reasons that motivate her. Take, for example, the case of Joel. Joel's career, his wife and her career, his friends, his Lakers' season tickets, his family, and his loves of surfing and of mountain climbing all tie him to Los Angeles. But Joel also loves chocolate-cayenne-cinnamon flavored ice cream, which he can only get in Madison, Wisconsin. The fact that he can only get it in Madison is a reason for Joel to live there (I'm imagining that he is crazy about it), but it is not a particularly great one. And there are fantastic reasons keeping Joel away from Madison. As I imagine Joel's case, he is disposed to find the facts about chocolate-cayenne-cinnamon ice cream salient, if ever he thinks about moving to Madison, but these thoughts would not actually motivate him to move, not even in any *pro tanto* sense—this disposition is masked by the presence of such clear motivations not to move to Madison. Joel, I think, is not a case of a conflicted psychology—even slightly. He feels no conflict at all—not even one that is very tiny—over only giving up his favorite ice cream.

I think that cases such as Joel's are easy to construct. It is not that I don't think Joel can be motivated to move to Madison. But I think you would have to change more about Joel than his state of information. I think you would have to remove his passion for his career, his dedication to his wife whose career also ties her to Los Angeles, his enjoyment of his friends, his craze over the Lakers, and his loves of surfing and of mountain-climbing, however, or at least some large portion of these things. If you first got Joel to stop caring about all of these things, then I have no doubt that you could motivate Joel to move to Madison. But if you are allowed to change all of those things about him in order to motivate him to act, then I don't know what you *couldn't* motivate him to do. After all, the most central features of Joel's psychology are his dedication to his wife, his passion for his career, and so on for the rest. Asking what Joel would do if we removed all these things is like asking what he would do if he had a totally different psychology. If we are allowed to do that, then I'm worried that it will trivialize Internalism about Reasons.

Add to Nate's and Joel's cases the straightforward cases of ordinary agents who are unmoved by their moral reasons.[5] Defenders of Internalism about Reasons contend that this only happens when agents are subject to some form of irrationality. But this move seems forced. Clearly agents who are unmotivated by their moral reasons are less morally good. But it is not obvious why this must be due to a failure in their rational capacities. For all these reasons, I think it is doubtful whether any version of Existence Internalism about Reasons seems likely to be true.

On the other hand, those who reject Internalism about Reasons typically draw the conclusion that there is no direct connection between reasons and motivation. But this also seems to miss out on something important. What internalists seem to get right, is that at some basic level, reasons are for acting on. That is what they are *for*. An agent who was incapable of responding to her reasons would be no agent at all. Hypotheticalism holds that there is an important and intimate connection between reasons and motivation, without holding that there is some neat subjunctive test for motivation that will apply in the case of every reason. For Hypotheticalism holds that every reason is connected to some desire, and that desires are, dispositionally, motivating states, motivation by which counts as acting for reasons. There are simply many ways in which these dispositions can fail to be realized—and particularly so, in the case of agent-neutral reasons such as those of morality.

One way in which they can fail to be realized is if the agent lacks relevant information or has false beliefs. If Ronnie doesn't know that there will be dancing at the party, then he won't go there for that reason. And if he falsely believes that he wasn't invited, then even if he realizes that there is dancing there, this may not move him—he has to be aware not only of

---

[5] Much of the literature about *judgment* internalism applies equally well on this score. Compare, for example, Stocker [1979] and Svavarsdottir [1999].

his reason, but of the enabling conditions of that reason helping to explain why going to the party will promote dancing.

9.2 Moral Motivation and Virtue

But another important way in which someone may fail to be motivated follows immediately from Desire. Even in cases in which some consideration helps to explain why X's doing A promotes P, where X desires that P, this connection may not be an obvious one, and Desire only provides that an agent will be motivated to act by the considerations that relatively obviously play this role. In fact, the Hypotheticalist account of agent-neutral reasons offered in Chapter 6 commits us to something much stronger: for though it allows us to explain genuinely agent-neutral reasons—reasons that are reasons for everyone, no matter what she desires—the connection of these reasons to any given agent's psychology may be extremely remote. It follows that we should expect agent-neutral reasons to be among the reasons that are subject to failures in motivation of this kind.

And that is convenient—for moral reasons are among the paradigm agent-neutral reasons. But moral reasons are notorious for being subject to failure to motivate agents who know about them. These failures of motivation are not only possible, according to Hypotheticalism. They can be explained. If the connections between some reason and your desires is only remote, then those desires will not prompt you to act on it.

Fortunately, most people we ordinarily meet happen to desire some thing or other which is less remotely connected with moral reasons than Mary's desire to buy new shoes. For example, people typically care about being able to justify their actions to others, and have at least some minimal desire that others not suffer. So ordinary agents, who care at least a little about these things, are typically motivated at least a little by moral reasons. And those who care about these things more will, other things being equal, be more motivated to act for these reasons.

If there really are agent-neutral reasons explained along the lines of the model advocated in Chapter 6, then all agents face a challenge about how to act for their reasons. In general, the failure of Proportionalism means that it can easily happen that one's motivation to act for some reason will not match the weight of that reason. How to do best at acting in accordance with one's reasons, then, is an engineering problem. What kind of agent would do best at acting for her reasons?

We have already begun to see. Agents who care at least a little bit about things that are more directly connected to moral reasons than just any arbitrary desire will do better at being motivated by moral reasons than those who have no such desires. And agents who care more about these things will be better motivated so to act. In general, having a desire that *matches* the weight of one's reason is what one needs in order to have one's motivation match the weight of the reason.

If the central moral reasons are agent-neutral, then they are reasons that everyone has, no matter what her desires. Still, agents who desire certain things that are closely connected to these reasons will do better at acting for those reasons. So since everyone has a reason to do those things, and having such desires is universally instrumental for doing so, it follows that everyone has a reason to have desires that are closely related to moral reasons.

Ideally, of course, in order to be motivated in proportion to the weight of one's reasons, one must not just desire the right things, but also desire them in proportion to one another—to the right degree. This, of course, is what Aristotle says about the person of virtue—that she desires the right things, and to the right degree. And I think it is true. Even though you would have some reason no matter what you desired, it is still important to desire the right things, for your desires are what motivate you to act. So it is important to desire the right things, and to the right degree. The person who has a collection of desires whose strengths match the weights of her independently existing reasons will do the best at acting for her moral reasons. And this, I think, is the person of virtue. The important connection between moral reasons and motivation is not that *everyone* acts for their moral reasons, or even that rational people do. It is that *virtuous* people do—to the extent that they are virtuous. Moreover, if virtue involves having the right desires, and to the right degree, then that explains why.

I think that this idea about virtue allows Hypotheticalism to explain not only why virtuous people are motivated by their moral reasons, but why, as Aristotle tells us, virtuous agents are better judges of moral questions. In section 9.3 I'll raise an important problem about the prospects for a reductive view helping with moral epistemology and show how Hypotheticalism's acceptance of the Attitude-Content view can help to solve this problem. And then in section 9.4 I'll introduce a general problem in moral epistemology and explain why I think Aristotle's idea that the virtuous are better moral judges goes some way toward solving it. And I'll use the results of sections 9.2 and 9.3 to offer a Hypotheticalist explanation of why Aristotle is right.

9.3   Reductive Moral Epistemology

The chief problem in the epistemology of the normative is to explain how it is possible to have knowledge about the normative. This is a big problem. In fact, it was once the main problem in metaethics, which was in turn often called 'moral epistemology'. Irrealists about the normative may not find this problem particularly hard, which is probably why normative epistemology has gotten much less attention since the non-cognitivist rage in the middle of the twentieth century. But realists find it hard, and that is why the main divide among realists between reductivists and non-reductivists used to be characterized as the dispute about whether *intuitionism* is true. For intuitionism is the epistemological view that has traditionally been wedded to non-reductivism.

Reductive views about the normative were traditionally supposed to have an advantage over non-reductive views when it came to answering epistemological questions. In fact, this was supposed to be one of the main motivations for reductive views.[6] For if the normative reduces to the non-normative, then plausibly it might seem that the epistemology of the normative can be reduced to the epistemology of the non-normative. How do you find out whether killing your brother is wrong? That might be hard to understand, if being wrong was just having the irreducible, *sui generis* property of *wrongness*, which is not even causally efficacious. But if *wrongness* is not irreducible after all—if it is just *failing to maximize overall happiness*, or some such thing, then it isn't hard to see how to find out whether something is wrong. You just find out whether it fails to maximize overall happiness.

But of course, we have to be more careful. Alisha may know that killing her brother will fail to maximize overall happiness, but not know whether

---

[6] Compare Harman [1977], chs. 1 and 2.

it is wrong. At least, so it seems. If a reduction can only help solve the problems of moral epistemology if it entails otherwise, therefore, then it falls to this version of the Open Question argument. The argument goes like this: if finding out that killing your brother fails to maximize overall happiness is sufficient for finding out that it is wrong, then it can't be possible to know that killing your brother fails to maximize overall happiness, but not know whether it is wrong. Yet that surely is possible. So it takes *more* to find out that killing your brother is wrong than simply discovering that it fails to maximize overall happiness. And the same argument applies *mutatis mutandis* for any other proposed candidate reduction of *wrongness*.

So the Open Question argument rules out the most straightforward application of reduction to the problems of normative epistemology. Notice that I haven't said that the Open Question argument rules out reduction. I obviously don't think so, since I've been endorsing Hypotheticalism, which I claim is a reductive view. But the Open Question argument seems to clearly establish that no reductive view can take this *easy* solution to the problem of normative epistemology—the easy solution that was originally supposed to be one of the main attractions of reductive views. And since getting an easy solution to the central problem of normative epistemology was traditionally supposed to be the main attraction of reductive views, this problem is significant. I think this problem is important. Reductive views *do* seem to have more resources for solving the central problems of normative epistemology. But it is very hard to see how they can be put to use.

The natural idea to have at this point is that *knowing* the truth of the reductive view—or at least its extensional equivalence—is precisely what Alisha needs, in order to find out that killing her brother is wrong. For if she *knows* that if it fails to maximize overall happiness, then it is wrong, then she can surely find out that it is wrong by finding out that it fails to maximize overall happiness, and simply applying *modus ponens*. So perhaps this is the right trick in order to get reduction to help us with our normative epistemology.

But this is still highly problematic for at least two important reasons. The first is the problem of Disagreement. The problem of Disagreement is that more people seem to have the capacity to acquire normative knowledge than can be gotten to agree about any principle general enough to explain the source of normative knowledge. The problem isn't simply that lots of people disagree about which things are right and wrong—some of them might be mistaken. The problem is that any principle general enough to explain the source of moral knowledge—like a reductive theory such as the one that *wrongness* just is *failing to maximize overall happiness*—is disagreed on by agents who—even if they are often wrong—are at least in principle *able* to figure out the answers to moral questions. But if all normative knowledge is possible by means of the application of knowledge about the correct reductive theory, then it should follow that those who disagree with the correct reductive theory can't acquire normative knowledge in this way. They can acquire normative knowledge only through testimony or the equivalent. They shouldn't be able to get any of their own—even about such uncontroversial questions as whether it is wrong to kill your brother. Yet I take it that even someone with the wrong reductive theory about the normative should be able to know that it is wrong to kill her brother without the need to be informed of such by those who *do* know the correct theory.

But there is a second reason why we should be worried about this attempted reductivist solution to the problems of normative epistemology. For on the face of it, this solution, all by itself, should be available even to the *non*-reductivist. Since the solution only appeals to the application of *modus ponens*, it isn't necessary to assume that for moral knowledge, people need to know that *wrongness* just is *failing to maximize overall happiness*. All that they have to know is that *if* some action fails to maximize overall happiness, then it is wrong. But *that* is something that the non-reductivist could have said. Even the non-reductivist could have said that the way that someone finds out whether killing her brother is wrong is by finding it out whether it fails to maximize overall happiness, and applying her general knowledge that if something fails to maximize overall happiness, then it is wrong.

So I take it that the advantage of the reductivist is not in how *this* part of the solution to how we can have moral knowledge works. I take it that the reductivist advantage is supposed to lie in the kind of explanation that can be given of how this *conditional* can be known. For the reductivist can appeal to the fact that the conditional follows directly from the reductive theory, in explaining how it can be known. But the non-reductivist, on this view, can offer no such explanation of the truth of the conditional.

Yet this gets the reductivist into hotter water. *How* could the fact that *wrongness* just is *failing to maximize overall happiness* explain how it is possible to know that if something fails to maximize overall happiness, then it is wrong? Perhaps it is because the reduction requires that anyone who is a competent user of the word 'wrong' believes this, or is disposed to accept it in certain circumstances. Or perhaps it is because the reduction requires that anyone who is able to have *thoughts* about whether something is wrong or not has to believe the conditional, or be disposed to accept it in certain circumstances. But any of these answers only *aggravates* the problem of Disagreement. For if one of these answers is right, then someone who on full reflection continues to disagree with the reductive theory not only fails to be in a position to know that killing one's brother is wrong without testimonial evidence, but actually must not count as having beliefs about whether it is wrong at all, or as incompetent with the word 'wrong'. And those are surely uncomfortable things to be forced to say.

If what I've argued here is right, then the Open Question and Disagreement problems, whether or not they make trouble for reduction in general, certainly make trouble for any easy or straightforward connection between reduction and a solution to the problems of moral epistemology. And if that is right, then even if the various brands of synthetic reduction currently available successfully address the Open Question and Disagreement problems, this doesn't put them in a position to take advantage of the reductivist's traditional aspirations for a straightforward solution to the problems of moral epistemology.

So does it follow that reduction can't help with normative epistemology? Not exactly. It just follows that it can't help in these straightforward ways—by means of being *known*. But now we can see that the problem of how a reduction can help with normative epistemology is a lot like that of how background conditions on a reason can make Ronnie act for it, without Ronnie having to know about them. I solved the puzzle about background conditions and acting for reasons by postulating that the background conditions on reasons are themselves motivationally efficacious, without being observed to obtain. A similar solution to the problem of normative epistemology would therefore have it that the reductive base of the normative is itself causally efficacious in producing knowledge about the normative, without being observed to obtain. How could this be?

The answer, I think, is the Attitude-Content view. In Chapter 8 I defended the Attitude-Content view, according to which desires involve seeing things as reasons. And although I did not set out a complete Hypotheticalist explanation of this view, I did argue that Hypotheticalism stands in better stead, in virtue of its reductive thesis, Reason, to be able to explain this than other sorts of view. But once we have used our reductive view to explain why desires involve seeing things as reasons, it is natural to hope that beliefs about reasons that are formed on the basis of this will turn out to be defeasibly justified in something very much like the way that basic perceptual beliefs are justified.

Take, for example, some consideration which strikes you in the salient way, which, I claimed, is being in a state with the content that that consideration is a reason for you. And suppose that it not only strikes you in this way, but you go on to form the *belief* that the consideration *is* a reason for you to act in the way that it prompts you to act. In my view, forming this belief on the basis of the consideration's *seeming* to you to be a reason is like forming the belief that there is something red in front of you, on the basis of a perceptual experience with the content that there is something red in front of you. I think that once we have the Attitude-Content view on the table, a good account of what makes the latter a source of knowledge about red things will translate into a good account of what makes the former a source of knowledge about reasons.

The reason-seemings explained by Reason and Desire are a reductivist's 'in' to solving the problems of normative epistemology. It explains how the kind of psychological state which is likely to lead us to form beliefs about reasons counts as having a content about reasons precisely because its genesis is structurally well enough connected up with the conditions under which there actually are such reasons. So when you want a cup of coffee, and your belief that there is coffee in the lounge is *true*, and so are your background beliefs that the coffee in the lounge is not being guarded by someone who will keep you from getting any if you go there, then it is in fact *true* that this fact is a reason for you to go to the lounge. And so forming beliefs about your reasons in this way can lead you to true beliefs about your reasons.

The challenge for reductive normative epistemology was to say how a reductive view can make normative epistemology any easier, once we give up on the idea that the reduction is widely known to obtain. I think this challenge is a hard one, and insufficiently appreciated. But the solution that I'm suggesting is simple. A reductive view, I suggested, can play a direct role in the acquisition of knowledge, even if it is not known to obtain. Hypotheticalism's acceptance of the Attitude-Content view puts it in a position to accept this solution. According to Hypotheticalism, the reduction of reasons to desires ensures that the saliences associated with desires come to have contents about reasons in a similar way to how certain events in your visual perceptual system come to have contents about redness. So beliefs formed on the basis of these saliences can potentially be justified in the same sort of way as beliefs formed on the basis of visual red experiences. In this way, the Attitude-Content view gives Hypotheticalism an 'in' to solving the central problems of normative epistemology—an edge over other kinds of view.

9.4 Moral Reliability

I think that these materials also enable us to gain ground in dealing with another important general problem in moral epistemology. The problem arises because of two phenomena. The first phenomenon is that there are no moral experts. Moral knowledge is not plausibly something that derives only from a few enlightened souls—everyone is in some position to acquire moral knowledge for themselves, to evaluate whether what they are being told is really on the right track or not, and so on. So whatever the ultimate source of moral knowledge, it should plausibly turn out to be something to which everyone has access. But on the other hand, moral disagreement is deep. There are many moral topics about which people disagree deeply, having come to completely different answers. How to count topics is controversial, but if we individuate finely, then the range of topics over which there is disagreement is immense.

These two facts create a puzzle about how anyone's moral beliefs could be justified. If everyone has access to the same source of moral knowledge, but people come to such divergent beliefs in such a wide variety of cases, that seems strongly to suggest that no one's source of moral knowledge is particularly reliable. And if the sources of moral knowledge are *that* unreliable, then it is unclear how anyone could ever be in a position to be justified in any moral belief.

The problem is that the no experts condition makes it look as though everyone must have access to the same sources of moral knowledge, but the existence of deep disagreement makes it look as though those sources can't be very good. What we need to get out of the dilemma is an explanation of why even though everyone has access to the same sources of moral knowledge, those sources are more reliable for some people than for others. For only if they are more reliable for some than for others, can they be particularly reliable for anyone, since the amount of disagreement means that many, many people are often wrong about the answers to moral questions. On such a view everyone has *in principle* access to the answers to moral questions, allowing for the no moral experts condition, but when some put these methods to work, they get more reliable results than others do. And that is why, on such a view, it does not follow from deep disagreement that no one is reliable—it only follows that at least some are unreliable.

Aristotle defended a view like this. He claimed that the person who is best suited to judge of moral questions is the person of virtue.[7] The virtuous person is the one who desires the right things, and to the right degrees. According to Aristotle, this enables her to judge correctly about cases, even though she has access to no underlying moral theory to which no one else has access. She is able to judge correctly about virtue because she is virtuous, rather than being virtuous because she independently knows the answers to moral questions. This kind of view accommodates the no moral experts condition, because no one has any basic store of moral knowledge to which others don't have access. But it also allows for deep disagreement without universal unreliability, because it creates the right kind of asymmetry between those who are more reliable in applying their moral judgment, and those who are less reliable, only getting the broad strokes of moral questions correctly.

The only thing that this hasty sketch of Aristotle's position lacks, I think, is an explanation of why it could be that desiring the right things and to the right degree would have any connection at all with moral judgment. Surely this is something that requires explanation! But given the suggestions of

---

[7] Aristotle repeatedly claims that virtue is the mean state as the person of practical wisdom or prudence (the phronimos) would choose it. But at 1178a16–18 Aristotle tells us that phronesis is both necessary and sufficient for virtue: '[b]esides, prudence [phronesis] is inseparable from virtue of character, and virtue of character from [phronesis].' So the person of virtue is a better judge of what it takes to be virtuous than the person without virtue. This is also why Aristotle tells us that virtue must be cultivated before it can be studied.

sections 9.2 and 9.3, we can now explain it. Our basic epistemic access to the answers to moral questions derives from our judgments about reasons, which are supported by the things which strike us as salient—which seem to us, according to the view defended in Chapter 8, to be reasons. But the psychological mechanism by which considerations strike us as salient is desire. Virtue, according to the view of section 9.2, involves desiring the right things, and to the right degree. I observed there that this enables the virtuous person to be reliably motivated by her moral reasons. But we can now see that it also enables her to reliably *notice* her moral reasons. If the virtuous person has desires that match the weight of her reasons and are obviously connected to those reasons, then her moral reasons will strike her as salient in the appropriate way, as well, and hence she will be on her way to moral knowledge. And all of this happens without her needing to accept any theory about reasons.

All the accounts in this chapter are short of detail, but the main ideas are simple. The failure of Proportionalism means that some people will fail to be motivated by their moral reasons. In a sense, this is a rational failing, because it is a failure to reason correctly—to place the correct weight on one's reasons. But it need not result from a failure of any rational capacity, for there is no perfect connection between reasons and motivation, and there is no further psychological faculty of Reason that is responsible for motivating us to act for our reasons. Given this fact, any agent has reason to have desires that are connected in obvious ways to the agent-neutral reasons that she would have anyway, but would not act on. Desiring these things, and to the right degree, will enable her to be more reliably motivated for the reasons that she has anyway, and I said that this is an important part of what is involved with virtue.[8]

I also raised two problems in moral epistemology. The first is a puzzle about how a reductive view could still, after the Open Question argument, really have an advantage over non-reductive views when it comes to explaining how we acquire moral knowledge, and I suggested that the Attitude-Content view may help lead to an attractive moral epistemology. And the second is the problem about how the basic source of moral knowledge could be reliable for anyone, if the same method is used by

---

[8] It does not follow, on my view, that the desires that constitute the virtues are merely instrumental desires. See Ch. 10 for discussion.

all and there is deep disagreement. To solve this problem, I suggested, we should want a principled story about why it is that some agents are more reliable judges than others, and I noticed that Hypotheticalism could explain this by appeal to its account of the source of moral knowledge and of the role of virtue. All of these are, I think, potentially advantages of Hypotheticalism. They suggest, I think, that it is better situated than many other views to account for important facts about moral motivation and moral epistemology. And I think that the ideas that they involve illustrate the versatility of the Humean Theory. If Hypotheticalism can vindicate and explain some of Aristotle's central ideas, but it is a version of the Humean Theory of Reasons, then we need to be cautious about stereotypes when evaluating such views.

We are nearing completion of the main argument of this book. In Chapter 10, I'll explain why Hypotheticalism is not committed to any objectionable form of *instrumentalism*. That it is, is a common and I think, confused objection. Seeing what is wrong with this objection will also allow us to explain why the virtues, even though they may be desires that one has for reasons that are themselves explained by desires, are not merely instrumental desires. This will answer an important possible objection to the account of the virtues from section 9.2. Then in Chapter 11 I'll turn to focus on why anyone should believe the Humean Theory of Reasons in the first place.

10

Instrumentalism

10.1 The Charge of Instrumentalism

In earlier chapters we have considered the charges that the Humean Theory of Reasons allows for Too Many Reasons or Too Few, is in one or another way literally incoherent, makes practical reasoning out to be Objectionably Self-Regarding, locates the explanation of reasons in the Wrong Place, or exhibits a deep kind of Chauvinism. These, I think, are the hard problems for a defender of the Humean Theory of Reasons to think about. But no defense of a version of the Humean Theory of Reasons could be complete without treating the considerable array of charges that the Humean theory is guilty of one or another of a variety of theses which make it count as objectionably *instrumentalist*. These charges are diverse, I think, but we now know enough about Hypotheticalism to be able to explain them away.

The kinds of charge which I now want to dispel—the *instrumentalist* charges—are not always even thought to be objections to the Humean Theory. They are often thought simply to be a, or *the*, central part of what the Humean Theory *is*: They say such things as:

According to this familiar model, desires are not conclusions of practical reasoning but starting points for it.[1]

The theory itself claims that there are no reasons for or against intrinsic desires; one just has them or one doesn't.[2]

Instrumentalism is an exclusionist view; if it is right, then while you can think about how to get what you want, you can't think about what to want in the first place.[3]

---

[1] Scanlon [1998: 43].　　[2] Dancy [2000: 33].

[3] Millgram [1997: 2]. Don't be misled by the fact that Millgram stipulatively defines Instrumentalism to be precisely this thesis, into thinking that he is not attributing this commitment to the Humean

And such claims *must* be denied by those who accept desire-based theories of reasons. On such theories, we cannot have reasons to want anything as an end, or for its own sake.[4]

The charge that the Humean Theory of Reasons amounts to an objectionable kind of instrumentalism includes (at the least) the charges that:

1   It is impossible to deliberate about what desires to have.

2   There are no reasons for or against having (intrinsic) desires.

3   There are at least some desires which are beyond the scope of rational criticism.

4   Every agent must have at least one desire she has no reason to have.

5   You can't have arrived at all of your present desires as a result of deliberation.

6   You can't have any reasons to act if you don't have any desires.

These theses are ordered, roughly, from strongest to weakest; I'll now explain why Hypotheticalism is only committed to the last. And that, I'll argue, is hardly objectionable.

The Humean is usually believed to be committed to 1, I take it, because he is believed to be committed to 2. If there are no reasons in favor or against desiring one or another thing, then there is nothing on the basis of which to deliberate. After all, as we agreed in Chapter 2, deliberation requires you to think about your reasons, so if there are no reasons for you to think about, there is no deliberation to do. But why is the Humean thought to be committed to 2?

According to Hypotheticalism, reasons weigh in favor of actions in some *very* broad sense. They weigh in favor of things that you can *do*, rather than things which can *be the case*. Desiring to dance is something that you can *do*. So by my estimation, there is so far no puzzle at all about how

theory. The main arguments in favour of Instrumentalism which he cites (pages 2 and 3) are really arguments for the Humean Theory of Reasons, including the elegant statement of the Classical Argument which I quoted in Ch. 1. Millgram clearly thinks that Instrumentalism, in his sense, is of a piece with the Humean Theory of Reasons, and that the way to refute the Humean Theory is to argue against Instrumentalism.

4   Parfit [forthcoming], manuscript, July 2006, 37.

a Humean could think that there are reasons which count in favor of or against desiring to dance—or desiring anything else, for that matter. The problem, I take it, is supposed to arise once we carefully distinguish between two *kinds* of desires—*intrinsic* desires, and *extrinsic* or *instrumental* desires. According to those who think that the Humean is committed to 2, I can only allow for reasons in favor of *extrinsic* or *instrumental* desires, and not for reasons in favor of *intrinsic* desires.

To evaluate this claim, we have to look at what this distinction between intrinsic and instrumental desires is supposed to be. One definition of instrumental desires that would do the right work, would be to define an instrumental desire as one which is had for a reason which is explained by some other desire. Since the Humean Theory holds that all reasons are explained by other desires, it follows that the Humean Theory can't allow for reasons to have desires which aren't instrumental, in this sense. But that's hardly interesting. If the objection to the Humean Theory is that it can't allow for reasons to have non-instrumental desires in *that* sense, then the objection simply amounts to asserting that there are reasons to have desires which don't themselves depend on desires. And that is simply a special case of the Too Few Reasons objection to the Humean Theory. So if there is to be some bite to this version of the instrumentalist objection, it will have to turn on an independent characterization of what the distinction is between intrinsic and instrumental desires.

According to another possible definition, an instrumental desire is one that you have for some reason explained by a further desire *and* which, further, does not give you any *additional* reason to do what promotes it, over and above the reasons that you have to do what promotes the original desire. This definition is a good candidate for what is often meant by the 'intrinsic'/'instrumental' distinction, but it doesn't do very well for supporting 2 as a commitment of the Humean Theory. For this idea still admits of two readings. It could really mean that instrumental desires do not by themselves allow for the explanation of reasons *at all*. But if that is what the distinction amounts to, then the problem for Hypotheticalism is not that it fails to account for reasons to have *intrinsic* desires. For by the lights of *this* distinction, Hypotheticalists believe *only* in intrinsic desires—at least so far as they have told us. After all, according to Hypotheticalism, *every* desire is capable of explaining reasons. So by the proposed definition of 'instrumental', none are instrumental. So if

Hypotheticalism can allow for reasons to desire at all, they must be reasons to have intrinsic desires.

On a different reading, however, this distinction proposes that instrumental desires must not explain reasons that add any *weight* to the reasons already explained by the desire that explains reasons to have these instrumental desires in the first place. But there is no reason to think that Hypotheticalism can't allow for *this* kind of distinction. Take any desire, that P, in favor of which there is some reason. And let us say that the desire which explains this reason is the desire whose object is Q. Must the desire whose object is P be instrumental? Well, by the lights of this distinction that depends on whether the weight of the set of reasons explained by the desire whose object is Q is the same or less than the weight of the set of reasons explained by either the desire for Q or the desire for P.

But according to Hypotheticalism, whether the weight of some set of reasons is greater than the weight of some other set of reasons simply depends on the weights of the sets of all reasons to place more weight on the first than the second and conversely. When the weights of these sets of reasons are the same, the weights of the original sets of reasons will be the same. And when they are different, the weights of the original sets will be different. In the former case, the desire for P will count as instrumental, and in the latter, it will count as intrinsic, by the lights of this distinction. Since we began by assuming that there was a reason to desire for P, it follows that the latter cases are ones in which there are reasons in favor of intrinsic desires, by the lights of this distinction. And this distinction gives us a perfectly good way of making sense of what instrumental desires might be.

I don't know how else to state what the distinction between intrinsic and extrinsic desires is supposed to be in a way that would both be faithful to the kind of thing people usually mean in making this distinction, and which would be helpful in establishing that the Humean Theory of Reasons is committed to 2. I don't have a knock-down argument that there is no other helpful way to make this distinction, either. But as we'll see in the next section, the Humean Theory is not even committed to the considerably weaker 3 and 4. If it's not even committed to 3 and 4, it is surely not committed to 1 and 2.

10.2 Millgram Instrumentalism

Statement 3 states the thesis of *Millgram Instrumentalism*—that there are at least some desires which are beyond the scope of rational criticism.[5] That is, there are some desires in favor of and against which there can be no reasons. Millgram Instrumentalism is apparently weaker than thesis 2, according to which *all* (intrinsic) desires are beyond the scope of rational criticism. It only claims that *some* desires are beyond the scope of such criticism. But as we'll see, it is actually hard to see why we should think that Humeans are committed to even this much.

The argument that they are, I take it, is supposed to go something like this: take some desire that you have, say, D_1. Either there is a reason for you to have D_1 or not. If there is, then according to the Humean Theory, that reason must be explained by some further desire, say, D_2. Again, either there is a reason for you to have D_2 or not. If there is, then according to the Humean Theory that reason must be explained by some further desire D_3. And so on. Now consider the sequence $D_1, D_2, D_3 \ldots$ One of three things must be true. It is either finite or infinite, and if it is infinite, it must either have recurrent members, or no recurrent members. According to the argument, the infinite possibilities are those of a vicious infinite regress and of vicious circularity, so the sequence must be finite. And since it is finite, there must be some desire that you have which you have no reasons to have or not to have. Namely, the last member in the series. *QED*.

This, I think, is a very bad argument. To begin with, it is not actually an argument for thesis 3, Millgram Instrumentalism, at all. It is rather an argument for thesis 4. It is consistent with the conclusion of the argument that you have no desire which is *incapable* of being supported by reasons. Consider an example. Suppose that you want to go out into the hallway because you want to get a drink of water, and there is a bubbler in the hallway. As far as the argument goes, this could be a desire that you have for no reason whatsoever. But that doesn't mean that it is *incapable* of being rationally criticized. Suppose, for example, that you start desiring to satisfy your thirst. This desire certainly supports reasons to desire to get a drink of water, and so having it supplies you with a reason to desire this thing

---

[5] Millgram [1997].

which you previously desired in the absence of any reason to. The example is, of course, oversimplistic. But it is enough to illustrate the point: that the argument isn't even of the right form to support thesis 3. At best, it is an argument for the weaker thesis 4, that everyone has at least one desire in favor of which she has no reasons.

What's more, I don't even think that the argument is a good argument for thesis 4. Whether it is, after all, turns on why we should think that either the infinite series or the circular one should count as *vicious*. Now, it's easy to formulate possible assumptions about the explanation of reasons by desires that sustain the claim of viciousness. But like all theories about *how* reasons are explained by desires, the important thing for us to keep in mind when employing these theories, is whether these views are ones that the Humean must *share*.

Consider, for example, a simple theory that I call the *trickle-down theory*. The trickle-down theory, like most views we have considered so far, is a theory about *how* a reason can be explained by a desire. The theory is that the reason gets explained by the desire only in company with a further reason to *have* that desire. Then, the idea goes, the force of the reason to have the desire 'trickles down' through the desire, to reasons to do what promotes that desire. We've encountered versions of the trickle-down theory already, in section 5.2. Korsgaard's theory that desires in the stipulative sense have to further be understood in terms of reasons was a version of the trickle-down theory. Her idea was that only if we appeal to further reasons to *be* in some kind of purely psychological state, can that psychological state itself help to explain the existence of further reasons.[6] And Darwall's view in that same section was very much like Korsgaard's, except that it arose from his 'wide scope' view about the connection between reasons and desires. On Darwall's view, a reason to have some desire is needed, in addition to the wide-scope reason to either do what promotes the desire or not have that desire, in order to derive conclusions about reasons to do what promotes the desire.[7] Since it holds that a reason to have the desire is needed in order to complete the explanation of a reason by that desire, it is also a version of the trickle-down theory.

So versions of the trickle-down theory are ubiquitous. Many philosophers find it a natural view to take about how desires can explain reasons. And

---

[6] Korsgaard [1997]. See section 5.2.   [7] Darwall [1983]. See section 5.2.

it seems to be what drives the conclusion that the circular and infinite series possibilities from the proposed argument from the Humean Theory to Millgram Instrumentalism must be *vicious*. After all, according to the trickle-down theory, desires can only explain reasons *because* there is some further reason to have that desire. And the trickle-down theory and the Humean Theory together imply that the infinite regress is an *explanatory* regress. Each item in the series is needed in order to explain the last, but the series never stops, and so nothing ultimately does the explaining. Likewise, the trickle-down theory and the Humean Theory together imply that the circular possibility is *vicious*. For each element in the resulting circle is supposed to explain the last, but this means that the first is supposed to explain the last, even though it is itself also ultimately supposed to be explained by it. And that is a vicious explanatory circle.

I hold, however, that this is a better argument understood as an argument to think that Humeans shouldn't be understood as accepting the trickle-down theory, than as an argument against the Humean Theory itself. After all, like all the other arguments against the Humean Theory that I've been considering, it turns on a controversial theory about *how* desires explain reasons. And in earlier chapters, I've set out Hypotheticalism in a way that makes clear that it is not committed to the trickle-down theory, and explained how to deal with the other kinds of problem, like the Too Many Reasons objection, that arise if we don't accept 'fixes' like Korsgaard's and Darwall's that commit us to the trickle-down theory.[8] Moreover, as I'll argue in the next section, the trickle-down theory is dangerously unstable, even if we *don't* accept the Humean Theory.

But first, I want to illustrate by means of an example how it is that rejecting the trickle-down theory leads to a plausible view on which someone can have two intrinsic desires, each of which supports a reason to have the other. This possibility is sufficient to rule out Humean commitment even to thesis 4. The example is the case of Bob. Bob likes metaphysics, and he desires to become a better metaphysician. It's useful, in doing metaphysics, to know a thing or two about epistemology. In fact, it's best to know quite a bit about epistemology. Bob would therefore be best off with respect to getting better as a metaphysician, if he desired to become a better epistemologist as well. In fact, he'd be best off if he actually

[8] Especially in Ch. 5.

cared about epistemology for its own sake, and not merely for the sake of metaphysics.[9] Some of the arcane distinctions made by epistemologists are ultimately important for metaphysics, but it's hard to see their importance if one is constantly preoccupied with how the question is eventually going to bear on metaphysics. Fortunately, Bob *does* care about epistemology for its own sake, and sincerely desires to become a better epistemologist. But things are good for Bob, since it would help him to become a better epistemologist if he knew a thing or two about metaphysics—in fact, if he cared about metaphysics for its own sake.

Since Bob desires to become a better metaphysician, there is a reason for him to desire to become a better epistemologist, and since he desires to become a better epistemologist, there is a reason for him to desire to become a better metaphysician. Bob has reasons for each of these two desires, but the *justification* for Bob's learning about metaphysics or about epistemology does not go around in a circle. It does not go around in a circle because the fact that Bob has a reason to desire to become a better metaphysician does not play a role in the explanation of why, given his desire to become a better metaphysician, there is a reason for him to desire to become a better epistemologist. The only thing that plays this role is Bob's actual desire. The *justification* for Bob to desire to learn about epistemology is just that sincerely caring about epistemology for its own sake will make him a better metaphysician. Full-stop. It doesn't trickle down from anywhere else.[10]

Bob has reasons to care about epistemology for its own sake, and to care about metaphysics for his own sake. That, at any rate, is the view taken by Hypotheticalism. Generalizing from Bob's example, it is consistent with Hypotheticalism that someone has reasons for each and every desire that she has. In other words, Hypotheticalism can reject all of theses 1 through 4. This is a far cry from the claim that some desires must be beyond rational criticism.[11]

---

[9] In the previous section I considered a handful of ways of making the distinction between intrinsic and instrumental desires; it doesn't matter for my purposes here how we make that distinction, so long as Bob's reason is to have an intrinsic desire.

[10] See Richardson [1997] for extended discussion.

[11] I take it that one historical reason why critics of the Humean Theory of Reasons are tempted to attribute the trickle-down theory and Millgram Instrumentalism to the Humean Theory of Reasons is the passage in Hume's *Treatise* in which he claims that the only sense in which a desire can be rationally criticizable is if it is merely an instrumental desire. I think, however, that this passage is

Finally, Bob's case illustrates what is wrong with the possible objection to the Hypotheticalist account of the virtues from section 9.2, that it makes the desires involved with virtue to be merely instrumental desires. In 9.2 I argued that desiring certain things, and to the right degree, is something that everyone has reason (given by their desires) to do. But this doesn't show that desires had for this reason would be merely instrumental desires—the argument, as in Bob's case, is that everyone has reason to desire these things *for their own sake*.

10.3 The Trickle-Down Theory

The trickle-down theory seems, in any case, not to be a particularly promising way of explaining one of the fundamental features of cases like that of Ronnie and Bradley. That is, Ronnie and Bradley's case seems to be one in which two agents actually *differ* with respect to what their reasons are, and a difference in their psychologies is supposed to be a candidate in order to explain where this difference comes from. But if the explanation must itself advert to a further reason, then the problem is that the actual psychological state seems like it makes no difference in the efficacy of this explanation. And if it does not, then by explaining the difference in Ronnie and Bradley's reasons to go to the party by appeal to Ronnie's reason to dance, we have merely passed the explanation of the difference in one reason off to a difference in some other reason. And then the question will arise all over again: what makes Ronnie and Bradley differ with respect to *that* reason?

So consider Darwall's version of the trickle-down theory.[12] Darwall claims that there is an agent-neutral reason to either go to the party or not desire to dance. And this reason, together with a reason for Ronnie

actually evidence that Hume didn't accept the Humean Theory of Reasons at all, nor any other theory about reasons for action or to have desires. (And this is why it pays to be careful in describing the theory as 'Humean'!) On my reading, Hume held that only beliefs could stand in the *reason* relation. That is why he says that strictly speaking, in the case of the instrumental desire it is not even the desire at all that is to be rationally criticized, but only the false belief on which it hinges: 'In short, a passion must be accompanied by some false judgment, in order to its being unreasonable; and even then 'tis not the passion, properly speaking, which is unreasonable, but the judgment' [1978: 416]. See Korsgaard [1997: 220–6], Rawls [2000]. But also compare Setiya [2004].

[12] There are, of course, other versions of the trickle-down theory, and this reasoning may not apply equally well to all of them.

to desire to dance, yields a complex reason for Ronnie to go to the party. The question however, is how does this distinguish Ronnie from Bradley? Ronnie's *actual* desire to dance plays no actual role in this explanation. Even if Ronnie didn't actually desire to dance, a reason for him *to* desire to dance and a reason to either go to the party or else not desire to dance would yield a reason for him to go to the party. So if Darwall is right about how Ronnie's reason gets explained, then that must be because Ronnie and Bradley differ in some way *other* than whether they desire to dance. They must differ with respect to whether they have a *reason* to desire to dance.

Yet now our search for an explanation of the difference in Ronnie's and Bradley's reasons starts all over again. We have two people who differ psychologically and who seem to have different reasons. One hypothesis was that some aspect of their psychological difference—stipulatively, what each *desires*—explains this difference in their reasons. And the trickle-down theory *succeeds* at substantiating the explanation of *Ronnie's* reason. But it does *too* well. It succeeds at explaining *too much*. Its appeal to a further reason to desire to dance also ends up explaining a reason for *Bradley* to go to the party, unless we posit a *further* difference in Ronnie's and Bradley's *reasons*, over and above the difference in their psychologies. And once we do that, we have to start all over again.

For this reason, the trickle-down theory seems not to be a particularly promising way to go about explaining ultimate differences in reasons between different agents. It seems, at least in this version, to force us to appeal to another difference in reasons, and we are no better situated to explain that difference than we were to explain the first one. So it seems anything but unmotivated to me to reject the trickle-down theory. Like the other theories that Hypotheticalism rejects, it is not a promising view about what is going on in Ronnie and Bradley's case.

10.4   Instrumentalism Again

If the Humean Theory of Reasons is not committed to any of theses 1 through 4, however, perhaps it is at least committed to thesis 5. Even if someone has reasons for each of her desires, it might seem, at the very least she can't desire all of those things *for* those reasons. Consider Bob's case.

Even if Bob has reasons both to care about epistemology for its own sake and to care about metaphysics for its own sake, one of these surely had to come *first*. He can't both have started by caring about metaphysics and then started to care about epistemology for this reason, *and* started to care about epistemology because he cared about metaphysics, and thus had a reason to care about epistemology. So perhaps at least the Humean is committed to thesis 5. And that is at least *some* kind of instrumentalist claim. It's broadly in the same family of claims as the other, stronger ones.

But even this, I think, is not right. For perhaps Bob *did* acquire all his present desires for reasons. Suppose, for example, that Bob started by caring about *ethics* for its own sake, and *this* gave him reasons to care about metaphysics for its own sake, and so he began to do so. And *then* he had reasons to care about epistemology for its own sake, and so he began to do so. Once he had started to care about epistemology for its own sake, however, *this* gave him reasons to keep caring about metaphysics for its own sake, and so when he stopped caring about ethics, he nevertheless continued to care about each of metaphysics and epistemology, neither of which he had started caring about for no reason at all, but in which he had deliberately cultivated an interest, on the basis of reasons. If that is the case, then none of Bob's present desires are states which originally merely 'assailed' him.[13] They are all things which he desires for reasons, and even which he *began* to desire for reasons.

Moreover, even putting this aside, it should be clear that whether Bob *now* cares about epistemology for some reason is simply not the same as whether Bob *originally* began to care about it for that reason. This point should be familiar from the epistemological literature. You can originally believe something on the basis of good evidence but only continue to believe it because doing so makes you feel better. Or you can originally believe something for bad evidence, but later acquire good evidence for it, and count as believing it for this reason. So even if Bob *began* to care about epistemology for no reason at all, it doesn't follow that he doesn't *now* believe it for a reason.

So if there is an 'instrumentalist' thesis to which the Humean Theory is committed, it can only be thesis 6, according to which no one has any reasons to do or to desire anything, if she has no desires whatsoever.

---

[13] Scanlon [1998: 39].

Obviously *this*, at least, *is* a commitment of the Humean Theory. If every reason needs to be explained by a desire, you can't have any reasons if you don't have any desires. But if *this* is an objectionable thesis, it must simply be because there is something objectionable about the Humean Theory in general. And I've now spent close to eight chapters trying to track down what this objectionable feature of the view is supposed to be, with (according to me, at least) little success.

It is important, after all, to keep two different claims straight. First, that there are reasons that one would have even in the absence of any *particular* desire. Such reasons have the strong modal status, and I explained how Hypotheticalism can account for them in Chapter 6. And second, that there are reasons that one would have even in the absence of *all* desires. This further thesis is the denial of thesis 6, to which the Humean Theory *is* committed. But we can't allow it to inherit any plausibility from the highly credible strong modal status thesis. Yet it is hard enough to carefully distinguish between these two theses that I suspect that at least some of the unintuitiveness of thesis 6 derives from the intuitiveness that some reasons have the strong modal status. And if that is right, very little should worry us about thesis 6.

Still, there is more that we can say. After all, I think that the *real* impetus for the idea that one ought to be able to step entirely outside one's desires and deliberate about which desires to have comes from a very real phenomenon related to deliberation. In deliberating about what to do, Ronnie will note that there is going to be dancing at the party. Though in many cases this will settle him on what to do, in moments of reflection[14] he *may* wonder *why* this is a reason for him to go. Noticing the difference between himself and Bradley, he may reasonably attribute the cause to his desire to dance. And sometimes things will stop there. But if Ronnie is feeling particularly reflective, this may cause him to step back and wonder whether or not he should really want to dance after all. (Imagine that though Ronnie loves dancing, he was brought up in a strict religious community which forbade it.) And this will lead Ronnie to start looking for reasons for and against wanting to dance.

I think that this deliberative phenomenon is real and robust. And I think that it does have some connection to how *strong* or *weighty* Ronnie's reason

---

[14] Korsgaard [1996].

is. Reasons to or not to desire to dance can have a bearing on how weighty Ronnie's reason to go to the party is, if they translate into reasons to place more or less weight on this reason. I've explained how in Chapter 7. So this does not seem to be cause to balk at Hypotheticalism. The fact that thinking about whether to go to the party can raise further questions for Ronnie about whether or not to desire to dance, does not by itself show that the force of his reason to go to the party could only have 'trickled down' from the force of a reason for him to desire to dance.

Hypotheticalism holds that Ronnie can always ask, of any desire, whether there is a reason for him to have that desire. And importantly, because it distinguishes between reasons and background conditions, it does not hold that in order to deliberate well in answering this question, Ronnie must think about any other desire that he has. This is why there can be a phenomenon of *seeming* to step outside one's desires and reason about what to desire. Though the reasons that one thinks about even in reasoning about what to desire are themselves *explained* by desires, they are not always so explained in obvious ways, and the desires themselves do not figure as part of these reasons. So people who are deliberating well about such questions will usually not be thinking about their desires at all. It is no wonder that they will feel as if they have stepped outside their desires and deliberated about what to desire without presupposing any desires. Their desires, as I argued in Chapter 8, are *efficacious* in their deliberations without being thought about. They figure only in the background.[15]

---

[15] In the useful terminology of Pettit and Smith [1990].

11

Why Be Humean?

11.1 Review

The biggest ideas of Hypotheticalism have been these:

1 Desires explain reasons because they are part of their analysis.

So there is a distinction between reasons and background conditions, allowing answers to the Self-Regarding and Wrong Place objections, and no further, more basic, desire is needed to explain reasons like Ronnie's, as is presupposed by the Incoherence and Chauvinism arguments based on the Standard Model.

2 It is important to distinguish between reasons and their weight.

Once we do so, we should be cautious about the intuitions underlying the Too Many Reasons objection. This also ultimately allows us a response to that objection. It introduces the same complication into the Too Few Reasons objection, and also allows a response to it.

3 Desires allow us to respond to reasons.

Scanlon is right that desires involve seeing things as reasons. But this is something that Hypotheticalism can explain. Desires allow us to act for reasons, and are our source of knowledge about the reasons that we have. Our grasp of the reasons that we have and motivation to act are more reliable when we desire the right things, and to the right degree.

These were the biggest ideas of Hypotheticalism. But along the way, we have also collected a number of important theses:

Agent-Neutral   For R to be a reason to do A is for R to be an agent-relational reason for all of [us] to do A. The scope of

'us' is contextually determined and may include every
possible agent.

According to Agent-Neutral, reasons are always reasons *for* someone. So
if we want to understand what makes something a reason, we have to
understand what makes it a reason *for* the persons for whom it is a reason.
This is what Hypotheticalism aspires to do. It aspires to find the link
between a reason and the agent for whom it is a reason. This link is one of
the agent's desires.

> **Reason**   For R to be a reason for X to do A is for there to be some p
> such that X has a desire whose object is p, and the truth of R
> is part of what explains why X's doing A promotes p.

This is the central analysis of the reason relation provided by Hypotheticalism. It is the heart of the view. According to it, the relation, R is a reason
for X to do A, is analyzed in terms of desire, promotion, and explanation.
Analysis, I said, is a matter of the structure of properties. Analyses tell us
what things have in common, underwrite constitutive explanations, and
explain why some ways of recombining that property with others are
metaphysically impossible.

> **Reason Basicness**   What it is to be normative, is to be analyzed in
> terms of reasons.

Reason Basicness is why many non-reductivists believe that normative properties, including the reason relation, must be irreducible to
non-normative properties and relations such as desire, promotion, and
explanation. They think that no such view can explain the *normativity* of
normative properties and relations. But they are wrong. Reason Basicness
makes normativity *easy* for reductive views to explain, so long as they are
reductive views about *reasons*.

> **Ought**   For it to be the case that X ought to do A is for it to be the
> case that $S_{X,A} \succ S_{X,\sim A}$, where $S_{X,A}$ is the set of all the reasons
> for X to do A and $S_{X,\sim A}$ is the set of all the reasons for X to
> not do A.

Oughts are analyzed in terms of reasons rather than conversely. You ought
to do what you have most reason to do. 'Ought', therefore, admits of

various restrictions. You morally ought to do what you have most moral reason to do, and you prudentially ought to do what you have most prudential reason to do.

Correct   For it to be correct to do A is for it to be the case that $S_A \succ S_{\sim A}$, where S_A is the set of all the right kind of reasons to do A and $S_{\sim A}$ is the set of all the right kind of reasons to not do A.

Correct generalizes on Ought, but correctness is not agent-relational. It is relative to an activity, and activities are governed by respective right kinds of reasons. Not just any reasons are relevant to just any activity. I also said something about *which* kind of reasons is the right kind for a given activity:

Right Kind of Reasons   The right kinds of reasons to do A are reasons that are shared by everyone engaged in the activity of doing A, such that the fact that they are engaged in doing A is sufficient to explain why these are reasons for them.

I'm not sure that this is exactly right, but I appealed to it in order to explain why Ryan's reason to help Katie is weighty and Aunt Margaret's reason to build her spacecraft is poor. If it turns out to be indefensible, what Hypotheticalism would need from some other account is that it turns out that all and only agent-neutral reasons are of the right kind, when it comes to placing weight in deliberation.

I also defended a recursive account of the weight of reasons:

Weight Base   One way for set of reasons A to be weightier than set of reasons B is for set B to be empty, but A non-empty.

Weight Recursion   The other way for set of reasons A to be weightier than set of reasons B is for the set of all the (right kind of) reasons to place more weight on A to be weightier than the set of all the (right kind of) reasons to place more weight on B.

The recursive account, along with the hypothesis that there is the right kind of reason to place more weight on reasons than on non-reasons, allowed us to explain the Attractive Idea:

Still Attractive   Set of reasons A is weightier than set of reasons B just in case it is *correct* to place more weight on A than on B.

And along with Ought, this was what we needed in order to explain why correct deliberation from full information will lead someone to do what she ought to do. It also allowed us, along with Correct, to explain how undercutting defeaters work. Undercutting defeaters, on this view, are the right kind of reason to place less weight on some reason. So they make it correct to place less weight on it, which makes it less weighty. Taking the *weightier than* ordering to hold among sets of reasons also gave us an elegant and attractive way of accounting for how the weight of reasons adds up. All in all, the account of the weight of reasons was well grounded in independent motivations.

And in Chapter 8 and Chapter 9 I defended some important theses about desire:

Desire   For X to have a desire whose object is P is for X to be in a psychological state grounding the following disposition: when for some action a and proposition r believed by X, given X's beliefs r obviously helps to explain why X's doing a promotes P, X finds r salient, and this tends to prompt X to do a, and X's attention is directed toward considerations like r.

This gave us an analysis of directed-attention desires that does not appeal to reasons in its analysis. But I argued that the parallel between the structure of Desire and of Reason made the following claim both defensible and explicable:

Attitude-Content   Action for reasons involves taking things to be reasons. The salient considerations associated with desires are things that the agent takes to be reasons. Their salience has the content that they are reasons.

This thesis, I agreed with Scanlon and Quinn, offers the best explanation of why motivation by desires is acting for—responding to—reasons, rather than mere caused behavior. But Reason and Desire give us the best prospects for explaining why it is true. Attitude-Content, I argued in Chapter 9, also allows us to give an attractive explanation of important facts about moral motivation and moral epistemology, where it led us to the following:

Aristotelian Doctrine   Responding appropriately to your reasons requires desiring the right things, to the right degree. When you desire the right things, to the right degree, your motivation to act will correspond to the weight of your reasons, absent false belief or missing information. Moreover, your judgments about reasons based on the considerations which strike you as salient will then be most reliable.

Because we rejected Proportionalism in Chapters 5 through 7, it does not turn out that there is a neat link between the strength of your desires (and hence of your motivation) and the weight of reasons that are explained by those desires. And in Chapter 6 I argued that there are reasons that are reasons for anyone, no matter what her desires, but that this does not mean that such a person will recognize such reasons or act on them. This happens when the connection between a reason and some desire is unobvious or remote. Nevertheless, they are still reasons for her. Since there are reasons that you have no matter what your desires, but will not necessarily act on, it helps to have desires that are more obviously connected to those reasons, and hence which *would* motivate you to act on them. And it would help to proportion these desires to the weight of the reasons that they motivate you to act on. You must desire the right things to the right degree. This is Hypotheticalism's Aristotelian Doctrine.

Hypotheticalism consists of these theses, together with the strategies that I have used in the last ten chapters to defend it against the various objections to the Humean Theory. Its central thesis is Reason, its analysis of reasons, but these are all parts of the view as a package. But because it includes Reason, it entails and hence is a version of the Humean Theory of Reasons:

HTR   Every reason is explained by a desire in the same way as Ronnie's is.

So if Hypotheticalism is attractive and defensible, then there exists a version of the Humean Theory of Reasons that is attractive and defensible. That

constitutes my existence proof for the defensibility of the Humean Theory
of Reasons.

11.2 Motivations

I have now spent ten chapters arguing that the Humean Theory of Reasons
is defensible, by arguing that Hypotheticalism is. But I have said less about
why we should believe it. This is deliberate; I don't believe that positive
arguments are easily had in philosophy. It is usual to trot out two-or
three-line arguments from premises that are supposed to be uncontroversial
as if, having settled in this way that a view is true, we may then go on to
explore its implications. But assessing such arguments usually turns out to
be as difficult as assessing the view in the first place. I don't think that this
is the right way to make progress in philosophy.

I think, rather, that the way to make progress in philosophical theorizing
is to assemble and categorize the costs and explanatory advantages of
the various theories that are available in some domain, keeping track of
which features of the views subject them to which costs and yield which
advantages, and doing our best to stick to arguments which may show less,
but whose merits are easier to evaluate. That is what I have been trying
to do in this book: there is a long list of putative costs of the Humean
Theory of Reasons, and I have been arguing throughout that these are
not costs of the Humean Theory as such, but rather of the combination
of the Humean Theory with various auxiliary theses about how Ronnie's
reason is explained. This is supposed to shed light not only on whether the
Humean Theory is subject to these objections, but on what does lead to
them, and why. I think that the light that it sheds on these issues can also be
put to work in assessing whether other kinds of ethical theory are subject to
Objectionable Reasoning, Wrong Place, Incoherence, Chauvinism, Too
Many Reasons, or Too Few Reasons objections.

I have also been trying to bring out some of the explanatory advantages
of Hypotheticalism, and where those come from. In the remainder of this
closing chapter, I will rehearse again what I think are the deepest and
most attractive explanatory advantages of Hypotheticalism and where they
come from. And then I will turn to the Humean Theory of Reasons more
generally, and explain why, if what I've argued so far is largely correct, it is

methodologically promising to look to the Humean Theory for a unified explanatory theory of what makes things reasons. Finally, I will explain why I think that any adequate explanatory theory of reasons will face the same general kinds of problems as the Humean Theory, and require similar sorts of tools to solve them.

The first class of explanatory advantages of Hypotheticalism derive from the fact that it is a reductive theory of reasons. The reducibility of the normative is not exactly the kind of datum on which to base a clever two-step argument for Hypotheticalism, of course. But it is an attractive hypothesis, I argued in Chapter 4, because it allows us to explain the supervenience of the normative on the non-normative, and in general all metaphysical impossibilities about recombining the normative with the non-normative. And reductive views are also potentially helpful in securing advantages in normative epistemology and the theory of content for normative terms and thought. So it is attractive both to think that reasons can be reduced to non-normative properties and relations, and to think that the same goes for every other normative property and relation. No non-reductive realist view has an explanation of these things, taking them as brute facts.[1] But metaphysical impossibilities are not the right kind of thing to be brute. All it takes to be possible is to be *possible*.

Hypotheticalism is a reductive view about reasons, and provides a strategy for reducing all of the normative. After all, if Reason Basicness is true (and many non-reductivists think that it is), then all normative properties and relations can be analyzed in terms of reasons. And so if reasons can be analyzed in terms of the non-normative, then so can every other normative property and relation. Moreover, if Reason Basicness is true, then only one strategy for reducing the normative to the non-normative will work—everything else must be reduced to reasons, and reasons must be reduced to the non-normative. Any other strategy would

---

[1] Shafer-Landau [2003] does claim to explain supervenience. He says that the non-normative properties *realize* the normative ones. I'm not sure exactly how to interpret his view, however. On one interpretation, all that he does is to name the problem: on this interpretation, 'realizes' is just a name for 'necessarily does not appear without'. On another interpretation, he accepts the Standard Model Theory, and thinks that the 'realizers' for 'wrong' are the things that are necessarily wrong. But then his explanation appeals to the fact that these things are necessarily wrong, which again involves postulating that it is impossible that they not be wrong. Either way, it explains some metaphysical impossibilities only by appealing to others.

be inconsistent with Reason Basicness, and hence with explaining the normativity of normative properties and relations.

There are also independent reasons to think that the most promising reductive views will treat reasons, rather than, say, value, as the basic normative property, to be analyzed directly in non-normative terms. One of the chief of these is that getting the right results about any other property looks so hard to do. It turns out to be very hard to obtain generalizations in non-normative terms that are really plausibly necessarily equivalent to any given normative claim. The most plausible such generalizations always receive normative hedges. But obviously a generalization subject to a normative hedge cannot form the basis for a reduction. Fortunately reasons, as I argued in Chapter 5, can be of very low weight. And our intuitions about whether there are reasons to do the things these reasons are in favor of are unreliable, I argued, for systematic reasons. This makes it more promising to think that we will be able to state necessary generalizations about reasons that are not subject to normative hedges. So even if Reason Basicness were not independently plausible, it would be more promising to reduce reasons in non-normative terms than, for example, value.

A second class of advantages of Hypotheticalism derives from its account of the weight of reasons. Among those advantages are the ones catalogued in Chapter 7. But Hypotheticalism's account of the weight of reasons also enables us to explain the apparent holism of the normative and the plausibility of Hume's Law. Gillian Russell has argued persuasively that Hume's Law has the same status as the other important 'inferential barrier' theses, from the past to the future, the actual to the necessary, and the particular to the general.[2] She has shown that it is subject to the same kinds of putative counterexample and is apparently plausible for the same kinds of reason. And she and Greg Restall have suggested that the relationship between the normative and the descriptive is analogous to that between these other domains: the future and the past, the necessary and the possible, and the general and the particular. They say that this is the truth in Hume's Law that no 'ought' follows from an 'is'.[3]

Jonathan Dancy, meanwhile, has argued for the holism of reasons. He characterizes this as the thesis that any consideration that is a reason

---

[2] Russell [forthcoming].   [3] Restall and Russell [forthcoming].

may be no reason at all, or even a reason to do a contrary thing, in some other circumstances.[4] But this characterization is too weak for what Dancy really needs. For on this characterization, it follows from the distinction between reasons and background conditions. Any reason that has background conditions, after all, would fail to be a reason in some other conditions—namely, if its background conditions were not satisfied.[5] Dancy really thinks something stronger: he thinks that the background conditions on a reason cannot be stated by any simple positive formula, for the list of potential defeaters is long and diverse. We have to know something about the whole world in order to know that there is no canceller for a given reason. That is why he thinks that the thesis is a kind of *holism*.

Hypotheticalism explains Russell's data and Dancy's data in the same way. Reasons, according to Hypotheticalism, are atomistic. The fact that some consideration is a reason is a particular fact that can be given an analysis in non-normative terms. But talk about reasons is typically talk about relatively *weighty* reasons. In fact, according to Hypotheticalism, every other interesting normative category is not analyzable in terms of reasons alone, but only in terms of reasons together with their weight, as with Ought and Correct. But the weight of reasons, according to Hypotheticalism, is not a matter of particular fact. It is a matter of *general* fact. The weight of a reason is fixed by the facts about *all* reasons of the right kind to place more or less weight on it. So facts about the weight of reasons are *general* facts, not particular ones.

That is why the normative seems holistic. It seems holistic, because it is a matter of general fact, not particular fact. Since all normative claims that we are interested in making—including the claims about reasons that we make in ordinary conversations—involve claims about how weighty some reason or another is, their truth depends on facts about *all* the reasons of some kind. And in general, these will only be guaranteed once we know how the whole world is. This explains what seems to be right about holism. And it explains what seems to be right about Hume's Law, at the same time. The relationship between the normative and the descriptive, according to this view, is not *analogous* to the relationship between the

---

[4] See e.g. Dancy [2005].
[5] Jackson, Pettit, and Smith [2000] make this observation, as do McKeever and Ridge [2005].

general and the particular—insofar as Hume's Law seems to be true, it is because the cases that we consider are *instances* of the relationship between the general and the particular.

Yet a third class of advantages of Hypotheticalism derive from its treatments of moral motivation and moral epistemology, catalogued in Chapter 8 and Chapter 9. The connection between reasons and desires posited by Hypotheticalism is strong enough to explain how we are able to respond to our reasons, and what it is about the psychology of virtuous agents that motivates them to act in the right kinds of way. But it is not as strong as views on which motivational internalism is a conceptual truth. It explains what there is to explain about the connection between normativity and motivation, without explaining too much. All metaethical theories should aspire to this.

Hypotheticalism also yields attractive explanatory benefits in moral epistemology. I argued in Chapter 9 that moral epistemology faces two important problems. The first derives from the fact that reductive views seem as though they ought to be able to help us explain how we get knowledge about morality—instead of morality being about some realm to which we have no causal access, it turns out to be grounded in features of the world in which we live and with which we causally interact. And one of the traditional motivations for reductive views is to help with moral epistemology. But once we allow that the correct reductive view may be synthetic rather than analytic, and that it may be one that no one knows, it becomes very hard to see how reduction helps with moral epistemology at all. None of the existing options in the literature seems to help with this problem. So the problem is: how can reduction help with moral epistemology, if it is one whose truth no one knows?

The second problem for moral epistemology is a general problem. However we get our knowledge about morality, it has to be a way that everyone shares. It is not plausible that moral knowledge derives only from moral experts, who then pass it on to others. We can all reason our way through moral questions at some level or another. But there is widespread and deep disagreement on a wide range of important moral questions. Given these two facts, it seems that our source of moral knowledge cannot be very good. Any way of coming to moral beliefs that everyone uses, and leads to such different results in such a wide range of cases, cannot be a very reliable method. And if it is so vastly unreliable, then it becomes hard to deny the conclusion that no one's justification for her moral beliefs is ever very good. So moral knowledge appears very hard to explain.

The solution to the first problem, I argued, is that rather than being something that agents use as a premise in acquiring moral knowledge, the true reductive view might be one that plays a direct role in the agent's acquisition of moral beliefs. The way that Hypotheticalism did that was simple. Since the basic normative facts are facts about reasons, and the reasons for some agent reduce to facts about her own psychology, that explained why certain psychological events could come to have contents about reasons. And that was my in. I claimed that beliefs formed on the basis of seeing things as reasons are therefore defeasibly justified in the same way as beliefs formed on the basis of ordinary visual perception. In order to construct such a story, the reductive base of moral properties must somehow include psychological properties of some kind. So this was an advantage of Hypotheticalism and an argument for preferring reductive views that appeal to psychological properties. (Together with the arguments that a reductive view should start with reasons, above, that amounts to an argument that the best reductive views will analyze reasons in terms of psychological states of some kind—which looks very close to the Humean Theory of Reasons.)

The solution to the second problem of moral epistemology, I argued, can only be that some agents really do acquire moral knowledge more reliably than others. This is what Aristotle thought: he held that virtue made someone a better judge of moral questions. But this is something that I argued that Hypotheticalism could *explain*. Together with the explanatory perceptual moral epistemology just mentioned, I take it that this provides Hypotheticalism with the central tools to solve the hardest problems of moral epistemology. They are tools that Hypotheticalism can *explain*, and these explanations turn on essential features of Hypotheticalism—its analysis of reasons in terms of desires, its analysis of desires, its response to the Too Few Reasons objection, and its rejection of Proportionalism.

I think that all of the advantages listed here are reasons to be attracted to Hypotheticalism, as are the answers that Hypotheticalism can give to many other questions, large and small. For every theory about the explanation of Ronnie's reason that Hypotheticalism rejected in the last ten chapters, I think it is an advantage of Hypotheticalism that it rejects such a view. It is the sum total of these advantages, together with a careful assessment of the costs remaining after my responses to all the objections considered here and any others that may come to light, which, together with a similar assessment of the advantages and costs of all competing theories, will ultimately tell us whether Hypotheticalism should carry our allegiance.

11.3 General Motivation for the Humean Theory

Nevertheless, I do think that we can say some very general things about why the Humean Theory is the kind of place that we should look, if what we want is a general explanatory theory of all reasons. Most moral theorizing, after all, aspires to be explanatory. Standard moral theories aspire to give general explanations of what we *ought* to do, which explain, for any agent who ought to do something on some occasion, why she ought to do it, then. General explanatory theories of reasons aspire to do the same kind of thing for reasons as these kinds of theory do for what we ought to do.

But I think that general methodological considerations can tell us a lot about how this project should best be pursued.[6] These general methodological considerations strongly suggest that the most promising strategy for investigating how *all* reasons get explained will not be to focus first and foremost on cases of agent-neutral reasons, and then try to generalize. Rather, the most promising strategy will be to focus on cases of merely agent-relational reasons like Ronnie's and Larry's. In the remainder of this section, I'll explain what these methodological considerations are, and why they motivate this. Then in section 11.4 I'll give several reasons why among merely agent-relational reasons, psychology-explained reasons like Ronnie's are the most promising place to look for features that will generalize to the explanation of all other reasons. Together, this yields a general strategy for motivating the Humean Theory of Reasons on general methodological grounds, given the requisite explanatory ambitions.

The motivation that I'm suggesting requires a methodological principle, which I'll uncover in two stages. First, suppose that you start noticing a lot of shapes like the ones at Fig. 11.1. These shapes seem to have something interesting in common, and if you investigate, you will be able to find all

---

[6] The following argument was first developed in my 'The Humean Theory of Reasons' [2007c].

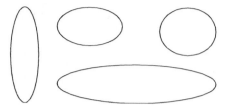

Figure 11.1

kinds of interesting things about them. They are, for example, the shape that objects which are actually circular occupy in our visual fields, and so if you are, for example, a painter, it would behoove you to learn more about what they really have distinctively in common that explains why they are *that* shape, rather than some other. It might, after all (indeed, it will), help you to recreate them accurately.

But you'll be going about things all wrong if you start trying to figure out what these shapes distinctively have in common that distinguishes them simply by looking at *them*. It will put you off on all sorts of wild-goose chases. For example, one of the first things you're likely to notice about your shapes is that they are all round. But what ellipses all have distinctively in common—for the shapes that you are trying to investigate are ellipses—is not simply that they are all round *plus something else*. You won't ever find something that you can add to their being round, to give you the right account of what sets them aside as a distinctive class of shapes. To discover the answer to that, you have to look not only at ellipses, but at *foils*—shapes that are like ellipses, but are not. In particular, you will want to look at egg-shapes and other non-elliptical ovals. Features that are shared by both ellipses and egg-shapes can be quickly set aside as irrelevant. The Methodological Principle, then, is this:

MP If you want to know what makes *P*s *P*s, compare *P*s to things that are not *P*s.

I want to take this carefully in order to be perfectly clear how uncontroversial the Methodological Principle should be, because I want to emphasize exactly how natural and forceful my motivation for the Humean Theory of Reasons is. But lest I be accused of belaboring the obvious, the Methodological Principle quickly generalizes once we start paying attention to the case of relations. And here my example will be slightly contrived. Suppose that having discovered what ellipses have in common[7] you notice that some people are the *ancestors* of other people, and decide that you want to discover the same thing about this relation, that you have discovered about the property of being an ellipse. It follows from a generalization of the Methodological Principle that some people are not going to be particularly worth investigating, if you are trying to discover what the common explanation is, of what makes one person the ancestor of another.

Eve, who is the ancestor of everyone (I warned you this would be *slightly* contrived) will not be a particularly good place to start, in investigating the *ancestor-of* relation. Since she is the ancestor of everyone, she has no non-descendants to compare to her descendants as foils. And so you will suffer from an embarrassment of riches, if you try to sort through all the things that all Eve's descendants have in common, in search of the one that makes them her descendants. Since every human being is one of Eve's descendants (as I stipulated), any feature that every human being shares will become a candidate, and you will have no way of ruling any of these out. So Eve's case gives you no privileged *insight* into the *ancestor-of* relation. Being descended from Eve is not being human *plus* anything else, any more than being an ellipse is being round plus something else.

So if you really want to investigate the ancestor-of relation, the generalization of our Methodological Principle tells us that you need to pay more attention to cases like that of Japheth. Japheth is the ancestor of many people, but he is also not the ancestor of many others. And so we have lots of non-descendants of Japheth to compare to lots of descendants of Japheth. With so many foils, we'll be able to rule out many more potential candidates for what it is that makes Japheth the ancestor of the people who are his descendants. In fact, it is quite likely that there will be *only one* natural candidate for what all Japheth's descendants have in common but his non-descendants lack: that they are people to whom he stands in the ancestral of the parent-of relation. So it is quite likely that Japheth's case is going to help you to zero in very quickly on the common explanation of what makes someone the ancestor of someone else. The Generalized

---

[7] They consist in the set of points whose summed distance from each of two fixed points is the same. (This knowledge *will* help you to depict them more accurately, if you really are a painter, because by tying a thread around two pins, you can use this knowledge to trace any ellipse you like with indefinite accuracy.)

Methodological Principle says, then, to pay attention to cases such as that of Japheth:

GMP   If you want to understand what makes $x_1 \ldots x_n$ stand in relation R, compare cases in which $A_1 \ldots A_n$ stand in relation R but B_1, $A_2 \ldots A_n$ do not, in which $A_1 \ldots A_n$ stand in relation R but A_1, B_2, $A_3 \ldots A_n$ do not, and so on.

Since everyone is a descendant of Eve, Eve's case sets an important *constraint* on a good account of the ancestor-of relation. The account will be wrong, if it yields the wrong predictions about her case. That is why it is a relief to check and see that Eve does, in fact, stand in the ancestral of the parent-of relation to everyone. But by the Generalized Methodological Principle, her case is not the right kind of case to give us any particular *insight* into what makes someone the ancestor of someone else. And that is because it leaves us with no useful foils. It allows us to see things that ancestor–descendant pairs have in common, but since it leaves no foils, focusing on this case is like trying to understand ellipses without comparing them to other shapes. It doesn't rule enough out.

My ancestor-of case is, as I noted, slightly contrived. It is highly unlikely, to say the least, that Eve is really the ancestor of *everyone*. To be so, she would have to be her own ancestor, which seems rather unlikely to be the case, stipulations aside. So to that extent, the ancestor-of relation really only approximates the troubles that beset us when we turn our attention to the *reason* relation. For one of the most philosophically salient features of the reason relation—and one that we should have fully in view, if we understand the puzzles about the objectivity of morality raised by the Humean Theory—is that there are some reasons that really *are* reasons for everyone, no matter who she is or what she is like. These *universal*, or *agent-neutral*, reasons of morality, about which the Humean Theory of Reasons is supposed to raise so many puzzles, are supposed to be such reasons. Agent-neutral reasons, in the uncontroversial sense, are like the case of Eve, in that they are reasons for everyone. They may place *constraints* on a good theory about the common explanation of reasons, but they can't give us any important *insight* into what makes some consideration a reason for someone to do something. For in their case we suffer from an embarrassment of riches. There are too many things that everyone has in common for the case to give us any insight into what distinguishes people for whom R is a reason to do A from those for whom it is not.

So by the Generalized Methodological Principle, it follows that if you want to know what the common explanation of all reasons is, agent-neutral reasons such as the reason to help Katie are not going to be a promising place to start. The *promising* place to start is with the case of reasons that are *merely agent-relational*: reasons for some people but not for others. Ronnie and Bradley's is such a case. And so Ronnie and Bradley's case is a much more promising place to look, in order to discover what makes reasons reasons, than the case of the agent-neutral reason to help Katie, or any of the other moral reasons.

And that is an interesting result. We might have thought that Humeans are obsessed with cases like that of Ronnie and Bradley because they begin with a pre-theoretic prejudice against such reasons as the one to help Katie. After all, as we saw in Chapter 3, Christine Korsgaard has claimed repeatedly that the very idea of a Humean Theory of Reasons *starts* with a special focus on such reasons as Ronnie's and a Chauvinistic attitude about other intuitive examples of reasons, such as the one to help Katie.[8] But the Generalized Methodological Principle explains why it is natural to be interested in cases like Ronnie and Bradley's. For according to the GMP, we *need* to focus on cases of reasons that are merely agent-relational, in order to see what role the agent-place plays in the three-place reason relation: R is a reason for X to do A.

But this observation is still insufficient to justify or even motivate the Humean Theory on the basis of our premises. The observation tells us that *merely agent-relational* reasons are the place that we need to look, in order to see what makes reasons reasons, but Ronnie and Bradley's case is only one *kind* of case of merely agent-relational reasons. The observation explains why the efforts of many philosophers to give explanatory accounts of reasons on the basis of paying special or exclusive attention to moral reasons are straightforwardly methodologically unpromising. But it does not justify paying any more attention to psychology-explained agent-relational reasons than to promise-explained agent-relational reasons, special-relation-explained agent-relational reasons, or any number of others, and that is why

---

[8] One such argument is the central line of argument in her [1986]; a distinct and more general argument to this effect is implicit in the opening pages of her [1997].

the methodological principle gives us only the *first* step in our motivation for the Humean Theory.

Compare: Anne is Larry's infant daughter. That is a reason for him to take care of her. But unless you are in Larry's family or a particularly close friend, it isn't a reason for you to take care of Anne. Now, you might have all manner of reasons to take care of Anne—she might, for example, have been abandoned by her father. But the fact that she is Larry's daughter is not among *your* reasons to take care of her. Here it is Larry's relationship to his daughter that seems to make for a difference between his reasons and yours. Other examples of merely agent-relational reasons include reasons deriving from voluntary obligations such as promises, reasons due to availability (when you are walking past a pond where a child is drowning you have reasons to save the child that others do not, simply because they are not close enough), and so on.

So examples of merely agent-relational reasons are ubiquitous. Our Methodological Principle tells us to look at what is distinctive of merely agent-relational reasons, in order to understand reasons in general. But that isn't yet enough to close in on the Humean idea of focusing on Ronnie and Bradley's case, in which the difference in reasons is due to some *psychological* feature. To do that, we need an argument that Ronnie and Bradley's case gives us a *better* insight into what is distinctive of the agent-place in the reason relation than does Larry's case or other cases of merely agent-relational reasons. That is, we need to establish an *asymmetry* thesis. My motivation for the Humean Theory of Reasons does not rest on ignoring cases like Larry's, or on taking Ronnie's case more seriously. It rests on establishing this Asymmetry Thesis, to which I turn in section 11.4.

11.4 The Asymmetry Thesis

The methodological principle enjoins us to look at cases of merely agent-relational reasons, if we want to find a unified explanatory theory of all reasons. But not all merely agent-relational reasons are on a par. There are a number of reasons why they are not all on a par. One reason is that some provide more promising candidates for generalization to account for all other reasons. It is hard, of course, to imagine how Ronnie's case can be generalized to account for all other reasons. We expended a great deal of effort over this in Chapters 6 and 7, in particular. But it is *harder*, I think, to see how to generalize the other cases.

Larry's reason, for example, is explained because he is a father. But surely it is harder to explain all reasons because their agents are fathers than to explain all reasons by desires. That sounds glib. But it is important. If we are going to generalize from some case of merely agent-relational reasons, we have to generalize the features of that case. Perhaps I focused on too specific a feature of Larry's case by focusing on fatherhood. Perhaps what explains Larry's reason is that he is related to her. But that doesn't seem to make it any easier to explain all reasons—they can't all be explained by who their agent is related to, either. But Larry's case is only helpful, if there is some obvious feature that distinguishes you from Larry, and which can be used to explain all other reasons. The prospects for this look dimmer to me than the prospects of finding a desire in the background of all other reasons, and I think similar reasoning goes for each other case: reasons explained by promises, reasons explained by availability, and so on. So even though it is definitely *hard* for the Humean Theory to solve the Too Few Reasons objection by accounting for all reasons, it still appears to be a more promising way to do this than looking to other kinds of merely agent-relational reasons.

Another important difference between cases like Ronnie's and those of other merely agent-relational reasons, is that I think the other kinds of reasons are better modeled by Standard Model explanations. In Chapter 6 I set aside Larry's case as a version of the Too Few Reasons objection, by subsuming it to the case of accounting for agent-neutral reasons. I did this by accepting a Standard Model explanation of Larry's reason—I said that it is explained by an agent-neutral reason to provide for whatever children one has. Among the agent-neutral reasons to do this is that they are moral subjects for whom one is causally responsible. Since we can use Standard Model explanations to treat these cases, we can reduce the project of explaining them to the project of explaining agent-neutral reasons.

But I argued in Chapter 3 that Standard Model explanations are harder to give for cases like Ronnie's. I rested the most weight, there, on my argument that the Standard Model cannot hold for the explanation of *all* reasons, and that cases of psychology-explained reasons like Ronnie's are the case where it looks worst. But I provided grounds for thinking that it does not work in such cases at all. And if not, then again, we have a relevant asymmetry between cases like Ronnie's and other kinds of case of merely agent-relational reasons. Because we can reduce the project of explaining the others to that of explaining agent-neutral reasons, but can't do so for reason's like Ronnie's, that makes cases like Ronnie's more promising to look at, if we are looking for a general explanation of all reasons.

Finally, the failure of the Standard Model to account for cases like Ronnie's leads to a third interesting argument for the Humean Theory. The substantive theory I provided in Chapter 4 about how the explanation of Ronnie's reason works, was partly motivated as an alternative to the Standard Model. But it was a reductive explanation. But if reasons reduce to desires, then every reason will require a desire. So if the constitutive model for normative explanations that I appealed to in Chapter 4 is the chief alternative to the Standard Model, then the failure of the Standard Model in Ronnie's case would itself be enough to provide motivation for the Humean Theory.

This conjecture, that the Standard Model and the constitutive model are the only real options for how explanations of normative phenomena might work, I call the Standard-Constitutive Conjecture. I am attracted to it, but there is insufficient space here to fully address its merits. Still, in the absence of a genuine alternative proposal, I think that this contributes to a picture of where the Humean Theory can find its motivation.

11.5 In Closing

It is important to emphasize that I think the problems facing the Humean Theory of Reasons are general problems in ethical theory. This is true in every case. Every explanatory moral theory is subject to objections that it is committed to a bad view about good practical reasoning, or that it locates the explanation of reasons or of what we ought to do in the wrong place. Every explanatory moral theory has to face up to the Standard Model Theory and explain why it is not either incoherent or Chauvinist. Every explanatory moral theory is subject to extensional counterexamples of one kind or another.

The tools that I've marshaled on behalf of Hypotheticalism can be used by any theory to deal with these kinds of objection. But they work best when paired with a view that looks very much like Hypotheticalism.

For a first example, I proposed to get out of the Objectionably Self-Regarding and Wrong Place objections by distinguishing between reasons and background conditions. And any explanatory theory of reasons can do that. But as we saw at the beginning of Chapter 8, this creates a puzzle about *how* agents are able to respond to reasons. Hypotheticalism solves that puzzle, because its background conditions include facts about the agent's motivational psychology—which are precisely the right kind of thing to motivate action without the agent having to think about or be aware of them. It is not clear how other explanatory theories of reasons which appealed to the distinction between reasons and background conditions would deal with this problem.

Second, I proposed to avoid the Incoherence and Chauvinism worries raised by the Standard Model Theory by insisting that my explanations of reasons were based on constitutive explanations, grounded in the right analysis of reasons. Again, I think that these are forceful objections, if we buy into the requisite assumptions. And any general explanatory moral theory is subject to similar objections. In principle, any theory can insist, as I do, that its explanations are grounded in the correct analysis of reasons. But then such theories must defend the view that their analysis is really correct. I explained in Chapter 4 why I think Hypotheticalism provides a promising analysis of reasons, but this task would be one that other theories would need to take up.

And third, I proposed to evade the Too Many Reasons and Too Few Reasons objections by distinguishing between reasons and their weight, and observing that there are general problems with our negative existential intuitions about reasons. This is obviously not a move that can be made by general explanatory theories about what someone ought to do, or about what is good. In principle, it is a move that can be made by any general explanatory theory of reasons, but it will not work equally well for any such view. For example, take the value-promoting theory that the reasons for X to do A are considerations that help to explain why X's doing A would promote some value. Putative Too Many Reasons counterexamples to this theory[9] can be explained away in my way, only if it is plausible to

---

[9] The formula for constructing such an example proceeds by looking at the ordinary constraint-like cases that are counterexamples to consequentialism. For example, suppose that Barry has a choice between helping his own daughter with her homework and ensuring that several other parents help their daughters with their homework. Things would be better if he took the latter course of action,

reject a corresponding Proportionalist thesis: that the weight of a reason that is explained by some value is proportional to that value and to how well the action promotes it. But this thesis might be more compelling than the version of Proportionalism that I rejected.

So the problems that I've been showing how to deal with are general ones, and so are the tools that I've been using to deal with them. But the tools work especially well for Hypotheticalism. This contributes to my sense that Hypotheticalism is on the right track.

Finally, I've been arguing in the last two sections that any general explanatory theory of reasons needs to focus on the case of merely agent-relational reasons. This is because reasons are always reasons *for* someone, even when they are also, as it happens, reasons for everyone else as well. So a satisfactory explanation of them will have to explain what makes a reason a reason *for* someone. It will have to locate the relationship between a consideration and an agent that makes that reason a reason for that agent. This can't be the mere fact that she is an agent, because reasons are not, in general, reasons for every agent. So there must be something further about the agent which explains why it is a reason for her. According to the Humean Theory, this is a fact about her psychology, and according to Hypotheticalism, it is a fact about her desires. This lands the Humean Theory with its hardest problems—stemming from the Too Few Reasons objection. But any feature of agents that we located would lead to similar problems. So I think that they are perfectly general problems, not problems for the Humean Theory, in particular.

The principal virtue of Hypotheticalism is that it confronts these problems head-on, rather than avoiding them. But everyone, I think, needs to understand why it is that some reasons are reasons for anyone, while others are reasons for only some. It is, I think, one of the most central problems of ethical theory. My best hope, here, is to have made some small progress in illustrating how this important problem can be attacked. If I haven't gotten anything exactly right, I at least hope that readers will find ideas here on which they can build.

but it is intelligible to resist, and think that this gives Barry no reason to do so, at least in this case. So-called 'agent-relative' theories of value can avoid counterexamples like these, but they have their own problems—see Schroeder [2007a].

References

Adams, Robert [1979]. 'Divine Command Ethics Modified Again'. *Journal of Religious Ethics* 7(1): 66–79.

Altham, J. E. J., and Harrison, Ross (eds.) [1995]. *World, Mind, and Ethics: Essays in Honor of Bernard Williams.* Cambridge: Cambridge University Press.

Anscombe, Elizabeth [1957]. *Intention.* Oxford: Basil Blackwell.

—— [1958]. 'Modern Moral Philosophy'. *Philosophy* 33(1): 1–19.

Bond, E. J. [1983]. *Reason and Value.* Cambridge: Cambridge University Press.

Boyd, Richard [1989]. 'How to Be a Moral Realist'. In Sayre-McCord [1989], 181–228.

Brandom, Robert [1994]. *Making It Explicit.* Cambridge, Mass.: Harvard University Press.

Brandt, Richard [1979]. *A Theory of the Good and the Right.* Oxford: Oxford University Press.

Brink, David [1989]. *Moral Realism and the Foundations of Ethics.* Cambridge: Cambridge University Press.

Broadie, Sarah [1990]. *Ethics with Aristotle.* Oxford: Oxford University Press.

Broome, John [1999]. 'Normative Requirements'. *Ratio* 12(4): 398–419.

—— [2004]. 'Reasons'. In Wallace et al. [2004], 28–55.

Brunero, John [2003]. 'Practical Reason and Motivational Imperfection'. *Philosophical Inquiry* 2(1–2): 219–28.

Chang, Ruth [2004]. 'Can Desires Provide Reasons for Action?' In Wallace et al. [2004], 56–90.

Copp, David [2001]. 'Against Internalism About Reasons—Gert's Rational Options'. *Philosophy and Phenomenological Research* 62(2): 455–61.

Cordner, Christopher [2001]. 'Ethical Necessity and Internal Reasons'. *Philosophy* 7(298): 541–60.

Crisp, Roger [2000]. 'Particularizing Particularism'. In Hooker and Little [2000], 23–47.

Cudworth, Ralph [1731]. *A Treatise Concerning Eternal and Immutable Morality.* Whitefish, Mont.: Kessinger.

Cullity, Garret, and Gaut, Berys (eds.) [1997]. *Ethics and Practical Reason.* Oxford: Oxford University Press.

Dancy, Jonathan [2000]. *Practical Reality.* Oxford: Oxford University Press.

—— [2004]. 'Enticing Reasons'. In Wallace et al. [2004], 91–118.

Dancy, Jonathan [2005]. *Ethics Without Principles*. Oxford: Oxford University Press.

D'Arms, Justin, and Jacobson, Daniel [2000]. 'The Moralistic Fallacy: On the Appropriateness of Emotions'. *Philosophy and Phenomenological Research* 61.

Darwall, Stephen [1983]. *Impartial Reason*. Ithaca: Cornell University Press.

Davidson, Donald [1973]. 'Freedom to Act'. Reprinted in Davidson [1980], 63–81.

—— [1980]. *Essays on Actions and Events*. Oxford: Oxford University Press.

Dreier, James [1990]. 'Internalism and Speaker Relativism'. *Ethics* 101(1): 6–25.

—— [1999]. 'Transforming Expressivism'. *Noûs* 33(4): 558–72.

Dretske, Fred [1981]. *Knowledge and the Flow of Information*. Cambridge, Mass.: MIT.

Egonsson, Dan, Josefsson, Jonas, Petterson, Björn, and Rønnow-Rasmussen, Toni (eds.) [2001]. *Exploring Practical Philosophy: From Action to Values*. Aldershot: Ashgate.

Enoch, David [2007]. 'An Argument for Robust Metanormative Realism'. *Oxford Studies in Metaethics*, ii.

Fine, Kit [1994]. 'Essence and Modality'. *Philosophical Perspectives* 8 (Logic and Language), 1–16.

Fitzpatrick, William [2004]. 'Reasons, Value and Particular Agents: Normative Relevance Without Motivational Internalism'. *Mind* 11(450): 285–318.

Fodor, Jerry [1987]. *Psychosemantics: The Problem of Meaning in the Philosophy of Mind*. Cambridge, Mass.: MIT.

—— [1990a]. 'A Theory of Content'. In Fodor [1990b], 51–136.

—— [1990b]. *A Theory of Content and Other Essays*. Cambridge, Mass.: MIT.

Foot, Philippa [1959]. 'Moral Beliefs'. Reprinted in Foot [2002], 110–31.

—— [1975]. 'Morality as a System of Hypothetical Imperatives'. Reprinted in Foot [2002]: 157–73.

—— [2001]. *Natural Goodness*. Oxford: Oxford University Press.

—— [2002]. *Virtues and Vices*. Oxford: Oxford University Press.

Frankfurt, Harry [1971]. 'Freedom of the Will and the Concept of a Person'. *Journal of Philosophy* 68(1): 5–20.

Gauthier, David [1986]. *Morals By Agreement*. Oxford: Oxford University Press.

Gensler, Harry [1985]. 'Ethical Consistency Principles'. *Philosophical Quarterly* 35(3): 156–70.

Gert, Joshua [2001]. 'Skepticism About Practical Reasons Internalism'. *Southern Journal of Philosophy* 39(1): 59–77.

Gibbard, Allan [2003]. *Thinking How to Live*. Cambridge, Mass.: Harvard University Press.

Greenspan, Patricia [1975]. 'Conditional Oughts and Hypothetical Imperatives'. *Journal of Philosophy* 72(10): 259–76.

Grice, H. P. [1967]. 'Logic and Conversation'. Reprinted in Grice [1991], 1–144.

—— [1991]. *Studies in the Way of Words.* Cambridge, Mass.: Harvard University Press.

Hamilton, Richard [2004]. 'Might There Be Legal Reasons?' *Res Publica* 1(4): 425–47.

Hampton, Jean [1998]. *The Authority of Reason.* Cambridge: Cambridge University Press.

Hare, R. M. [1952]. *The Language of Morals.* Oxford: Oxford University Press.

Harman, Gilbert [1975]. 'Moral Relativism Defended'. Reprinted in Harman [2000], 3–19.

—— [1977]. *The Nature of Morality.* Oxford: Oxford University Press.

—— [1978]. 'Relativistic Ethics: Morality as Politics'. Reprinted in Harman [2000], 39–57.

—— [1982]. 'Conceptual Role Semantics.' *Notre Dame Journal of Formal Logic* 23: 242–56.

—— [1985]. 'Is There A Single True Morality?' Reprinted in Harman [2000], 77–99.

—— [1987]. '(Nonsolipsistic) Conceptual Role Semantics'. In Lepore [1987], 55–81.

—— [2000]. *Explaining Value and Other Essays in Moral Philosophy.* Oxford: Oxford University Press.

—— [2002]. 'Practical Aspects of Theoretical Reasoning'. In Al Mele and Piers Rawling (eds.), *The Oxford Handbook to Rationality.* Oxford: Oxford University Press.

Heuer, Ulrike [2004]. 'Reasons for Actions and Desires'. *Philosophical Studies* 121(1): 43–63.

Hieronymi, Pamela [2005]. 'The Wrong Kind of Reason'. *Journal of Philosophy* 102(9): 437–57.

Hill, Thomas [1973]. 'The Hypothetical Imperative?' *The Philosophical Review* 82(4): 429–50.

Hooker, Brad [1987]. 'Williams' Argument Against External Reasons'. *Analysis* 47(1): 42–4.

—— and Little, Margaret (eds.) [2000]. *Moral Particularism.* Oxford: Oxford University Press.

Horty, John [2007]. 'Reasons as Defaults'. *Philosophers' Imprint* 7(3), <www.philosophersimprint.org/007003/>.

Hubin, Donald [1999]. 'What's Special about Humeanism', *Noûs* 33: 30–45.

Huemer, Michael [2005]. *Ethical Intuitionism.* New York: Palgrave Macmillan.

Hume, David [1978]. *A Treatise Concerning Human Nature*, ed. P. H. Nidditch. Oxford: Oxford University Press.

Hurley, Susan [2001]. 'Reason and Motivation: The Wrong Distinction?' *Analysis* 61(2): 151–5.

Jackson, Frank [1997]. *From Metaphysics to Ethics*. Oxford: Oxford University Press.

—— [1999]. 'Non-Cognitivism, Normativity, and Belief'. *Ratio* 12(4): 420–35.

—— Pettit, Philip, and Smith, Michael [2000]. 'Ethical Particularism and Patterns'. In Hooker and Little (eds.), *Moral Particularism*. Oxford: Oxford University Press, 79–99.

Johnston, Mark [2001]. 'The Authority of Affect'. *Philosophy and Phenomenological Research* 6(1): 181–214.

Joyce, Richard [2001]. *The Myth of Morality*. Cambridge: Cambridge University Press.

Kant, Immanuel [1997]. *Groundwork of the Metaphysics of Morals*, trans. Mary Gregor. Cambridge: Cambridge University Press.

Kim, Jaegwon [1984]. 'Concepts of Supervenience'. Reprinted in Kim [1993], 53–78.

—— [1993]. *Supervenience and Mind*. Cambridge: Cambridge University Press.

King, Jeff [1995]. 'Structured Propositions and Complex Predicates.' *Noûs* 29(4): 516–535.

—— [1998]. 'What is a Philosophical Analysis?' *Philosophical Studies* 90: 155–79.

—— [2002]. 'Two Sorts of Claim about "Logical Form"'. In Gerhard Preyer (ed.), *Logical Form and Language*. Oxford: Oxford University Press.

Korsgaard, Christine [1986]. 'Skepticism About Practical Reason'. *Journal of Philosophy* 83(1): 5–25.

—— [1996]. *The Sources of Normativity*. Cambridge: Cambridge University Press.

—— [1997]. 'The Normativity of Instrumental Reason'. In Cullity and Gaut [1997], 215–54.

Kriegel, Uriah [1999]. 'Normativity and Rationality: Bernard Williams on Reasons for Action'. *Iyyun: The Jerusalem Philosophical Quarterly* 4: 281–92.

Lavin, Douglas [2004]. 'Practical Reason and the Possibility of Error'. *Ethics* 114(3): 424–57.

Lehrer, Keith, and Paxson, Thomas [1969]. 'Knowledge: Undefeated Justified True Belief'. *Journal of Philosophy* 66(4): 225–37.

Lepore, Ernest (ed.) [1987]. *New Directions in Semantics*. London: Academic Press.

Lewis, David [1986]. *On the Plurality of Worlds*. Oxford: Basil Blackwell.

—— [1989]. 'Dispositional Theories of Value'. *Proceedings of the Aristotelian Society*, Supp. 63: 113–37.

Lillehammer, Halvard [2000]. 'The Doctrine of Internal Reasons'. *Journal of Value Inquiry* 34(4): 507–16.

McDowell, John [1995]. 'Might There be External Reasons?' In Altham [1995], 68–85.

McKeever, Sean, and Ridge, Michael [2005]. 'What Does Holism Have to Do with Moral Particularism?' *Ratio* 18(1): 93–103.

McNaughton, David [1989]. *Moral Vision*. Oxford: Basil Blackwell.

_____ and Rawling, Piers [1991]. 'Agent-Relativity and the Doing–Happening Distinction'. *Philosophical Studies* 63: 167–85.

Mackie, J. L. [1977]. *Ethics: Inventing Right and Wrong*. New York: Penguin.

Millgram, Elijah [1996]. 'Williams' Argument Against External Reasons'. *Noûs* 30(2): 197–220.

_____ [1997]. *Practical Induction*. Princeton: Princeton University Press.

_____ (ed.) [2001]. *The Varieties of Practical Reason*. Cambridge, Mass.: MIT.

Millikan, Ruth [1984]. *Language, Thought, and Other Biological Categories: New Foundations for Realism*. Cambridge, Mass.: MIT.

Moreau, Sophia [2005]. 'Reasons and Character'. *Ethics* 115(2): 272–305.

Nagel, Thomas [1970]. *The Possibility of Altruism*. Princeton: Princeton University Press.

_____ [1986]. *The View from Nowhere*. Oxford: Oxford University Press.

Neander, Karen [1991]. 'The Teleological Notion of Function'. *Australasian Journal of Philosophy* 69: 454–68.

Oddie, Graham [2005]. *Value, Reality, and Desire*. Oxford: Oxford University Press.

Olson, Jonas [2004]. 'Buck-Passing and the Wrong Kind of Reasons'. *Philosophical Quarterly* 54(215): 295–300.

Papineau, David [1987]. *Reality and Representation*. Oxford: Basil Blackwell.

Parfit, Derek [2001]. 'Rationality and Reasons'. In Egonsson et al. [2001], 17–39.

_____ [forthcoming]. *Climbing the Mountain*. Oxford University Press.

Peacocke, Christopher [1992]. *A Study of Concepts*. Cambridge, Mass.: MIT.

Pettit, Philip, and Smith, Michael [1990]. 'Backgrounding Desire'. *Philosophical Review* 90(4): 565–92.

Piller, Christian [2001]. 'Normative Practical Reasoning'. *Proceedings of the Aristotelian Society* 75 Supp. 1.

_____ [2006]. 'Content-Related and Attitude-Related Reasons for Preferences'. *Philosophy* 81(1).

Plantinga, Alvin [1986]. 'Reply to Kit Fine'. In Tomberlin [1986], 329–49.

Pollock, John, and Cruz, Joseph [1999]. *Contemporary Theories of Knowledge, 2nd edn*. Savage, Md.: Rowman & Littlefield.

Price, Richard [1948]. *A Review of the Principal Questions in Morals*, ed. D. D. Raphael. Oxford: Clarendon.

Price, Terry [1999]. 'Are Williams's Reasons Problematically External After All?' *Southern Journal of Philosophy* 3(3): 461–78.

Prichard, H. A. [1912]. 'Does Moral Philosophy Rest on a Mistake?' Reprinted in Prichard [2002]: 7–20.

――― [2002]. *Moral Writings*, ed. Jim MacAdam. Oxford: Oxford University Press.

Prior, Arthur [1960]. 'The Autonomy of Ethics'. *Australasian Journal of Philosophy*. 38: 199–206.

Putnam, Hilary [1990]. 'Beyond the Fact/Value Dichotomy'. In *Realism with a Human Face*, ed. James Conant. Cambridge, Mass.: Harvard University Press, 135–41.

Quinn, Warren [1993a]. *Morality and Action*. Cambridge: Cambridge University Press.

――― [1993b]. 'Putting Rationality in its Place'. In Quinn [1993a], 228–54.

Rabinowicz, Wlodek, and Rønnow-Rasmussen, Toni [2004]. 'The Strike of the Demon: On Fitting Pro-attitudes and Value'. *Ethics* 114(3): 391–423.

Railton, Peter [1984]. 'Alienation, Consequentialism, and the Demands of Morality'. *Philosophy and Public Affairs* 13(1): 134–71.

――― [1986]. 'Moral Realism'. Reprinted in Railton [2003], 3–42.

――― [1997]. 'On the Hypothetical and Non-Hypothetical in Reasoning About Belief and About Action'. In Cullity and Gaut [1997], 53–79.

――― [2003]. *Facts, Values, and Norms*. Cambridge: Cambridge University Press.

Rawls, John [1971]. *A Theory of Justice*. Oxford: Oxford University Press.

――― [2000]. *Lectures on the History of Moral Philosophy*. Cambridge, Mass.: Harvard University Press.

Raz, Joseph [1975]. *Practical Reason and Norms*. Oxford: Oxford University Press.

――― [1999a]. *Engaging Reason*. Oxford: Oxford University Press.

――― [1999b]. 'Explaining Normativity: On Rationality and the Justification of Reason'. Reprinted in Raz [1999a], 67–89.

――― [1999c]. 'The Truth in Particularism'. Reprinted in Raz [1999a], 218–46.

Restall, Greg, and Russell, Gillian [forthcoming]. 'Barriers to Inference'. In *Hume, 'Is' and 'Ought': New Essays*, ed. Charles Pigden. Rochester, NY: Rochester University Press.

Richardson, Henry [1997]. *Practical Reasoning About Final Ends*. Cambridge: Cambridge University Press.

Robertson, Teresa [2003]. 'Internalism, (Super)fragile Reasons, and the Conditional Fallacy'. *Philosophical Papers* 3(2): 171–84.

Russell, Gillian [forthcoming]. 'In Defence of Hume's Law'. Forthcoming in *Hume, 'Is' and 'Ought': New Essays*, ed. Charles Pigden. Rochester: Rochester University Press.

Sayre-McCord, Geoffrey [1989]. *Essays on Moral Realism*. Ithaca: Cornell University Press.

Scanlon, T. M. [1998]. *What We Owe to Each Other*. Cambridge, Mass.: Harvard University Press.

Schroeder, Mark [2004]. 'The Scope of Instrumental Reason'. *Philosophical Perspectives* 18 (Ethics): 337–64.

____ [2005a]. 'Realism and Reduction: The Quest for Robustness'. *Philosophers' Imprint* 5(1), <www.philosophersimprint.org/005001/>.

____ [2005b]. 'The Hypothetical Imperative?' *Australasian Journal of Philosophy* 83(3): 357–72.

____ [2005c]. 'Instrumental Mythology'. *Journal of Ethics and Social Philosophy*, <www.jesp.org>, symposium 1.

____ [2005d]. 'Cudworth and Normative Explanations'. *Journal of Ethics and Social Philosophy* 3(1), <www.jesp.org>.

____ [2007a]. 'Teleology, Agent-Relative Value, and "Good"'. *Ethics* 117(2): 265–95.

____ [2007b]. 'Reasons and Agent-Neutrality'. *Philosophical Studies*, 135(2): 279–306.

____ [2007c]. 'The Humean Theory of Reasons'. *Oxford Studies in Metaethics*, ii. 195–219.

____ [2008]. 'Having Reasons'. *Philosophical Studies*, 139(1): 57–71.

Setiya, Kieran [2004]. 'Hume on Practical Reason'. *Philosophical Perspectives* 18 (Ethics), 365–89.

Shafer-Landau, Russ [2003]. *Moral Realism: A Defence*. Oxford: Oxford University Press.

Shelton, Mark [2004]. 'What's Wrong with External Reasons?' *Philosophical Studies* 11(3): 365–94.

Skorupski, John [1997]. 'Reasons and Reason'. In Cullity and Gaut [1997], 345–68.

Smith, Michael [1994]. *The Moral Problem*. Oxford: Blackwell.

____ [1995]. 'Internal Reasons'. *Philosophy and Phenomenological Research* 55(1): 109–31.

Sobel, David [2001]. 'Explanation, Internalism, and Reasons for Action'. *Social Philosophy and Policy* 18(2): 218–35.

Sober, Elliott, and Wilson, David Sloan [1998]. *Unto Others*. Cambridge, Mass.: Harvard University Press.

Stocker, Michael [1979]. 'Desiring the Bad'. *Journal of Philosophy* 76(12): 738–53.

Svavarsdottir, Sigrun [1999]. 'Moral Cognitivism and Motivation'. *Philosophical Review* 108(2): 161–219.

Thomas, Alan [2002]. 'Internal Reasons and Contractualist Impartiality'. *Utilitas* 1(2): 135–54.

Tiffany, Evan [2003]. 'Alienation and Internal Reasons for Action'. *Social Theory and Practice* 2(3): 387–418.

Timmons, Mark [1999]. *Morality Without Foundations*. Oxford: Oxford University Press.

Tomberlin, James (ed.) [1986]. *Alvin Plantinga*. Dordrecht: Reidel.

Toulmin, Stephen [1950]. *Reason in Ethics*. Cambridge: Cambridge University Press.

Velleman, David [1989]. *Practical Reflection*. Princeton: Princeton University Press.

—— [1996]. 'The Possibility of Practical Reason'. Reprinted in Velleman [2000*b*], 170–99.

—— [2000*a*]. 'The Aim of Belief'. In Velleman [2000*b*]: 244–81.

—— [2000*b*]. *The Possibility of Practical Reason*. Oxford: Oxford University Press.

Wallace, Jay [2001]. 'Normativity, Commitment, and Instrumental Reason'. *Philosophers' Imprint* 1(3), <http://www.philosophersimprint.org/001003>.

—— Pettit, Philip, Scheffler, Samuel, and Smith, Michael (eds.) [2004]. *Reason and Value: Themes from the Moral Philosophy of Joseph Raz*. Oxford: Oxford University Press.

Watson, Gary [1975]. 'Free Agency'. *The Journal of Philosophy* 72(8): 205–20.

Wedgwood, Ralph [2006]. 'The Meaning of "Ought"'. *Oxford Studies in Metaethics*, i. 12–60.

Williams, Bernard [1973]. *Utilitarianism: For and Against*. Cambridge: Cambridge University Press.

—— [1981*a*]. 'Internal and External Reasons.' Reprinted in Williams [1981*b*], 100–10.

—— [1981*b*]. *Moral Luck*. Cambridge: Cambridge University Press.

—— [2001]. 'Some Further Notes Concerning Internal and External Reasons'. In Millgram [2001].

Index